CW00530439

ISBN 978-1-333-46669-5
PIBN 10508002

PREFACE.

THE recital of the story of a Native life of our times, may be compared to a journey through a barren tract in which the relieving green spots are few and far between. Again, a man's biography is mostly his contemporaneous history. These two facts must be the apology for the imperfections of the following sketch.

In "the sap-consuming winter" of his age, the fruit of one's labors is likely to taste unsavoury. But the thoughts liable to objection by his countrymen in their present humour, have been obtruded with no other than the benevolent motive of promoting national good.

The necessary materials were supplied chiefly by the industrious researches of Babu Raj Jogeshur Mitter of Bhabanipur, who is well informed on most questions of public interest. He also kindly undertook the supervision of the work at the Press.

CONTENTS.

CHAPTER I.

	PAGE.
Birth and Ancestry	1—5

CHAPTER II.

Patshala, School, and College Life . . .	6—12

CHAPTER III.

Marriage, Tutorship and other services .	13—18

CHAPTER IV.

The Managery. The Hare Memorial Meeting. Death of Raja Kissen Nath Roy.	19—25

CHAPTER V.

Manufactures and Trade. The Commercial crisis in 1847. The fall of the Union Bank	26—31

CHAPTER VI.

Zamindari status—The British Indian Association	32—38

CONTENTS.

CHAPTER VII.

Beginning of Public Life—The Charter Memorial 39—48

CHAPTER VIII.

The Black Act Meeting . . . . . . 49—75

CHAPTER IX.

Stock Speculations—The Municipal Commission—The Latour Memorials —The Income Tax Conference . 76—90

CHAPTER X.

The Harish Memorial Meeting—The Monster Wells Meeting—The Sati Case . . . . 91—102

CHAPTER XI.

The Epidemic Fever in Bengal—The Epidemic Commission . . . . . . 103—124

CHAPTER XII.

The First Career in the Bengal Council —The Great Rent Case . . . . . 125—135

CHAPTER XIII.

The Ganga-Jatra Case—The Orissa Famine—The Hook-Swinging Bill— The Inoculation Prohibition Bill . . 136—149

CHAPTER XIV.

Exemption from Attendance in Civil Courts—The Orissa Revenue Settlement—The Mela Question . . . 150—161

CHAPTER XV.

The British Indian Association Clique—The Age of Brandy and the Age of Brag—The Second Career in the Bengal Council, and the Irrigation and Drainage Bill . . . 162—177

CHAPTER XVI.

Meeting in Honor of Sir William Grey—The Anti-Cess Meeting—The Road Cess Bill . . . . 178—194

CHAPTER XVII.

The Mayo Memorial Speech—The Fawcett Memorial Meeting—The Third Career in the Bengal Council—The Epidemic Theory—The Embankment Bill—The Abkari Acts. . 195—209

CHAPTER XVIII.

The Presidentship of the B. I. Association—The Agrarian Riot in Pabna—The Famine of 1874—The Advent of the Prince of Wales—The Star of India Chapter—The Northbrook Meeting—The District Appellate Benches Question—The Epidemic Commission . . . 210—227

CHAPTER XIX.

The Provincial Public Works Cess Meeting—The Investiture Darbar—Interregnum in the B. I. Association—The Maharaja Roma Nath Tagore Memorial Meeting—The Expenditure and Taxation Meeting . . 228—241

CHAPTER XX.

The Last Illness and Death—The Lieutenant-Governor's Condolence Letter—Obituary Notices—Committee Resolutions—The British Indian Association's Refusal of a Memorial Portrait—Friendly Reminiscences . 242—259

CHAPTER XXI.

Personal Appearance and Characteristics — His Zamindarship.—His Young Bengalism—His Political Opinions. His Public Character and Private Beneficence — His Spiritualism . . . . 260—277

CHAPTER XXII.

Characteristics as a Writer and a Speaker. Summary of Character. . 278—283

CHAPTER XXIII.

The Family and Heirs . . . . . 284—286

Appendices . . . . . . i—lxxiii

ERRATA AND EMENDATIONS.

Page 16, line 12, for resolute and persevering *read* resolute and enterprising.
,, 38, ,, 2, ,, "loving themselves the last" *read* "loving themselves last."
,, 42, ,, 15, ,, never raised their voice before now *read* never raised their voice independently before now.
,, 43, ,, 11, ,, acted in consultation *read* acted in consultation with.
,, 48, ,, 7, ,, that takes the vast compass *read* that takes in the vast compass.
,, 50, ,, 3, ,, and which scarcely find *read* which scarcely find.
,, 54, ,, 1, ,, salts of their nation *read* salt of the nation.
,, 55, ,, 2, ,, first of all tried to carry out the recommendation of the Directors by subjecting the Europeans, in 1836, *read* tried to carry out the recommendation of the Directors by subjecting the Europeans, in 1836, first of all.
,, 59, ,, 21 ,, sincerer approachment *read* sincere rapproachment.
,, 72, ,, 13, ,, than that of the Covenanted Judges *read* than those of the Covenanted Judges.
,, ,, last line ,, 36 per cent confirmed *read* 36 per cent. were confirmed.
,, 74, line 6, ,, 31st. August 1859 *read* 31st. August 1861.
,, 74, last line,,, no approachment *read* no rapproachment.
,, 92, line 3, ,, giving half-holiday *read* giving a half-holiday.
,, 105, ,, 12, ,, if not identical with, was of the same class as, *read* was not identical with, though of the same class as.
,, 108, last line ,, dysentry *read* dysentery.
109, line 2, ,, anoemic *read* anæmic.
,, ,, ,, 8, ,, people taking it *read* people taking the illness.
,, 121, ,, 26, ,, transversly *read* transversely.
126, ,, 26, ,, parvenues *read* parvenus.
,, 144, ,, 11, ,, superstitious ears *read* superstitious fears.
,, 145, ,, 3, ,, suffered more from deficiency *read* suffered from deficiency more.
,, 153, ,, 20, ,, emanaations *read* emanations.
,, 161, last line, ,, held there in the present year, *read* held there last year.
,, 166, ,, 22, ,, that we were in a begging *read* their being in a begging.
,, 168, ,, 28, ,, it was the Railway *read* it was the Railways.
,, 233, ,, 12, ,, there were abatements, but the country still suffered from its outbreak in its malignity, *read* there were abatements in its malignity, but the country still suffered from its outbreak.
,, 248, ,, 2 ,, maintion *read* maintain.
286, last line ,, that awaits all useful and honorable career *read* that awaits a useful and honorable career.

Raja Digambar Mitra.

CHAPTER I.

BIRTH AND ANCESTRY.

IN his speech at the Harish Memorial Meeting, Babu Ramgopal Ghosh remarked :—" In a country like this, and under a Government such as they had, it was impossible to expect native talent and native genius to be appreciated and promoted. They were not living in a free country ; or under a representative government. He did not find fault with the existing rule ; perhaps it was the best they could have under present circumstances ; but with an exclusive Civil Service and no outlet for career there was no stimulus to exertion." Thus, the influences that tend to elevate a people and perpetuate its qualifications being withdrawn, the natural law of degeneration has commenced its work. Until the setting in of a re-action, and regeneration under a more favourable set of circumstances—under more care and encouragement, we must bid adieu to our expectation of such prodigies as grace our past history ; and with Ranjit Singh has ceased our last great mind for many years to come. But for long does the law of heredity continue to operate against the law of Reversion to Type and the retrograde principle in our being, and therefore we have had our Ram Mohan Roy and Iswara Chandra Vidyasagara. The policy of administrative outlawry is undoing the past—the old garden is running to waste. But, nevertheless, pines and oaks fail not to spring forth from the virtue in their seeds—only they have a dwarfed growth and a stinted development. To such, or to the first rays in the dawn of a nation, may be likened those men of our times who by their abilities placed themselves in the fore-rank of their countrymen, and left an impress of biographical importance upon their careers. One of these men was the subject of our sketch. He "did the State some service," and made himself a man of mark. His life-story reads a lesson, and it shall be told as simply and soberly as it ought to be without any exaggeration or omission.

Digambar Mitra was born at Konnagara, in 1817. His horoscope having perished, the date of his birth cannot be given. The village of Konnagara is on the right bank of the Hughli, nearly midway between Calcutta and Serampur. Half a century ago or more, Konnagara was something like a colony of the Mitra-Kayasthas. Of the three families honored as Kulins by Ballala Sena, the Mitra-Kayasthas have produced most men of note In native Calcutta-history, we have the well-known names of Govindaram Mitra —the "Black Zemindar" of Holwell; of Abhay Charan Mitra—celebrated for his *Nari;* of Gokul Mitra and Pitambar Mitra; of Ramchandra Mitra, Peary Chand Mitra, Kissory Chand Mitra, and Gopi Kissen Mitra—all of them more or less literary men; of Dwarkanath Mitra and Romesh Chandra Mitra—the two Judges of the High Court; and, lastly, of Rajendra Lalla Mitra—"a Brahman and hereditary Pandit" of Dr. Max Muller.

The most noted Mitras of Konnagara were the *Mandira-Bati-Mitras*, who were a wealthy and respectable family. They were so called from having built those conspicuous *Mandirs*, or temples, which draw the eye of all people sailing by the place. In this family Digambar was born. He had a very long pedigree, which carries us back to one of those Kayastha followers who accompanied the Brahmans invited by Adisura from Kanauj, in the 10th century. Traced from this ancient progenitor, he numbered the 28th *pary-yaya* (generation), or the 23rd from the ancestor who first received the honour of Kulinism. Born in a Kulin family, he had "gentle blood" in the esteem of Hindu society.* His grandfather,

* In his account of the *Sena Rajas of Bengal,* Rajendra Lalla Mitra calls the Kulin Kayasthas the "hereditary nobility" of that land.

Ramchandra Mitra, was employed as Cashier in the mercantile firm of Messrs.———, who afterwards became Messrs. Leyburn and Co. He died leaving Rs. 50,000 to three sons, Siva Chandra Mitra, Sambhu Chandra Mitra, and Rajkrista Mitra, who were all employed in the said firm. Siva Chandra was in charge of the Import Godown; Sambhu Chandra was the Cashier; and Rajkrista Mitra was an Assistant in out-door business. Being the eldest, Siva Chandra was the head of the joint-family. His son was Digambar, who was the elder of two boys.

It is now some twenty minutes journey from Konnagara to Calcutta by rail. But for years people had to come from there and return to it daily in swift-sailing *pansways*, that took away much of their time, interfered with their punctual attendance at office, exposed them to Nor-Westers, and obliged them on mornings of adverse tide to be content with cold rice cooked over night. In consideration of these several inconveniences, Siva Chandra took up his abode in Calcutta. He bought a house at Raja Navakrishna's Street, in Sova Bazar, that stood on the same grounds on which Raja Prasanna Narana Deb afterwards built his noble residence. In this neighbourhood he became intimately acquainted with Rajas Gopimohan Deb and Radhakanta Deb.

Two generations ago, the business of a Godown Sarkar was of considerable emolument. There are traditions that metal-goods, such as copper and iron, in mercantile ware-houses turned out short in weight from *dry-age*, and Godown-Sarkars made their fortunes. To this day, theirs is the coveted post next to those of the Banian and Sadar-Mate in a commercial firm. Siva Chandra was an earning man, but not economical. His class in the community is proverbially known to be wanting in saving-habits. It is a common thing to find a well-off Kayastha drained by fifty kindred drones fattening upon his acquirements. This happened to Siva Chandra, who also by nature was expensive in his tastes. He was an orthodox Hindu disposed largely to the observance of religious festivals. He celebrated all the principal *pujas*—Durga Puja, Dola-Jatra, Ratha-Jatra, and others. The Durga Puja was performed by him both at Calcutta and Konnagara. Living in this style at last led him out of his depth. His earning not sufficing, he spent away the patrimony left to him and to his brothers. Late in life he got into trouble. His brother Rajkrista, calling for his one-third share, went to law against him. Managing to get out of his embarrassments, Siva Chandra finally retired to Benares, the sacred abode for a Hindu in the last stage of his life.

CHAPTER II.

PATHSHALA, SCHOOL, AND COLLEGE LIFE.

LITTLE is known of Digambar's early life. His childhood was spent at Calcutta, where, according to Kristodas Pal, he "was reared up at his maternal uncle's house at Shambazar" Commonly, the fifth year of a Hindu boy is his abecedarian year. No doubt, Digambar, in orthodox style, commenced chalking his native alphabet in that year of his life, either under the household *Gurumahasaya*, or in the *Pathshala* of the neighbourhood. Now-a-days, the vernacular *pathshalas* have been improved on the model of European schools. But in the old *pathshalas*, fifty or sixty years ago, boys learned only ciphering and letter-writing. The utmost they were taught to read, consisted of a few lessons in *Chanakya slokas* and *Gurudakshina*.

Going through his initial Bengali training, Digambar took to his study of English. Two years before his birth, in 1815, the movement for our English education had commenced. Ram Mohan Roy had submitted an appeal in its favor to the Governor-General of the day. David Hare had begun his labors in its cause. In 1817, the Hindu College was opened. The School Society was also founded. In 1823, the Government came to the pecuniary aid of the Hindu College. By January, 1825, it was located in the new buildings on the north of the College Square. Under Dr. H. H. Wilson's supervision, it prospered to be the most noted seat of learning in the town. Opposite to it, on the south of the Square, was the School Society's school, generally called Hare's School. In this school Digambar began his study of English. He was then in his tenth year. On Babu Ramtanu Lahiri's authority, we state that "he and Digambar were admitted in Mr. Hare's school on the same day, in 1827. He was Digambar's senior in age, but they were both placed in the same class." Reading together for about three years, they became entitled to the privilege of being passed into the Hindu College, where they were admitted into Mr. Derozio's class. Rarely have pupils been so fortunate in a preceptor as those who enjoyed their tuition under Mr. Derozio. He was a gifted young man, hardly passed his twentieth year, who, had he lived to mature age, would have proved the intellectual and literary ornament of the East Indian community. The story of his first transforming the cold superstitious Bengali into an ardent reformer, transcends all stories of the kind. In November, 1826, he became a junior teacher in the Hindu College. Possessing affable manners, and entering into the feelings of his pupils with the fervour of a poetic mind, he grew extremely popular, and was followed as their leading master-spirit. With unwonted enthusiasm "he used to impress upon his pupils the sacred duty of thinking for themselves—to be in no way influenced by any of the *idols* mentioned by Bacon —to live and die for truth—to cultivate all the virtues, shunning vice in every shape. He often read examples from ancient history of the love of justice, patriotism, philanthropy and self-abnegation, and the way in which he set forth the points stirred up the minds of his pupils. Some were impressed with the excellence of justice, some with the paramount importance of truth, some with patriotism, some with philanthropy."* How he admitted his pupils to the precious treasures of Shakespeare, Milton, and Byron; how he charmed and excited the youths who listened to his clever metaphysical and religious lectures; how he breathed the love of virtue into them, developed new faculties within them, and opened a new future to them, are best portrayed in the following sonnet from his own pen.

"Expanding, like the petals of young flowers
I watch the gentle opening of your minds,

* Biographical Sketch of David Hare by Babu Peary Chand Mitra.

And the sweet loosening of the spell that binds
Your intellectual energies and powers,
That stretch, (like young birds in soft summer hours)
Their wings to try their strength O! how the winds
Of circumstance, and freshening April showers
Of early knowledge, and unnumbered kinds
Of new perceptions shed their influence ;
And how you worship Truth's omnipotence !
What joyance rains upon me, when I see
Fame, in the mirror of futurity,
Weaving the chaplets you are yet to gain
And then I feel I have not lived in vain.'

Such were the great advantages possessed by the students under Mr. Derozio. "The pupils," to quote again Babu Peary Chand Mitra, "who constantly sought for Derozio's company were Krishna Mohan Banerjea, Russik Krishna Mullick, Dakhina Ranjan Mukerjea, Ram Gopal Ghosh, Madhava Chandra Mullick, Ramtanu Lahiri, Mohesh Chandra Ghosh, Siva Chandra Deb, Hara Chandra Ghosh, Radha Nath Sikdar, Govind Chandra Bysack, Amrita Lall Mitra, and others, who may be called the *Young Calcutta.*" Digambar Mitra does not appear in this list. His friend Ramtanu is there, but his name is not mentioned. Most likely Babu Peary Chand has given the names of only those who were the most advanced and prominent, and has kept Digambar, who coming late in 1830 had not yet become particularly distinguished, in the mystery of "others." But, no doubt, he was the intimate fellow and friend of many of them, and was one of the "four hundred young men that attended Mr. Derozio's course of lectures on metaphysics in Hare's school." He must also have frequented the famous debates of the Academic Association, and was more or less interested in the liberal movements of the youthful hopes and leaders of that day. Those who were his most noted college contemporaries and comrades, and in whose association he imbibed noble sentiments and principles, have all joined the majority. The only surviving exception is Babu Ramtanu Lahiri. Born in 1813, he is now, in his 80th year, a hoary and venerable oracle for reference. He hath not been a leader like Krishna Mohan, a writer like Russik Krishna, or a speaker like Ramgopal. Babu Ramtanu Lahiri "hath borne his faculties meekly" is most remarkable for his overflowing "milk of human kindness." He is a moral hero, whose "virtues plead trumpet-tongued."

By the year 1830, when Digambar was transferred to the Hindu College, Derozio's lessons had accumulated in a body of stirring sentiment and thought. They had ignited the moral fusee that burnt slowly but surely to produce an explosion. Hindu Conservatism took alarm. The "root of the evil" being traced to Mr. Derozio, his dismissal was resolved upon. But he anticipated the resolution of the Managing Committee by tendering his resignation on the 25th April, 1831. Thus, in a twelve month, Digambar lost the advantages of his valuable instruction. But a room yet retains the odour though the flower has been removed ; a sound repeats itself in echoes after it has died away ; and a fire leaves its warmth when it has ceased to burn. So it was with Derozio, who left behind an enduring mark on the arena of his tuition. The spirit he had raised continued to exercise an influence for many a day to come. He had called forth a Frankenstein, which "grew with its growth and strengthened with its strength."

In the College, Digambar "would do whatever he liked. He was fond of sport, and so he walk ed about, jumped about, played about with the utmost freedom."* But he failed rot to make a noted progress in his studies. No anecdote of his educational life is remembered, excepting that he had on an occasion written a remarkably good essay. Mr. Hare thought so well of it that he brought it to the notice of Mr. J. C. C. Sutherland, who was Secretary to the General Committee of Public Instruction in those days, and as such occasionally visited the College. Mr. Sutherland liked it much, and, marking Digambar as a promising lad, looked upon him with a favourable eye from that day, and promoted his views in after-life. His friend Ramtanu left the College in 1833. Digambar remained till 1834. There were no scholarships in his time. The students then chiefly distinguished themselves in literature, and particularly so under the well-known D. L. R. With a view to

* The *Hindu Patriot's* obituary.

bring them up in general proficiency, the Junior and Senior scholarships were instituted in 1842. The early system, leaving a boy to his inclinations, imparted mostly a literary education. He was brought up in the study of poetry, rhetoric, history, geography, and philosophy; and he was exercised also in composition. But his reading being desultory, he acquired little more than a tone and taste. No professional knowledge paved his way to the world. He came out of the college-walls with "the key to the chest of learning" as Captain Richardson used to say, and was left to make use of the varied treasures it contained by self-exertion in after-days. The foundation for the future superstructure was sufficiently laid. In one important respect, however, the early batches were distinguished. They acquired a *principle*, upon which they seldom failed to act. Digambar came out with one, to which he held fast through good and evil with an unshaken constancy

CHAPTER III.

MARRIAGE, TUTORSHIP, AND OTHER SERVICES.

THE marriage of a Hindu boy in Bengal generally takes place in his teens, when he is too young to have all the necessary considerations about that important step in life, and many a time too modest to express an opinion about it himself. The choice of a match, therefore, is left to the parents and elders. Again, in a Kulin family, the observance of *Kul*, or marriage in a house of equal Kulinism, is so imperative a caste-rule as to override all other considerations. Out of the large community of the Kayasthas, Ballala Sena honored only three families with Kulinism—the Ghoshes, the Boses, and the Mitras. The first look-out of these families is confined to such a matrimonial connection as entailed no degradation in caste-rank. After due enquiry, a match was selected in an old well-to-do Bose-family of

Calcutta. In 1832, at his fifteenth year, while carrying on his collegiate studies, Digambar married the daughter of Babu Chunilal Bose, near the Cornwallis Square. This first wife dying in three or four years he married a second girl, the daughter of Babu Ballaram Sarkar, of Chorebagan.

By 1834, Digambar left his College. His father had now retired from business upon the little left after the wreck of his fortune. His younger brother was then in school. He had burthened himself with a wife. In this situation, it became necessary for him to commence life without delay. Though only seventeen years old, he was qualified in many respects for entering upon the hard business of the world. Bodily, he was made of strong nerves. He possessed an excellent capacity. His mind was formed by noble teachings. The example of his eminent college-predecessors and associates was his cynosure. And he was held in good opinion by all who knew him.

But, in those days, the outlook of an educated Native youth was confined to a small limited circle. He was not prepared like a young man of the present generation to take to the professions of law, or medicine, or civil engineering. The Chartar of 1833 had but recently given to the natives the privilege "of holding any office or employment under the government of the Company." Under this concession, "Chunder Saikur

Deb, Russik Krishna Mullick, Siva Chandra Deb, Govind Bysack, and Madhava Chunder Mullick were employed as Deputy Collectors." Hara-chunder Ghosh became a Munsif. They were the most meritorious and eligible candidates for first reward. Digambar could scarcely put forth his claim before his seniors. He had therefore to commence the great and important chapter that follows collegiate life with an humble start. He began with a tutorship. In this, he had before him the examples of Krishna Mohan Banerjea and his friend Ramtanu Lahiri, who served as teachers—the one at Hare's School, and the other in the Hindu College. There being no opening at Calcutta, Digambar went out upon a Mofasil appointment at the Nizamat School, in Murshidabad.

Between the years 1825 and 1837, the Nabob Nazim of Bengal was Humayunja. He was contemporaneous with Lords Amherst, Bentinck, and Auckland. In his time, the Nizamat School was established to teach Persian and Arabic to the members of the families in the service of the Nabob. An English class was afterwards opened, very probably on the Legislative enactment, in February 1835, for the use of the English language with Persian and Bengali in judicial proceedings and pleadings; and on Lord William Bentinck's famous Resolution of 7th March 1835 for "the promotion of European literature and science among the natives of India." Digambar was appointed to teach this English class. He owed the appointment to his patron Mr. Sutherland, who, as Secretary to the Education Committee, had the post at his disposal. The Nizamat School of old is now the High School of Murshidabad.

The time is not precisely known, but before long, Digambar resigned his employment in the Nizamat School. Tutorship was not to his liking. The pay was poor. The line was humble. It led not to progressive advancement—it promised not competence. He wanted to emerge from obscurity into distinction. In this state of mind, we behold the early indication of that resolute and persevering spirit which insured him success in after-life. Continuing for a year or so, he retired from schoolmastery, and, going over to Rampur Beauleah, took service under the Magistrate and Collector of Rajshai, as his Head Clerk, on a salary of Rs. 100 a month. This adventure also did not suit his taste. He returned in some six months back to Murshidabad, and tried a new berth—that of a Teshildar in the Government Khas Mehal This period of his history is involved in darkness. Scarcely any body is living who can throw light upon the interval. One or two conflicting reports have gained currency. According to Kristo Das Pal, he was now "an Amin, and worked for some years under we believe Mr. Russel, the Collector of Murshedabad. Mr. Russel was an Indian Nabob of the olden type, did very little work himself, and, as he found Digambar very intelligent and useful, he left almost the whole work of his office to him. It was here Digambar laid the basis of that accurate and comprehensive knowledge of the revenue system for which he afterwards became famous." According to the anonymous correspondent of the *Indian Mirror*, he was Tashildar of Hidaramdaspur, under Mr. Robert Torrens. During this Tashildari incumbency he got into a scrape. A subordinate Amin of his tampering with the records, altered the entry of certain "*bastu* or habitable lands for *garas* or unculturable holes." Digambar became liable to account for the offence. He made good his defence, and was honourably acquitted. But deeply feeling the injustice of the prosecution, he left his employment in the Collectorate, and served next as a clerk in the Native Infantry Lines at Berhampur.

This drifting from post to pillar lasted for three to four years. It did him one good. He got seasoned under vicissitudes, and schooled in varied experience. Towards the end of 1838, he met for a period with smooth sailing or respite from the buffets of a rugged life. Raja Kissen Nath Roy, of Kasimbazar, was then about to attain his majority. He was heir to the vast Zamindari estates left by Kanta Babu, the Banian, or personal Dewan, of Warren Hastings—the same that now belong to Maharani Sarnamoyi, and enable her to make her munificent donations and charities. The young Raja wanted an intelligent and upright Manager. Babu Digambar was on the spot, keenly looking out to come upon a rich vein. The Managership promised the means of living comfortably and honourably. Kristodas Pal says, he was "invited by the Raja's family." But it is more probable that he made the necessary interests, procured warm recommendations, got himself introduced to the Raja, and making a favourable impression carried away the prize.

The outside public is under the impression that Babu Digambar first became a tutor, and then stepped up to the position of the Manager. But he was not tutor as a drilling pedagogue, but a tutor like Mentor—a "guide, philosopher, and friend" of the young Raja, who stood not so much in need of lessons in black letter lore, as of being brought up in proper habits and well directed pursuits. The tutor under whom he learnt his English, was one Mr. Lambric, who was afterwards engaged to look after a Press, and publish a paper, in English and Bengali, called the *Murshedabad News.**

* The little information about Raja Digambar's Murshedabad life has been derived from certain letters of Babu Nilmoney Bysack to Babu Gobin Chandra Bysack that were kindly lent us by Babu Nilcamal Bysack for our perusal.

CHAPTER. IV.

THE MANAGERY. THE HARE MEMORIAL MEETING. DEATH OF RAJA KISSENNATH.

THE annals of Bengal point to many landed aristocracies in the last century—to Vishunpur, Birbhum, Bardwan, Krishnagar, Jessor, and Nator. Most of these ancient houses survive to this day, but shorn of their opulence. Their impoverishment resulted from a complication of causes. In our generation, negligence and supineness have ruined many Zamindars. But maladministration of the estates during minority, is the great evil from which several landed families have suffered. Its remedial measure called into existence the Court of Wards. In the times under consideration, the object of this beneficent institution was in a great measure carried out by a Manager combining intelligence with an administrative capacity. Such a character was Babu Digambar. Before the Hindu Wills and Majority Acts were law, one attained his majority in his 16th year. At this age, a young man of wealth is least inclined to any other thing than amusements and pleasures. Confiding his rich inheritance to Babu Digambar's management, the youthful Raja Kissen Nath, noted for his addiction to animated sports, kept a large kennel and stud, and was abroad on his vast estates, four or five days together, riding, hunting, and shooting.

Babu Digambar was at first taken into the service of the Raja on the monthly pay of 100 rupees. He became Manager on an increased allowance in the year 1840, on the Raja's majority. Certainly, in his 22nd year, he could scarcely have had the experience of those ex-official pensioner-Babus whose services are now engaged at high premiums. But he was a man of the right stamp, who, bringing his whole soul to the work, soon got over his short-comings. Raja Kissen Nath's appointment of a qualified Manager to administer his estates, is remarkable as the first precedent of its kind in Zamindari history. It was next improved to an imitation of the Councils of Government by Maharaja Mahatabchand of Bardwan, who had a body of enlightened advisers about him. Babu Digambar now lived at Kasimbazar. The Ranis bore him little good feeling. But he was a great favourite with the Raja. From time to time he had to come down to Calcutta, sometimes upon business, and sometimes with the Raja. He then used to travel by dawk, which brought him down in twenty-four hours.

For upwards of five years he went through the management, devoting to it the whole of his time and energy, and admirably fulfilling the trust reposed in him. An account of his administration would have been interesting, if the needed information were procurable. Little more can now be stated about it than that his measures and exertions laid the foundation of that prosperity, the benefit of which is now being reaped by the lady-proprietrix at present representing the family. This reasonable presumption is borne out and emphasised by the splendid reward of his services. The Raja was so well pleased with them, and felt so great a sense of obligation to him, that he made him the unprecedented present of a lac of rupees. We remember well the noise it made in its day. In the circles of his friends, he was thought to have made his fortune by one prodigious leap.

One of the occasions on which he came down with the Raja to Calcutta, was in June, 1842. It was shortly after Mr. David Hare's death, which occurred on the first of that month. No doubt, he came down expressly for the purpose of doing justice to the memory of his own and his country's great benefactor—to the man to whom we owe the most lasting debt of gratitude for "breaking our chains." No doubt, he brought down the Raja with him to enlist him in the cause of that justice. There cannot be a doubt also, that, at his suggestion, the young Raja called the Memorial Meeting of which the following account is given by Babu Peary Chand Mitra;—"On the 17th june 1842, Raja Kissennath Roy called a public meeting at the theatre of the Medical College, for the purpose of determining on the most suitable testimonial to be voted to the memory of David Hare. The meeting was numerously attended. Babu Prosanna Coomar Tagore took the chair. Babu Digambar Mitra, Captain D. L. Richardson, Babu Kissory Chand Mitra, and the Reverend K. M. Banerjea spoke at some length on the invaluable serviccs rendered by the deceased to the cause of native education, and on the warm interest taken by him in the general welfare and advancement of the natives. After some discussion it was resolved to vote a statue by a public subscription to be raised from among the Native community, and to appoint a Committee of the following gentlemen with power to add to their number

Raja Kissen Nath Roy.
Raja Satwa Charn Ghosal.
Babu Debendra Nath Tagore.
,, Nandalal Singhi.
,, Hara Chandra Ghosh.
,, Srikissen Singhi.
,, Baicanta Nath Roy Choudhary.
,, Ramgopal Ghosh.
Reverend K. M. Banerjea.
Babu Tarachand Chackrabarti.
,, Digambar Mitra.
,, Ramaprasad Roy.

Thus, with the Hare Memorial Meeting, which bore fruition in the noble statue that at first graced the Sanskrit College quadrangle, and now graces the compound between Hare's School and the Presidency College, is dated the earliest instance of Babu Digambar's public appearance, and his taking a part in public proceedings. No exertion has been spared to reproduce the first initial speech made on this occasion, but all attempt at exhumation has proved vain. Perhaps it did not see the light; and, left to languish in the obscurity of manuscript, it has irrecoverably perished.

Two yearsand four months after the above date, Calcutta, one morning, was startled with the news of a sensational occurrence. The nephew of an influential Native gentleman had been newly appointed the Sub-divisional Deputy Magistrate of Lalbag, in the district of Murshedabad. In his desire to distinguish himself by remarkable zeal, the novice over-acted his part. He made the most strenuous endeavours to drag Raja Kissennath to his court under a process of arrest. Pushed to a corner, the Raja secured his person from apprehension by taking refuge, in his Calcutta house at Jorasanko, from the jurisdiction of Mofasil law. He was there left alone to himself a prey to gloomy thoughts. Thinking it hopeless, in his own judgment, to get out of his toils, he preferred death to disgrace. He made up his mind, rode out early in the morning, returned home and, seating himself upon a chair with the muzzle of his gun beneath his chin, he pulled at the trigger with his feet and blew out his brains, which were found to have bespattered the ceilings of the room. Such is the melancholy story of the suicide of Raja Kissennath, on the 31st of October, 1844. It is a question whether he would have thus succumbed, if he had had the benefit of Babu Digambar's advice in his critical situation. The Babu had got him out from many serious scrapes. He was not at his elbow this time, or most probably he would have got him off once more. His absence is to be accounted for by the fact, that some time before this his connection had been dissolved, and he had bidden his farewell to the Raja. There had ensued a coldness, under which he had retired from the Managership. The story of that coldness, is simply the story of a disagreement occurring between a young aristocrat by birth, and an aristocrat by nature who would not act upon the maxim of Sadi :—"Should the prince at noonday say, it is night, declare that you behold the moon and stars." It is not that the Raja was merely generous out of the abundance of his wealth. He held the Manager in respectful regard, lived upon familiar terms with him, ate and drank off the same table with him. But Babu Digambar would not sink into a parasite—would not don his lord's livery. In the course of living together, he had many a time pointed out the laches in his conduct. His reproofs rankled in the mind of the Raja, who at last broke out in explosion caused by a trifling circumstance. On an occasion, the Raja had indented some wines from Calcutta, Liking them himself, he asked for Babu Digambar's opinion. Instead of a flattering response, he uncourteously pronounced them to be otherwise. The Raja took his fastidious objections in ill-humour. He alluded to his fault-finding discourteous spirit, and, in a fit of resentful out-spokenness, said that they could no more pull together. Babu Digamber at once bowed his conge, and left Kasimbazar. This incident happened about the middle of 1844. No statement has ever oozed out to the public as to the reasons for which Babu Digambar gave up his connection with the Raja. The anecdote published by us for the first time is not very likely, but it rests on the authority of a friend who heard it from Digambar himself.

CHAPTER V.

MANUFACTURES AND TRADE. THE COMMERCIAL CRISIS IN 1847. THE FALL OF THE UNION BANK.

THE Managership was an important era in Babu Digambar's life. In the outset, he had no definite object of pursuit—no particular aim in his view. He therefore took to any thing that came in his way. The Managership was a sphere in which he received a new education and development,—where he imbibed new ideas and experiences that determined the color of his future years. In the exercise of that office, his attention was not confined wholly to the tenures, revenues, and litigations of the Zamindari. Its administration opened a large field which he studied from many points of view. The indigo grown on the estates drew his notice. The patches of mulberry cultivation caught his eye. He noted the large silk-trade at Kasimbazar and its neighbourhood. He became acquainted with many dealers, mahajans, and bankers. They were all looked into not merely in a spirit of liberal enquiry, but with a prospective calculation and a purpose of future utilization. The fund of knowledge thus acquired prepared him for new lines—it provided him with a reserve to do service in case of an untoward contingency.

Such a thing happened by his resignation of the managery. It pitched him once more into one of those "downs" of life, that reduced him to the necessity of looking out for fresh fields and pastures. Leaving the Raja, he retired for a time to home-life in Calcutta But he was not the man to rust idly—he did not remain long without a decision, and a fresh cast of the die. Against service of any kind he had become deeply prejudiced. Naturally enterprising, he resolved upon following the bent of his mind, and trying the resources of his own energy. Trade had a great attraction in his view. Many of his contemporaries—Tarachand Chakrabarti, Peary Chand Mitra, Ramgopal Ghosh, and others, had taken to that pursuit of honourable fortune. He had laid in a large stock of information about its operations. The rich gift of the Raja had put capital into his pocket. Making up his mind as to the future course of his life, he made his start upon a new high-road towards the end of 1844.

The enterprise he launched upon was the manufacture of indigo and silk. Little business was done in Indian seeds before the Crimean war. Cotton and Jute thrived after the settlement of the Slavery-question in America. Equalization of duty had brought on the ruin of our sugar trade. Tea cultivation was not taken up till a quarter of a century afterwards. In Digambar's young days, the two most important trades were indigo and silk. The teeming number of factories noted on Tassein's old map, attests to the extent of the culture of those articles in those days. Considerable improvement in indigo had taken place under European process. It was then grown chiefly upon the alluvial tracts of Jessor, Krishnagur, and Murshedabad, in Lower Bengal. The factors held farms on long leases, and engaged cultivators by advances upon the crops. In their turn, they took advances upon the same terms from the Banks and Agency houses in Calcutta. The Union Bank did this sort of business very largely. Babu Digambar turned an indigo planter and manufacturer much in the style of his times. He carried on a factory in the vicinity of Murshedabad. But he made only the legitimate profits of the trade--and none by *zulm*. His dye was not stained "with human gore."

His silk business was on a much larger scale. This industry had also much improved under the commercial investments of the East India Company. But the charter of 1833 finally took away their trade-privileges. Their filatures were put up for sale. Scarcely was a private adventurer prepared to take them up. By 1840, the export of Bengal silk touched a very low figure Then came a re-action. In this state of the trade, Babu Digambar took to his silk business with a fair chance of success. He worked three filatures at Ramkhola, Rajapati, and Daulat Bazar in the district of Murshedabad, and set up a fourth concern at Sankar Mirzapur, near Jungypur. His silk was prepared and assorted after the European method. He had his own trade-mark bearing his initials DM., under which it was placed for sale in the market. It became a well known mark that readily found buyers, and fetched prices next to the qualities produced by Messrs. Watson & Co., the great silk merchants with whom lay his principal competition.

Babu Digambar never did a thing with a half heart. He devoted his whole soul to his new business. He spent the manufacturing months in the Mofasil, where he went through a personal supervision of his factories. During the sale-season, he came down to Calcutta for the disposal of his goods. In the course of his mercantile transactions, he became "familiar with the Gordons and Calders." Mr. Gordon was the Secretary of the Union Bank—a speculation in which people then largely put in their money. Babu Digambar followed the example of others. His dealings brought him in contact with Babu Dwarkanath Tagore, who had a large interest in the said Bank. He now became acquainted also with Babus Ramanath Tagore and Prasanna Coomar Tagore. Babu Dwarkanath Tagore was an enlightened native gentleman, who took a great interest in all intelligent and enterprising young men, and forwarded their views in a most liberal spirit. Babu Digambar greatly attached himself to him, and frequented his society. It was the best element in which he could move, and improve in "habit, thought, and spirit."

For about three years his business went on prosperously. But, in 1847, a great commercial crisis overtook the world. Several hundred bankruptcies occurred in England. In Calcutta, there were failures with the exception of one single firm. The fall of the Union Bank was the beaviest in the crash. Nearly all its stock was lent out and buried in Indigo Concerns. And in a state of general collapse, the out-turn of the season mostly sold for a song--for Rupees 50 a maund. Three fourths of its capital became a dead loss. Numbers lost their deposits. Public credit sustained a terrible shock. The law of Limited Liability was not then recognised in the commercial world. Joint-Stock Companies in those days incurred liabilities to make good the loss caused by their bad speculations. The Bank went into liquidation, and its shareholders were called upon to contribute quotas for payment to creditors. Many opulent native houses were drained by the heavy assessments. One family —reputed to be a millionaire one—making *benamis* to evade the payment, was so overwhelmed with ruin as to have become reduced now to the verge of beggary.

Babu Digambar was a heavy sufferer—so much so that he was nearly impoverished. He lost three-fourths of his lac invested in the shares of the Bank. But a calm after a storm, a tide after an ebb, an abundance after a scarcity, an excitement after a depression, is the law of nature. In other words, there came a re-action after the collapse. New firms rose on the ashes of the old ones. Credit flourished in rejuvenescence. Trade shook off its torpidity, and moved under a new impetus. Opportunities came on the wake of difficulties. Girding up his loins, Babu Digambar battled on with renewed efforts. His perseverence bore fruit in his laying by a purse after many shifting fortunes.

CHAPTER VI.

ZEMINDARI STATUS. THE BRITISH INDIAN ASSOCIATION.

PASSING, from 1834 to 1850, through a series of reverses and losses, Babu Digambar, after sixteen long years, came to the end of his hard struggles. Not that he was landed in luxurious affluence, without the desire of any further increments—without any more thirst of gold. In quest of wealth, the first object is the attainment of a competency. And this first goal was gained by him. Left by his father in straitened circumstances, he so far mended his lot as to have secured the means of an easy decent living. No more was he at tugs with fortune. His stars henceforth shed a gentler influence on his path.

Babu Digambar Mitra was now upwards of thirty years old. Hitherto, his time had been spent mostly in the Mofaşil. He now looked forward to living permanently in Calcutta. In carrying this intention into effect, he had not to close his business, but leaving his filatures in charge of his cousin Peary Mohan Mitra, son of his uncle Rajkrista Mitra, he shifted the scene of his career to Calcutta, in 1850-51. His father having parted with the house in Raja Navakrishna's Street, he took up his residence in the Bagmari garden, near Manicktala, in the suburbs, which was the only inheritance left to him in the shape of landed property.

Before the days of rail-roads and river-steamers, of educational institutions and press-publications, of libraries and literate associations, life in the Mofasil amounted nearly to a life in exile. The educated Calcutta-Babu languished there out of his element, and contracted a taint of rusticity from rural surroundings. Babu Digambar may have resided in Murshedabad and Kasimbazar---a quondam capital, where lived the Nabob Nazim and the descendants of Jagat Sett, where eminent Zamindars, and Mahajans, and ancient families made a polite society. But still it was a provincial theatre, where they lived in "dilettant speculations," with an absolute deadness of progressive opinions. The imperial metropolis then was far ahead of all other portions of the empire in intellectual progress, and Murshedabad comparatively was in the depths of moral torpor. In the Mofasil Babu Digambar missed the inestimable advantages of living in the Presidency. He missed the pleasures of association in the Society for the Acquisition of General Knowledge. He missed the pleasures of literary exercises in the *Gyananashan* and the *Bengal Spectator*. He missed the rich treat of George Thompson's political lectures to "the Chuckerbutty Faction," the nickname then given to Young Bengal by Mr. Marshman, in his *Friend of India*; and who compared the thundering speeches poured at the Fouzdari Balakhana to the actual thunderings then going on at the Bala Hissar, in Kabul. They who heard George Thompson M. P., heard in India what Parliamentary oratory was. David Hare had prepared the soil, on which George Thompson planted the first seed of Native political education in our country. His countrymen may have styled him Thompson the *Grievance-monger*, but to him is due the credit of having given the start to our political institutions. Returning to the society of Calcutta, and taking to the routine of metropolitan-life, Digambar rubbed away his Mofasil rust by companionship with his old chums, made new friendships, associated with the Tagores, frequented all those whom he valued and who esteemed him, and moved in the circles of "men of light and leading."

He had not returned to Calcutta for many months before his cousin Peary Mohan died of cholera, when he was obliged to retire from his silk-business, for want of a man on whom he could depend. But he did not wholly give up all business-life, and spend his time in idle cockneyism.

He took to a new field--to stock-dealing, in which he embarked most cautiously on the safest speculations. His active mind also led him to move on another tack. During his managership, he had not studied only the agriculture and industries going on about him. He had, at the same time, revolved in his mind the idea of utilizing his Zamindari experience by becoming a Zamindar himself, if ever he saw a chance that way in his prospect. This reasonable ambition was now gratified. A few years before this his patron, Mr. Sutherland, dying stricken down by apoplexy in bed, had left a landed property, Lot Dabipur, in the Twenty-Four-Parganas. Being put up for sale by his executor, Mr. Garstin, Babu Digambar, by a strange irony of fate, became its purchaser, in July, 1851. Not having the full amount of the necessary funds, he had to part with his Bagmari garden, and live in a rented house, in Lichi-Bagan, on the Circular Road. From this place he removed to a house in Bachu Chatterjea's Lane, where he resided until the purchase of his premises in Jhamapukur Lane, in 1853.

Babu Digambar very timely became a Zamindar on the eve of the foundation of the Zamindars' Association. There was the Landholders' Society, started by Babu Dwarkanath Tagore, with the object of protecting Zamindari rights and interests. Then there was the Bengal British India Society, which, in response to a Society of similar designa tion in England, had, on Thursday, the 20th April, 1843, been ushered into existence by the joint efforts of Mr. George Thompson, and of that small but determined band of rising-men, called Young Bengal—the Society which marked an era in native history by its being the earliest pioneer in the path of our political life. The one represented the aristocracy of wealth, the other the aristocracy of intelligence. The two bodies existed under different names, though many of their members were the same men, and who agreed on many points in their common purpose of political amelioration. Happily for the country, the hour of awakening had arrived, and they who languished mutually came to be of the opinion that disintegration was weakness, and union strength. So they turned their attention to the convergence of their efforts, and the reciprocated overtures for an alliance and amalgamation met with welcome from all concerned. The preliminaries being settled, the two bodies, dropping their different names, and bringing each to the other a reinforcement of strength, coalesced and merged themselves into one, under the common designation of the British Indian Association. This famous Native political institution, the parent of all political institutions in India, was founded on the 31st of October, 1851. The men, who, by drawing more closely to each other, effected its organization and turned over a new leaf, may well be judged of from the names of the members forming the first Committee. They are—

Raja Radhakanta Deb, *President.*
Raja Kalikrishna Deb, *Vice-President.*

Raja Satya Charan Ghosal, *Member.*
Babu Hara Cumar Tagore,
Babu Prosanna Kumar Tagore, ,,
Babu Ramanath Tagore.
Babu Joykissen Mukerjea,
Babu Ashutosh Dey,
Babu Harimohan Sen,
Babu Ramgopal Ghosh,
Babu Womesh Chander Dutt. ,,
Babu Krishna Kisar Ghosh,
Babu Jagadanand Mukerjea,
Babu Peary Chand Mitra,
Babu Sambhunath Pandit, ,,
Babu Debendranath Tagore, *Hony. Secretary.*
Babu Digambar Mitra, *Assistant Secretary.*

The amalgamation was a wise step, that invested the body with weight and authority in the public eye. No more could Government urge that there was a split between orthodoxy and enlightenment—between conservatism and liberalism, the two distinguished elements of native society. The vocation of the Association was also highly loyal. It proposed to be the interpreter between the rulers and the ruled—the only course left to a subject-people to deal in politics. Nothing could be nobler than its original starting-principle of broad humanity; and could the body always adhere to it with faithful allegiance, how worthy of all praise would it have been. But, in time, they began to prefer being distinguished by evanescent liveries and emblazonings to the approval of their consciences; and, merging their generous sympathies in Ego, they, instead of "loving themselves the last," as Shakspeare has put the words in the mouth of Wolsey, chose to love themselves in the first instance, and have, in their present phase, eventually degenerated into a "bunch of imbecility," who retain only an antiquarian flavour—who are fossil treasures without any intellectual vitality. Never has the country been so disappointed.

CHAPTER VII.

BEGINNING OF PUBLIC LIFE. THE CHARTER MEMORIAL.

HITHERTO our narrative has consisted of the incidents relating to Digambar learning in school ; to Digambar acting as a Manager, and getting trained for the part he was afterwards to enact ; to Digambar plying his trade ; to Digambar the private man. But we have now reached a period when the future pages of our biography shall contain an entirely new kind of interest. We shall see Digambar now as a public man influencing the policy of the State, and labouring effectually for the welfare of his country.

The career of Babu Digambar as a public man, dates from towards the end of the year 1851. It commenced with the establishment of the British Indian Association, with which he made his connection as much from ties of friendship and community of sentiment, as from the instincts of his natural liberalism. The Assistant Secretaryship appears to be a humble initiative, but, in fact, his office was the most important, because it required the capacity, energy, and judgment which few could bring to bear upon the discharge of its duties. In his exile and isolation in the Mofasil for a number of years, he may have got rusticated by provincialisms, and dropped behind in the race. But he did not return to his compeers of sharpened intellect and refined perceptions, as an exhumed mummy, or an obsolete letter, or an out-of-date uncurrent coin. The disadvantages he incurred, were amply compensated by his acquirement of that accurate knowledge of the details of inner life and of that diversified experience, for which there was no opportunity in the circles of cockneydom, and which could be picked up only in out-of-home life in the interior. He therefore proved a desirable colleague and valuable recruit to that representative conclave, in which none other was to be found like him. They gladly availed themselves of his services, and he made his connection with them serviceable in effecting his introduction into active public life.

It has already been stated, that the British Indian Association was the outcome of the fusion of composite groups of men, who wanted to move in harmonious action. The foremost men of wealth and influence, and the best of native tongues and pens were enlisted in its interest. A brilliant metamorphose of Crœsuses and

Brutuses with a new era of vitality, its success was immediate. It became popular almost in its very bud, and a recognised factor in its "mewling and puking" state. With the gaze of the community centred on their proud pre-eminence, and bound by their patriotic promises, the members could not sit down listlessly spending their time in dull association and volubility, but had to go straight to the discussion of the causes of the moral and political evils which they saw around them and lamented. In a little time, they had the accession of the famous journalist, Harish Chandra Mukerjea, into their body, and the benefit of his *Hindu Patriot* as a serviceable instrument for expressing their sentiments and acting on public opinion. Babu Digambar was a regular frequenter, who gave all the time he could spare from his other occupations to the furtherance of his country's cause.

One of the important questions, which, in the early stage of its existence, engaged the attention of the Association, was the approaching renewal of the East India Company's Charter, in 1853. It was a stirring event, which aroused all classes of people to come forward with their proposals. The earliest attempt at interference with the rights of the Company, was made by Fox's East India Bill, which, involving the virtual abrogation of their charter, failed in its purpose. It was Pitt who first inserted the thin end of the wedge by the institution of the Board of Control. Not, however, till the year 1813, did the first great inroad on the Company's exclusive privileges take place, by negativing their commercial monopoly, and throwing open the India trade to the general competition of the English nation. In 1833, the triumph of free trade principles did away with their monopoly of China trade. By 1853, improvements in the territorial administration of the Company engaged the consideration of the British Parliament. It appointed Select Committees of both the Houses to go into evidence. Petitions poured in from various quarters, praying for removal of grievances and suggesting reforms. The Indians, unused to public spirit in the furtherance of public objects, had never raised their voice before now. Having become awakened to the sense of their rights, they came in with their protests and demands. The British Indian Association took advantage of the opportunity to justify their promises by undertaking the advocacy. Its members ventured on an expression of their opinion, and submitted a humble memorial to the House of Commons. Babu Digambar, as Assistant Secretary, had mainly to draw this memorial. Babu Ramgopal Sanyal, in his *Biography of Bengal Celebrities*, states :—"We have the authority of no less a personage than the late Babu Ramgopal Ghosh, who, in his speech on the death of Harish Chandra Mukerjea, said that the famous petition sent from India protesting against the renewal of the Charter of the East India Company in 1853, was 'drawn up' by Harish Chandra himself." But, Babu Ramgopal Ghosh did not say anything more than the following :—"As the Editor of the

Hindoo Patriot he did an immense good. When that paper was first started, a great question came under discussion, namely, the Charter Act. In the elucidation of that measure he took an active and prominent part." * Besides, we have on our side the authority of Babu Kristodas Pal, who seldom erred in such matters. One important fact that gives weight to our statement, is that the duty of drawing the memorial lay with the Assistant Secretary, who certainly acted in consultation, and worked upon the suggestions of his colleagues. We have no doubt that Babu Harish Chandra largely advised in the matter.

The following extract from it, is put in as an interesting specimen of the Association's earliest proceedings, at the same time that it fitly claims space in our pages in connection with the subject of our sketch. Proceeding with the following preliminary representation

That your petitioners are desirous of bringing to the notice of your Hon'ble House the sentiments entertained by themselves, and the most intelligent part of their native fellow-subjects all over the country, on those points which, in their humble opinion, ought to be taken into consideration at the period of the termination of the Charter, granted to the East India Company, by the Act passed in the reign of His late Majesty King William the Fourth, entitled an Act for effecting an arrangement with the East India Company and for the better Government of His Majesty's Indian territories, till the 30th day of April, 1854. As subjects of the Crown of Great Britain, the Natives of this country entertain the deepest sentiments of loyalty and fidelity to Her Majesty, and sincerely desire the permanence of the British supremacy in India, which has ensured to them freedom from foreign incursions and

* The *Hindoo Patriot*, July 17th, 1861.

intestine dissensions, and security from spoliation by lawless power. Placed by the wisdom of Parliament, for a limited time and on certain conditions, under the administration of the East India Company, they have enjoyed the blessings of an improved form of Government, and received many of the advantages incidental to their connection with one of the greatest and most prosperous nations. They are impressed with a sense of the value and importance of these and similar benefits and of their obligations to the nation from which they have, under Providence, derived them. They cannot but feel, however, that they have not profited by their connection with Great Britain to the extent which they had a right to look for. Under the influence of such a feeling, they regarded with deep interest the enquiries conducted by Committees of both Houses of Parliament, between the years 1831 and 1833, preparatory to the passing of the last Charter Act. The fact of such enquiries being on foot, suggestive as it was of great administrative reforms, induced the people, who were unaccustomed to make any demonstration of their sentiments respecting the acts and measures of their rulers, to wait the result of the deliberations of the Imperial Parliament.

2. That the principal changes made by the above-mentioned enactment, consisted in the increase of the powers of the Crown and the Board of Control over the Court of Directors, and those of the Supreme Government over the Subordinate Governments ; in the power of legislating for all classes which was confined in the Supreme Government, and, as auxiliary thereto, the appointment of a Law Commission and of one member not of the Civil Service to the Supreme Council ; in the extension of the powers of the Governor-General when absent from the Council ; in the admission of British subjects to trade in China, and to hold lands in India ; and in the increase of the ecclesiastical establishment, for the benefit of professors of the Christian religion, at the expense of the general revenue of the country. But no provision was made for introducing those benefits which the circumstances of India notoriously required ; such as the relaxation of the pressure of the revenue system by lightening the land tax where it was variable, or erecting public works of utility,

calculated to develop the resources of the country and promote the growth and increase of commerce and manufactures;—the improvement of the system of judicial administration, by the selection of qualified officers, the appointment of proper ministerial officers, the abolition of stamps in law proceedings, and other salutary measures: the protection of life and property by the employment of a police adequate to the purpose in point of numbers and discipline, under the control of a proper number of experienced magistrates;—relief from the gigantic monopolies which the East India Company maintained very inconsistently with their position as rulers;—the encouragement of the manufactures and commerce of the country, which had been greatly depressed in consequence of throwing open the trade with India;—the education of the people on an adequate scale, for which the grant of a lac of rupees, authorised by Parliament, in 1813, was manifestly insufficient; arrangements for the appointment to the higher offices of persons better qualified by their experience, capacity, and knowledge of the languages and laws of the country, than those who were heretofore sent out, usually before they had emerged from the state of adolescence;—and the admission of the natives to a participation in those rights which are conceded by all constitutional Governments, and which would qualify them to enjoy the benefit of free institutions at a future period. The only privilege conferred on the natives was the declaration in Section 89 of the above mentioned Act "that no native of the said territories, or any natural born subject of His Majesty resident therein, shall, by reason only of his religion. place of birth, descent, colour, or any of them, be disabled from holding any place, office or employment under the said Company."

3. That the natives of this country were disappointed in the expectation they had formed, that the Charter of the Company, if renewed, would be so modified as to provide for some of those administrative reforms which were called for, and also to secure to them some of those civil and political rights, which they considered themselves entitled to, even without reference to their position as subjects of the British Crown. That feeling of disappointment has been, if possible, deepened by their perceiving that, notwithstanding the declaration just

recited, the natives of India, with one or two exceptions of very recent date. have not been appointed to any but subordinate offices under the Company, such as were very inferior in point of repectability and emolument to the posts held by the youngest of their civil servants.

4. That after being in much uncertainty as to the intentions of Her Majesty's Government to make enquiries into the affairs of India, with reference to the approaching termination of the Company's Charter, your petitioners have learnt with satisfaction of the appointment of Committees of both Houses of Parliament, to take into consideration the mode in which the Government of the British possessions in India is in future to be conducted. They cannot disguise from themselves the difficulties which those Committees will experience, in endeavouring to ascertain the nature and results of the administration of the East India Company. The evidence acessible to them will be chiefly of parties, who are more or less interested in the maintenance of the present system of the British Indian administration, and, who cannot be expected, even were some of them free from a natural bias, to enter into the feelings and wants of a people widely differing from them in religion, manners and habits. But your petitioners rely on the wisdom and justice of your Hon'ble House, to give due consideration to the representation which they are emboldened to submit by the consciousness that, though differing in religion and color, they are your fellow-subjects and that their claims as such will not be disallowed.

5. That your petitioners submit that it is for many reasons fit and proper that the period of such arrangements should be shortened, in order to bring the merits and working of them sooner under the review of Parliament. The Governments of remote dependencies of the Empire are generally liable to be ill-conducted, particulary when those dependencies are of the magnitude to which Her Majesty's dominions in India have at this day attained, and when there are various and dependent boards, and the grounds of their proceedings cannot be scrutinized by the public, except by the publication of correspondence by order of Parliament. It seems of paramount importance, therefore, that the administration of India should be more frequently brought under the revision

of the Supreme authority. An appeal to facts will corroborate the argument. By the last three Charters, the government of the British Indian territories was continued to the East Indian Company, for terms of twenty years; but however urgently reforms and improvements in the system of Government might seem to be required, none could virtually be introduced till the expiration of that long period. Accordingly, it required that period before British subjects were permitted to exercise their natural right of residing in, or even of trading with, this part of their sovereign's dominions, and another like period before they were permitted to enter into the trade with China, which was open to all other nations. If British subjects had to wait such protracted periods in breaking through a monopoly, the natives of India cannot have a better prospect of obtaining reforms which they may pray for, or rights which may be admitted to be unjustly withheld from them. Your petitioners are therefore most anxious that the term of the arrangements which may be next entered upon for the government of this country should not be extended beyond one year

the memorial next dwells particularly on the several heads then demanding urgent consideration. The amplified details swelling out into a lengthened statement, we have, out of regard to the readers' patience, thought proper barely to allude to those heads, which refer seriatim to the following important matters.

(1) The Home Government (2) The Government of India (3) Relations of the Governor-General with the Council (4) The Legislative Council (5) Laws made by the Executive in disregard of remonstrances (6) Plan of the Legislative Council (7) Powers of the Legislative Council and the Supreme Council (8) Control of Parliament (9) Declaration of non-interference with the religion of the natives (10) Local Governors (11) Appeals from the Governors (12) Economy in the Public Service (13) The Civil Service (14) The Judicial system (15) Union of the Supreme and Sudder Courts (16) Courts in the interior (17) The Police and Magistracy (18) Monopolies (19) Revenue officers (20) Education (21) Eccleciastical Establishment

In its entirety, the paper is not without merit. It may not be remarkable for attic elegance of language, or sonorous stilted periods. But judging from the selection and summary, the clear statement of facts, and the complete mastery of details, it is a clever matter-of-fact review that takes the vast compass of the question, with reference to all the points then bearing on the requirements of the country, and necessary to form the subject of inquiry.

It is not known, how far regard was paid to this Native memorial sent from India. But some of the points urged therein appear to have effectually influenced legislation. Formerly, the Company's charter used to be renewed every time for twenty years. But, in 1853, it was renewed for so long as Parliament should see fit, and not for a definite period. In spite of the provision, made in unqualified terms by the Charter Act of 1833' for the unlimited eligibility of the Natives of India to all offices whatsoever without exclusion of any person on account of caste, color, or creed, the Court of Directors had set it at nought and made it unfructuous by reserving the Covenanted Civil Service of India exclusively for the Europeans. But on this occasion, the monopoly of patronage in their hands was taken away to make room for the principle of open competition, and the days of evasion and abuse were numbered.

CHAPTER VIII.

THE BLACK ACT MEETING.

"IN early life," Kristodas Pal says, "Digambar mixed more with the non-official Europeans. He was familiar with the Gordons and the Calders, the Stocquelers and the Hurrys, and took an active part with them in the political warfare of the day. He generally fought unseen, for he did not like to push himself forward, and rarely came to the fore." In time, he threw off his anonymous veil, and openly took to the arena. His first undisguised public effort, in concert with his colleagues, was the Charter-memorial, in 1853. Not, till after the lapse of four years, had he an opportunity to make his first public appearance as a speaker, on the occasion of the great Black Act Meeting. The proper understanding of this subject, requires it to be introduced by a cursory retrospect of facts referring to the origin and progress of the quarrel, and which scarcely find a historian. The battle of Plassey laid Bengal open to the territorial sway of the British. But thirty years passed in vacillation between the Company as Dewan and the Nabob as Nazim—between a masked administration and the open assumption of the responsibilities of empire—between the experiments of Native and European agencies in alternation, during which the country suffered from endless disorders and abuses of the English rule. Little patch-work reform was attempted by the Regulating Act of 1774. But the years of Warren Hastings' rule, were years of one long misrule from the native point of view. Up to his time, the country was administered by Naib Dewans such as Mahomed Reza Khan and Sitab Roy, who received nine lacs of rupees a year. There was the Native Fouzdar, Raja Nandakumar, who annually drew 60 to 70 thousand rupees for his salary. There were native Kazis, Muftis, and Pandits, such as those that sit at the feet of Warren Hastings' statue at the Town Hall, for administering civil justice. But Lord Cornwallis decided upon employing European functionaries, and closed the door of public service to the Bengalis; and from 1793 "the highest salary given to a Native did not exceed a hundred rupees monthly." This law of exclusion, ignoring all native talent and ambition, was inexorably acted upon till 1831, when there was a fresh epoch under Lord William Bentinck. Impressed by the impolicy and injustice of Cornwallis' Code, his Lordship introduced a more generous system, and, by tentative admission of Natives to various offices, relieved the country from the dead-weight of many indolent and incompetent European Official-Nabobs. In endorsement of his Lordship's views, the Charter of 1833 also enacted that "no native, nor natural born subject of His Majesty, resident in India, shall by reason of his religion, place of birth, descent, or colour, be disabled from hold ing any office or employment under the government of the Company." The gate to public service being thus re-opened, the law began to operate by the admission of educated natives to high judicial posts, with increase of their jurisdiction and salaries.

With the enlistment of Native ability, the Charter also created the Legislative Council, and a Law Commission for improved legislation. The well-known Macaulay came out entrusted with the codification of a uniform body of laws for all India. About Macaulay, there prevails a mis-impression that needs removal. Writing from person al knowledge not extending beyond Chowringhee, he penned that "deceit is to the Bengali, what the paw is to the lion, or the sting is to the bee." The iron of his trenchant remark pierced the soul of Young Bengal, and to this day they wax wroth at the antiquated libel left standing on record. But they should magnanimously forgive and forget the sting in the immense good that has accrued from his noble advocacy of our education in the wholesome literature and science of Europe. It was Macaulay also, who, in the course of his law-making, proved his true devotion to the British Themis by, first of all, looking with an equal eye upon the conqueror and the conquered, and endeavouring to efface the humiliating distinction that existed between the Europeans and Natives in the dispensation of Justice. His enunciation of the right-minded principle does him the highest honor : the moral courage to do it calls forth our admiration. But it was one thing to carry on the championship in the battle of the Anglicists and Orientalists, and another to achieve the enforcement of his convictions. By the year 1837, he fulfilled his legislative mission by the completion of that Penal Code, which now has the force of Criminal Law throughout British India. He had given his closest attention to its construction, and enriched it with all those improved and enlightened principles of criminal jurisprudence, which had been elaborated by the ablest jurists in Europe and America. But it shared the unpopularity attached to his name, and was unscrupulously and indiscriminately assailed by his countrymen. They acknowledged him to be a brilliant rhetorician but not a lawyer, and denounced his levelling-principle of equality as ultra-liberal. The irritated Turtons, Dickenses, and Clarkes of the day censured his theory in no measured terms. They cried down his Act as the Black Act, a cant that for the first time now came into fashion. Such was the success of the agitation, that the code was at once shelved as a failure, and not mentioned for years without contempt.

Under the Company's rule every vice, which is the offspring of unchecked authority and insatiable avarice, had grown rampant in India. The principles of upright government were made subservient to selfish necessities. To secure money was the first concern: to show mercy and do justice the second. Brought up, from the days of Clive's double-treaty, in the traditions of aggression, dethronement, spoliation, and extortion, the British adventurers in India consider high-handed proceedings, with immunity from their consquences, as their time-honored privilege grown out of the strange and anomalous way in which the British Indian Empire has come into being, and which has gradually acquired the force of prescription from long enjoyment. In human nature, this privilege cannot but be dearly prized where avarice, coupled with authority, has to steal a march with giant steps, and where society, full of anomalies and gross abuses, makes light of unrighteous proceedings. Hence, every attempt to tamper with it has been systematically, resolutely, and vehemently opposed by successive generations of Anglo-Indians with murmurs and remonstrances. To part with it, would be to part with the greatest resource in raising fortunes out of the substance of ruined aliens—to lose the philosopher's stone.

But, ever and anon, there were those upright

and fearless few—the salts of their nation, who deeply regretted the inequality of law and expostulated against its injustice. The Supreme Court of Judicature was the first outcome of this righteous feeling, and the first fetter put upon licence. Next, by an Act passed in 1813, the British Parliament enacted that, for the better protection of the Natives of the country, the Anglo-Indians, hitherto entirely exempt from the jurisdiction of the Company's Criminal Courts, should be liable to be tried in them, and punished with fines to the extent of 500 Rs. in all cases of assault, forcible entry, or other injury accompanied with force. Then, by the Charter of 1833, the permission for Europeans to purchase lands and settle in India, was taken care of to be accompanied with the institution of the Legislative Council, which was empowered to make laws for all courts, all persons, and in all matters, upon principles of equity. The Court of Directors also lost no time in writing to the Indian Government, that, "in their view, it would be impossible to fulfil the obligation of protecting the natives of India from insult and outrage, unless both Natives and Europeans were rendered responsible to the same judicial control. There can be no equality of protection, where justice is not not equally, and on equal terms, accessible to all." In those days, the Anglo-Indian community, amenable only to the jurisdiction of the Supreme Court in the Presidency, enjoyed complete immunity of trial, both in civil and criminal matters, by the judicial and magisterial officers of the

Company. The Legislative Council, entering upon its duties, first of all tried to carry out the recommendation of the Directors by subjecting the Europeans, in 1836, to the civil jurisdiction of the Company's Courts. Loud was their outcry to appear before native Munsifs and Sadar Amins. But half the strength of Sampson was broken by this first step. He "champed the bit, and foamed in fetters," till, in time, he became reconciled to the inevitable.

Subsequently, three or four Acts were passed in the spirit of those instructions, and directed to the same object. One of these was the *Mochalka* Act, passed in 1848, to enable "a magistrate to take penal recognizances from British subjects, not convicted of any specific offence, whenever he may have good reason to apprehend any breach of the peace. In default of any such recognizances, parties may be committed to the civil jail. The object of this very proper enactment was, to enable men charged with the preservation of life, property, and the public peace, in a large district, to prevent those disgraceful outrages, by which in Lower Bengal especially, men have long insulted the civil power. Of course there was the usual amount of clamour raised against the Act by the Europeans, who hate subjection of all kinds, and who only begin to discover the inefficiency of the courts when those courts are likely to check their turbulence and insubordination. But the working of the law has proved its own vindication. There is an appeal from decisions passed under this Act. No man has been unjustly confined under its operation. British subjects have been more circumspect and amenable to reason. Affrays have been more rare. No sensible man now makes this law his grievance." *

In 1849, there was an important enactment for the trial of felony, murder, and other aggravated offences, committed by British subjects in the territories of a foreign or independent Prince.

Thus, step by step, with unwavering steadiness, the ground was broken, and gyves were laid on. But the shackles of civil enactments were not enough. The half-pinioned Indo-Britisher was still invincible. His strength lay stored in his exemption from criminal jurisdiction. Under this ægis, he kept law at arm's length, and seldom came to trial for his excesses and outrages. The truculent Mahomedan or Mahratta, was, in his day, a tyrant from fitful caprice, from lax police and unchecked licence. The cold, calculating Anglo-Indian, is a tyrant from prescience—from his consciousness of being able to give the slip to law. The individual Mahomedan, without knowledge and organization, was a petty tyrant, within a petty circle. But the individual Britisher, with his superior intelligence and energy, *sultanises* every-where in the interior as an infinitesimal representative of the sovereign : † "when he be-

* Marshman, *Calcutta Review.*

† Sir James Mackintosh called Lord Wellesley "a Sultanised Anglo-Indian."

comes the tyrant, the tyrant is everywhere; it is the universal presence of a universal Tiberius." Hardened in the creed that high-handedness and bahadooring are indispensables in an Indian career, and armed in his panoply of privilege, the European in India stands ready booted and spurred to ride, surrounded by thousands ready saddled and bridled to be ridden. He is scarcely withheld by scruples from the temptation of wrong, when wrong promises to be an accessory of success. It happened that his frailties overpowered his judgment many a time, and the country suffered from the oppression of knowledge over ignorance, of wealth over poverty, with a resort now and then to a brace of pistols. His misdeeds seldom transpired to the public, and almost invariably escaped without penalty. His murders were out in one instance out of ten—and that one commonly broke down in trial and turned out to be either a case of spleen-rupture from a kick under provocation, or death from a stray shot without malice. The enormous distances which the bulk of suitors and witnesses had to travel, and the delays at the seat of law to which alone the culprit was liable, formed impediments highly to his favor and convenience. In this state of things, the thought uppermost in the minds of the wisest and ablest servants of the Government, was to do away with the remaining half of the privilege, and make British subjects amenable to the Magistrates and Criminal Courts of the Company. The subject had been long under discussion, and the

Members of the Council and Law Commission, together with the Judges of the several Supreme Courts, at last pronounced their opinion decisively, though tardily, that the anomaly, rooted in self-interest, should be permitted no longer to exist. The year 1849-50 is most remarkable for this legislation, and for the political controversy of no common interest and importance it occasioned. In that year, the Legislative Council put forth the Drafts of four Acts, all purporting to bring British-born subjects under the jurisdiction of the East India Company's Courts, and the laws administered by them.* Alarmed Anglo-Britishism at once started up in arms. The anti-reform party, with wrath heated to the boiling temperature, rose to a man throughout the Indo-European non-official world to guard their privilege with inflexible pride against encroachment. The Presidency towns rang with indignant declamation abounding with sophisms. The party-press was full of diatribes. A large meeting was held in Calcutta, at which the conduct of Government was vehemently denounced, and the Acts were styled the Black Acts. It was determined to memorialize the Home authorities and the Parliament against the atrocious measures. A subscription was opened, and the sum of 36,000 Rs. was subscribed to meet

* 1. Draft of an Act for abolishing exemption from the jurisdiction of the East India Company's Criminal Courts

2. Draft of Act declaring the Law as to the privileges of Her Majesty's European subjects.

3. Draft of an Act for the protection of Judicial Officers.

4. Draft of an Act for trial by Jury in the Company's Courts.

the expenses. Mr. Theobald, the Prothonotary, and Mr. Seton-Karr, a Civilian, came out in the *Calcutta Review*—the first with a paper on the "Bengal Penal Code," and the other, with a paper on "Our Judicial System," both expressing temperate views. The only Native pen taken up on the occasion, was that of Babu Ramgopal Ghosh, who recorded "A few remarks on certain Draft Acts, commonly called the Black Acts," and opposed himself to express the current of Native feeling on the subject. Seldom was excitement more clamorous, or misrepresentation more effectual. Hitherto, the natives and non-officials had borne love to each other—they were at one and friends. Of their class was David Hare, the greatest benefactor of India. But after this event, punctilious national pride on the one hand, and heart-burning on the other, have converted them into bitter foes, and the antagonism between the races has become so intensified as to permit no sincerer approachment.

High rants and vituperative harangues once more succeeded to prolong the day of privilege, and defer that of justice. The memorialists won their game. Orders came out from the Home authorities suspending the Black Acts. They in England considered that India was not ripe yet for those Acts. The exemption being perpetuated, the storm subsided. Three years passed away in quiet, when a fresh fetter was forged for those who held that they carried about with them from the Thames to the Hughli, ready packed up with their out-fit, the indefeasible rights and privileges of Englishmen. "The first remarkable law of the year 1853," says Marshman, "is one, against which there would have been a tremendous out-cry formerly, but which passed without even a muttered growl. It is in reality the first of the Black Acts, which made British subjects liable to the same duties and punishments as Natives, in respect of public charges and duties in aid of the police. This is the introduction of the thin end of the wedge, and we have no doubt, that in due time, Planters and Zamindars, Native and European, will be placed on a much more equal footing in their respective dealings with the Mofasil courts."

The objections most vehemently urged and emphasised by the memorialists, were the absence of improved Courts, and the want of an enlightened code of Criminal Law for India The Courts existed very much as they did. The Indian Criminal Statute Book was "a patch-work of Mahomedan precepts, British Regulations, and legal precedents." This motley collection was not a code in accordance with the progress, the spirit, or the wants of the age. The last desideratum was at once sought to be removed. There lay the Macaulay Code, slumbering for years on the shelf of the Legislative Council. That code, the product of a philosophical genius, was taken down, and, on examination, was discovered to be admirably adapted to the wants of India, after its revision by the first lawyers in the service of the Crown and the Company. Lord

Dalhousie determined to utilize the labors of Macaulay, by placing his revised code in the hands of the Legislative Council for fresh revision and publication. The Council assiduously went through the task for its speedy submission to His Excellency, and for transmission to the public authorities in England.

At the same time that they were engaged upon the completion of the Penal Code, they proceeded also with the preparation of a Criminal Procedure Code, without which the former could not come into operation. The last was ready by January 1857, when the Hon'ble Mr. Peacock, then at the head of the Law Commission, moved the first reading of a Bill "for extending the jurisdiction of the Courts of Criminal Judicature of the East India Company in Bengal, for simplifying the Procedure thereof, and for investing other Courts with Criminal Jurisdiction." In that Bill was a clause that laid the axe at the root of their ancient privilege, and meant to exact from the British-born subjects a rigorous account for all defaults and sins from which they had hitherto escaped scot-free. It was the old attempt, and there was the old game of opposition, and the old blatant cry. The Chamber of Commerce, the Trades Association, the Indigo Planters' Association, and all European British subjects interested in the agitation, unanimously called a meeting at the Town Hall. Harangues, the out-come of minds distempered by party-spirit, were poured forth in profusion. The

Anglo-Indian Press, lacking argument, took to abuse, and in virulent articles styled the Company's Magistrates and Judges "full-fledged Civilian Eagles." Legal gentlemen got up an indictment, wholly ignoring that the burden of proof lay with them. Their cause was taken up in the Legislative Council Chamber by Sir Arthur Buller, a Supreme Court judge, in whose fervid description the Mofasil Jails were "cutcha-hovels in Feverpur or Cholerabad."

But as the inevitable had now arrived—as legislation would no longer tolerate inequality of justice, the discontent and chafing evaporated in petitions praying "against so much of the Bill as proposes to entrust powers of imprisonment to Native Officers in the two lower Courts, and for such amendments as will ensure competent and independent Judges in the two higher Courts." It was no more the old cue. They no more trod the old ground, but gave a new direction to their apprehensions. The question was now made to turn upon a new pivot. It now hinged upon pride of birth and domination of race. Representing themselves to be surrounded by envenomed aliens, they prayed to be safe from their tender mercies by means of legal hedges and precautions —they insinuated that they should be protected by fellow-feeling and favouritism. The petitions were referred to the Select Committee on the Bill. They were followed by one from the Armenians of Calcutta and Dacca—*Et tu Brute*, praying that "whatever Criminal Law may be passed for

British-born subjects may be extended to the Armenians domiciled and inhabiting within the territories of British India."

More than one reason led the Native community to bestir themselves on the occasion. It had been dropped by Sir Arthur Buller, in the course of his speech, that the Natives "were inspired with no traditionary reverence for equal laws or incorruptible justice;" that they "found in the existing Courts a safeguard far better than any that their forefathers ever enjoyed or dreamt of, and were content with them;" that they were "not animated by the feelings of an Englishman against privileges"; that they "felt no grievance at British subjects being tried by Juries;" and that if they objected, they did it not "from any constitutioual or philosophical enthusiasm in favor of an abstract principle, but simply because they saw and felt that it had become a practical nuisance."

Indeed, "the Bengalis are reticent, self-contained, distrustful of foreign observation, in a degree without parallel among other equally civilized nations. The Bengali bears existence with a composure that neither accident nor chance can ruffle. He becomes silently rich or uncomplainingly poor. The emotional part of his nature is in strict subjection; his resentment enduring, but unspoken; his gratitude of the sort that silently descends from generation to generation. Their taciturnity is maintained to such lengths that during the famine of 1866, it was found impossible to render public charity available to the female members of the respectable classes, and many a rural household starved slowly to death without uttering a complaint or making a sign."* But in Calcutta, they retain little of this old national characteristic. Instead of being reticent, Young Bengal have become demonstrative and garrulous to a degree. On the occasion under notice, they did not idly sit by under the reproach of apathetic silence, but braced themselves up for a worthy effort. The British Indian Association could not allow it to pass unchallenged. They resolved to be outspoken, and entered on the onslaught. In reply to the meeting of the European community, they held a counter-meeting of their own countrymen in the Town Hall, on the 6th of April, 1857. It was the great Native Black Act Meeting, otherwise called the Non-Exemption Meeting, held in support of the Bill then before the Legislative Council. The assemblage was as numerous, as it was conspicuous by the presence of the elite of the Native Community. There were present all those who represented the wealth and rank of the country, and that band of intellectual athletes who were then most noted for their enlightenment and public spirit. Besides, there were a few European gentlemen, among whom was Mr. George Thompson, who had occasion to come out a second time to India. From unavoidable circumstances Raja Radhakanta Deb had been obliged

* Hunter's *Annals of Rural Bengal.*

to be absent, and the meeting was therefore presided over by Raja Kalikrishna Deb. But Raja Radhakanta failed not in expressing his cordial sympathy with the meeting through the medium of the following public letter, which is remarkable as much for the moderation as for the urbanity of its language, and holds in preservation the opinion of a most dispassionate authority on the subject.

The object of our meeting is to consider the propriety of supporting that portion of the Draft of a Law now before the Legislative Council of India, which refers to the extension of the Criminal jurisdiction of the Moffasil Courts to all classes of Her Majesty's subjects without respect of religion, race, or place of birth.

The Penal Code of India, with reference to the jurisdiction of the Company's Criminal Courts as it now exists, is of a most objectionable character. It would not, I believe, be irrelevant to state here its principal features.

1st. Natives and all Europeans (not British-born subjects) are amenable to the authority of the Magistrates and Sessions Courts, within whose jurisdiction they are apprehended and brought to trial. But European British subjects, for all acts of a criminal nature, are amenable only to Her Majesty's Supreme Courts, and exempted from the jurisdiction of the local authorities in the administration of the Penal Enactments of the Government of India—53. Geo. III. Chapter. 155 Sec. 105 Beng : Reg. II, 1796 Sec. 2 Cl. 1.—Ceded Prov. Reg. VI, 1803 Sec. 19, Cl. 1 and Const No. 1296.

2nd. In the event of any charges being preferred against European British subjects which may render them liable to a Criminal prosecution in Her Majesty's Courts, the process is so circuitous, dilatory, expensive, and productive of such infinite inconvenience and trouble to the prosecutors and witnesses, especially if they belong to the class of poor Rayats and cultivators, that they (the European British-born subjects) are virtually allowed to commit crimes of the most heinous nature with impunity.

3rd. There are some petty offences for which, indeed, a European British subject can be tried by a Moffasil Magistrate, but convictions in such cases are removable by a Writ of Certiorari to the Supreme Court —53 Geo: III Chap. 155, Sec. 105.

4th. So great is the privilege of a European British subject that if a Native, happily, happen to be a brother felon with him, the Magistrate will not be able to try him (the Native) without a reference to the Nizamut—C. O. No. 79 Vol I.

5th. The Magisterial authorities have not even the power to interrogate a European British subject before them, for any alleged offence upon matters charged against them—C. O. No. 99 Vol III.

Such are some of the most odious features of a Law, unworthy the enlightened principles of the liberal Government of one of the most civilized nations in the world, which the proposed humane enactment intends to obliterate from the Penal Code.

It is indeed strange that the British Legislature should have delayed so long to pass a law founded upon the broadest principles of justice and humanity, and stranger still that many of the British inhabitants of India should protest against the enactment, and stigmatize it by christening it "the Black Act."

The Law proposed would strike at the foundation of an inhuman principle. Far from deserving the epithet "Black Act," I would call it the "White Act." It should be likened to the sun in his meridian splendour shedding the refulgent beams of justice on all classes of people equally, and dim indeed are their eyes with prejudice who cannot behold its genuine lustre. A celebrated Persian poet has aptly said :—

> "If bats' eyes cannot see in the day—
> What fault is there in the rays of the sun ?

Desirest thou the truth ? It is better that a thousand eyes were thus blind, than the sun dark."

There needs no argument to prove the necessity of a law dictating that justice should be administered without distinction of creed, color, or caste. Our most cordial and grateful thanks are due to the Hon'ble Mr. Peacock, who has wisely and with a feeling of noble disinterestedness framed an Act which proposes to render administration of justice uniform to the British subjects of India at large. But as there are always two sides of a question, we should examine the sum total of the objections raised against the passing of the Act by the oppositionists : it is no other than the standing imperfections of the Moffasil Courts.

I admit there are many serious defects in the constitution of these Courts, and I have all along both privately and publicly expressed this my opinion, but this circumstance should not, in any wise, interfere with the question at issue, which is simply this,—Whether there should be one Penal Code for the "Whites," and another for the "Blacks?"—one for the Christians, another for the Heathens? What unbiased individual would not answer in the negative? What man of common sense would not see the injustice of a *Shaheb* in the Moffasil maltreating a Native under the most aggravating circumstances, and going unpunished owing to the difficulties of a prosecution in the Supreme Court? Who would not call it a strange perversion of justice, that, whilst a Native is amenable to the local courts in Civil and Criminal cases, a European British subject can be tried there only in matters of certain civil controversy, and would be penally liable to the jurisdiction of Her Majesty's Courts. The defects of the Moffasil Courts should be enquired into and corrected by the Legislature, but because they are not yet reformed, it is no reason that justice should be made to assume a mild form for the conquering, and a harsh one for the conquered race.

* * * *

I beg our fellow British subjects would not regard our proceedings with a hostile feeling ; it is not our wish that they should in any respect suffer ; all that we look for is that justice should be dispensed with an even hand to all classes of Her Majesty's subjects.

The Natives sufficiently vindicated themselves from the charge of reserve by several eloquent speeches, in which there was no abuse, or acrimony, or the artifices of rhetoric, but sober argument founded upon incontrovertible facts. Babu Digambar took a leading part in the proceedings of the meeting—being one engaged in the fore-front of the agitation. He was prominently concerned to move the second Resolution, which was as follows :—

That this meeting, having regard to the well-known and marked improvements that have taken place in Moffasil judicature since the extension of native agency in the administration of the law, and to the numerous testimonies which have been voluntarily borne on the subject by many eminent Indian statesmen and rulers, would record their opinion that the uncovenanted judicial officers of the Government are entitled generally to the respect and confidence of the community.

It was the most important of all the Resolutions, the one which went directly to meet the new charge of the enemy. The European memorialists had laid the most emphatic stress on their distrust of the Native Deputy Magistrates. The Supreme Court Judges also had alluded to this want of confidence. The very framers of the code had put in a clause, exempting the Europeans in service from the jurisdiction of the Native Courts. No point, involved in the discussion of the question, was of more concern than to overcome the tide of scorn and scurrility that had set in—nothing was so imperatively necessary to be urged in defence, as a resolution vindicating the Uncovenanted Judicial Officers of the Government from unjust revilings, and establishing their title to respect and confidence. Babu Digambar moved the Resolution entrusted to him with a speech adapted to the pressing subject of the hour. He gave utterance to thoughts with a statement of testimonial evidence, which challenged the voice of racial and political prejudices raised against his countrymen. It was what is in common colloquy called his maiden speech, which was delivered in the following words.

GENTLEMEN,—I have been asked to move the second Resolution. In submitting this Resolution for your acceptance, I must crave your indulgence to a brief statement of the reasons, which have rendered such an expression of public opinion as is embodied in this Resolution necessary. You are aware, I presume, that at a meeting lately held of the British subjects, resident in Calcutta and elsewhere, sundry speeches were delivered animadverting in no measured terms of severity upon native character and native agency in the administration of justice.

In a Resolution adopted on the occasion, it was urged that the native judicial officers, to a want of legal training equally applicable to their covenanted superiors, added antagonism of race and prejudice of caste which rendered them totally unfit to be impartial judges in cases in which the British subjects were concerned.

However unfounded these alleged causes of disqualification might be, and however bitter the language in which they were set forth in the several speeches delivered on the occasion, I could, nevertheless, find ample jusification for such gross departures from truth, and I may say even decency, in the hollowness of the cause, which taxed the ingenuity of the speakers. (Cheers.)

A drowned man, they say, will catch at a straw. It is not to be wondered at, that the only plausible ground for the continuance of a privilege which our fellow British subjects have hitherto enjoyed (I wish I could say without prejudice to the rest of the community), (hear,

hear) would be made most of, and that they would struggle with the tenacity characteristic of the race, for the protection of what they imagine to be their birth-rights.

Gentlemen, I say I have nothing to complain against ; on the contrary, I fully sympathize with what I cannot but regard as the convulsive efforts of an expiring man. (Loud cheers.) But what excuse can you find for a man who, from his high and sacred position of a member of the Legislative Council for all India and its dependencies, descends to that of a special pleader, (hear, hear) and in the course of an elaborate, and as it has been aptly characterized by our worthy Chief justice, an ingenious speech, affirms on the authority of his clients and the *Friend of India,* the utter incompetency of the native Judicial officers to administer justice, in cases wherein his highly civilized clients are concerned, and as a sort of compromise between the vindication of a just principle, and the clamours of an unreasonable but an influential suitor, recommends that such cases should be treated only in courts presided over by the covenanted judges. But mark the logic which has helped him to arrive at this, as he would feign make it appear, satisfactory solution of the difficulties. (Hear, hear).

He finds to his horror that the Code of Criminal Procedure as framed by the Commissioners and which is now before the Legislative Council in the shape of a Bill, while professing to abolish on principle all distinctions between Europeans and natives, invents new distinctions, inasmuch as it provides, that four classes of public officers enumerated in the Bill are to be triable only at the Sessions Court. This certainly is a most offensive provision, and well might Sir Arthur say that he could not believe his own eyes when he first saw it in the blue book. But how does he propose to clear the code of this objectionable feature? Not as you would in your simplicity suppose by expunging it from the Bill, but simply by including his clamorous clients in the category of exemptions (Hear, hear). Now, gentlemen, you have the authority of a member of the Legislative Council and the judge of the Supreme Court to believe that two blacks made one white, and dare if you can gainsay it (continued laughter and cheers.) Again, the Company's judges, Covenanted and Uncovenanted. are totally unfit by want of legal training to administer justice. The Sessions judge abours under an additional disqualification by reason of his ignorance of the language of the country. He is therefore the fittest man to try cases in which the British subjects are implicated. So you see gentle. men, that the learned rule of Lindlay Murray, two negatives destroy one another, holds equally true in legislation, since it is the negation of two requisites to the administration of justice, which renders the Covenanted Judge qualified, which cannot be insisted on for native Judges whose disqualification rested on a want of legal training alone, (Loud cheers.) Well may the Indigo planters exclaim, save us from our friends.

But, gentlemen, what is the fact? Why that the native Judicial officers, as the experience of twenty years has placed beyond the shadow of a doubt, combine all the requisite qualifications towards an efficient administration of justice in their own country. They are quite competent to grasp the most intricate question of law or fact, and that their decisions (as I shall presently show) have in a much larger proportion been upheld by the highest appellate court in the country than that of their covenanted superiors (Hear, hear.) Gentlemen, it was Lord William Bentinck, that far-seeing and most liberal-minded of the Statesmen that ever ruled the destiny of this Empire, that first discovered in the natives of the land, important elements which might be successfully and cheaply employed in the administration of the country. With him to decide was to act, and he gave effect to his decision by that memorable enactment, the charter of our administrative rights—I mean Reg. 5 of 1831 (Continued cheers.) Since then his successors one and all have borne testimony to the justice, wisdom, and soundness of the measure by a more extensive introduction of the native agency in the different departments of the public service; in none of which has it failed to realize the most sanguine expectations entertained of it (Hear, hear).

Gentlemen, that these are not idle declamations, or the convictions of my own humble individual experience, though that experience extends over a period of 20 years, mostly spent in the Moffasil in active and multifarious duties—I put in proof a Pamphlet of 95 pages compiled some years ago under the direction of the British Indian Association, entitled "Evidences relating to the Efficiency of the Native Agency in India," bearing on every page testimony of the most beneficial results arising from the employment of the native agency in the administration of the country, and by men whose official position and local experience entitled them in the highest degree to speak authoritatively on the subject (Hear, hear). Out of this mass of valuable testimony I shall occupy your time only by reading the remaks of the Sudder Court in their report on the administration of Civil Justice in territories subject to the Government of Bengal during the year 1841.

I shall now redeem my promise by proving to you from a figured statement in the Pamphlet, that the decisions of the Native Judges have in a much larger proportion been confirmed by the Sudder Court than that of the Covenanted Judges. Vide Page 94.*

Such, gentlemen, is the useful and valuable class of the Public service that has been attempted to be cried down, and such is the character of the valuable mass of evidence which its opponents have ignored. (Continued cheers.)

With reference to this speech, Kristodas Pal says, "there were four Mitter speakers at the meeting, of whom Digambar was dubbed No. 1 by Mr. Cobb Hurry," the Editor of the *Englishman*. The four speakers were Babu Kissory Chand Mitra, Babu Digambar Mitra, Babu Rajendra Lala Mitra, and Babu Peary Chand Mitra. The last Babu simply moved the fifth Resolution, without a single word in addition. Babu Rajendra Lala made his first public ora-

* This statement, which is carefully prepared from the published reports of the Sudder Decisions, embraces a period of seven years, viz., from 1845 to 1851, showing that of 1126 decisions of the Covenanted Judges appealed against during that period, 215, or nearly 20 per cent, were confirmed, and 911, or 80 per cent, reversed, modified or remanded, whilst of the 1561 decisions of the Uncovenanted Judges, 559, or nearly 36 per cent, confirmed, and 1002 or 64 per cent reversed or modified. (Hear, hear.)

torical attempt, giving a promise of his future distinction. Babu Kissory Chand Mitra certainly made the greatest forensic display by a studied, ornate, and eloquent speech. But Babu Digambar favourably impressed his audience by a quiet, practical, and humorous speech, such as is liked most by Europeans.

His Resolution was seconded by Mr. G. Thompson, who, in a speech of as much eloquence as of generous sentiment, thoroughly repudiated the charges of "antagonism of race, prejudice of caste, and entire want of independence of mind," brought against the Native officials—taking up each point, and tearing to shreds the representation made in the European memorial.

Babu Joykissen Mukerjea supported the Resolution by a bold manly speech, that may be said to have sounded the first note of preparation for the Indigo Crisis of 1860.

The Native population adopted a memorial, which was subscribed by eighteen hundred names. But, in six weeks after their meeting, the Mutiny came on. It was a period when the land resounded with the din of war, and thousands of lives were being shot or sabred into death. Nothing could be attended to in the agony of the long fight, excepting what concerned immediately. Every irrelevant question lay postponed to placid times. Not till the fall of Delhi in September, did the season of composure return. In consequence of the disturbances, the presentation of the Native memorial had been delayed. But the Court of Directors having referred to it in one of their despatches, it was submitted on the 27th November, 1857. The Bill remained pending under consideration till the 31st of August 1859, and received the assent of the Governor-General on the 5th September of that year.

The public discussions that arose concerning the Black Acts, form an important socio-political event that is seldom noticed. They brought about that final decision which pronounced the doom of privileges and exemptions. The morbid growth of laissez-faire legislation, it was now removed by the legislation of an advanced age to the relief of the country from long years of misery and sorrow. But there was not a decided crowning triumph. Things were done by halves. The Legislature compromised the question by abolishing the privilege, but retaining the immunity of trial from the Native Courts. The great moral evil of this half-measure, has resulted in weakening the sympathy between the ruling and ruled populations. There can be little room for mutual regard where a few persons are allowed to arrogate superiority, and others have to brook their humiliation in sullen discontent. The standing estrangement has caused a soreness between the two peoples, which has rankled down to the present generation. Worked upon by a heritage of passions that has deadened every feeling for fellow-ship, no approachment since made has ever proceeded from the heart of either race. The Native endures what he cannot cure. He will never be reconciled until he meets upon equal terms, and moves on equal ground. Where "some are puffed up, and others depressed, all are morally deteriorated."

CHAPTER IX.

STOCK SPECULATIONS. THE MUNICIPAL COMMISSION. THE LATOUR MEMORIALS. THE INCOME TAX CONFERENCE.

DURING the Mutiny, the Government Securities underwent a great depreciation. The discount went up as the danger increased in magnitude. Owing to the low state of funds in its coffers, the Bank of Bengal refused loans upon them. This gave a rude shock to the faith in which they were held. Papers esteemed to idolatry now left their repose in iron-safes to change hands. Hundreds being anxious to part with them, the discount rose to more than thirty per cent. It was an opportunity for bold and long-sighted speculators in stocks. Shrewdly calculating that anarchism had no chance against an orderly regime—that the odds were overwhelmingly against the Sepoys, Babu Digambar took advantage, amid the depression of this most depressing period, to reap considerable profits from his stock-business. His capital increasing, he began to lay out money in profitable investments. By this means, as well as by a careful and judicious management of his Zamindaris, which in a few years from this time included the profitable estate of Patamundi in Katak and other properties in Jesor and the Sunderbunds, Digambar steadily grew into a rich man.

To quote Babu Kristodas Pal:—"It would be difficult to enumerate the public measures, for the last fifteen years, which did not receive important amendments under the influence of his advice given through the medium of the British Indian Association, the Bengal Council, or this or that Committee on which Digambar served." As far back as we have been able to trace, this career of public usefulness dates from the year 1861. By this time, he was no more the Assistant Secretary, but "a most intelligent and active member of the Committee of the British Indian Association in which his various experience lent much weight to his counsels." The first public cause in which he was called upon to act, was the Municipal Commission appointed in May, 1861. There was a Municipal Act in 1847 for the improvement of Calcutta. The Act for the Conservancy of Calcutta was passed in 1850. In 1851, there was another Municipal Act. But none of these fulfilled the objects for which they were framed. The defective administration of the

Municipality of Calcutta became a general public complaint and grievance by the year 1861. The *Hindu Patriot* of that day wrote as follows:—

> The patience of the inhabitants is tired, and there is a general craving for change. There is a lamentable scarcity of water in the town, and the inhabitants complain that nobody looks after their wants. The late showers have exhibited the road-works of the Municipal Triumvirate in all their glory, and the inhabitants are indignant that their rates are not properly employed. There is stench all over the Native town and mortality fearfully raging, and the inhabitants cry that their money is vainly frittered away upon impracticable drainage works which will come to a smash as soon as Mr. Clarke goes home.*

It was felt that the absence of representation of the rate-payers in the Municipal Board was at the root of the evil. A representation was made to the Government of Bengal, and Sir Cecil Beadon, who was at the head of the Government at that time, was induced to appoint a Commission composed of officials and non-officials to enquire into the subject, and to devise a better scheme of administration. The Committee of the British Indian Association addressed a letter to the Government of Bengal, suggesting the desirableness of so constituting the Commission as to secure a due representation of the Native interest. The Government in reply wrote to the Committee that Babu Prosana Kumar Tagore had been appointed to represent the Native Community, but if the Association did not feel themsel ves sufficiently represented by him, the Lieute nant-Governor would be prepared to appoint a

* The *Hindoo Patriot,* May 20th, 1861.

non-official native member. To this letter the Committee replied by suggesting the appointment of two non-official native members. But the Government agreed to the appointment of one member, and requested them to nominate their representative They accordingly returned their colleague Babu Digambar Mitra, who, on account of his late nomination, could not join the Commission until their work was considerably advanced. He was however serviceable in advising on the report adopted by the Commission. The Government of Bengal acquiesced in the plan proposed by the Commission, as one worthy of trial, and the Government of India as the supreme local authority expressed a similar acquiesence. A Bill was accordingly introduced into the Bengal Council to amend the Municipal constitution of Calcutta, which after many additions and alterations was passed in 1863. Under this Bill, Babu Digambar became a Justice of the Peace and an Honorary Magistrate of Calcutta.

We come next to a singularly remarkable incident, the like of which does not occur in the his tory of a Native life. It is a patent fact that the abject and timorous Bengali is an avowed worshipper of the Sahib, on whom he looks as an incarnation, or a representative type of the sovereign. Overawed, he tamely puts up with mal-administration, and suffers wrongs without a whisper. He never allows himself to overstep this constitutional line of conduct. He never thinks of bringing him to reason, though his forbearance be presumed upon to the utmost strain. In short, his indulgence in submissive humour knows no limit. But it was widely different with Digambar, who broke through the rule, and not only ventured to cry out, but manfully withstood to obtain redress. He was so bold and audacious as to go to the length of undertaking the impeachment of a Civilian, Mr. Edward Latour, the Judge of the Twenty-four Parganas. Mr. Latour was a Civilian of that old school, who would govern his district little according to the letter and spirit of the law, and much according to the dictates of his own will. He had his likes and dislikes—his prepossessions and prejudices. In the vexed question between the Zamindar and the Rayat then before the public, he seems to have been schooled in the opinions against the Zamindar, whom Mr. Marshman persistently represented in his *Friend of India* as the great wrong-doer in Bengal. To the Rayat, he was a one-sided partial umpire, who adjudged in favor of the weaker party by jumping to foregone conclusions. The Zamindar, left to his tender mercies, found in him a stern arbitrator. Many a time had Babu Digambar to come before Mr. Latour as a litigant against his Dabipur tenants. Invariably he lost his suits because of his being the Landholder, and therefore in the wrong box. Suffering for years, his patience was at last worn out, when he took the manly resolution of crossing the Rubicon. He conceived the project of protesting against his course, and bringing the proud, self-willed, and self-opinionated Judge under a restraint from his perverseness. Far from being dismayed, he thought it was a duty which he owed to himself and to others in a similar condition. The difficulty of executing it can be estimated when it is considered how others used to bear uncomplainingly were found reluctant to join him in the unprecedented undertaking. Great credit is due to him to have formed an opposition out of spiritless hesitating men brought up in blind respect to authority. He must be admitted to have prevailed upon them with the most skilful persuasive powers. Having succeeded to enlist some fellow-sufferers in the cause, Digambar, towards the end of May, 1861, laid the following petition before the Lieutenant-Governor of Bengal :—

To

THE HON'BLE JOHN PETER GRANT,

LIEUTENANT-GOVERNOR OF BENGAL.

The humble petition of the undersigned Landholders and Residents in the 24 Parganas.

Sheweth,

That your petitioners have for sometime past viewed with distrust, alarm, and dissatisfaction, the manner in which the law is administered in the district of the 24 Parganas by Mr. Edward Latour, the present Civil and Sessions Judge, whose extreme prejudices and other grave deficiencies have been of late so frequently exhibited, that it is impossible for your petitioners to have any confidence in his judgment, integrity, or honesty of purpose.

To explain the ground on which the prayer of this petition is based, it will be necessary for your petitioners to bring to Your Honor's notice Mr. Latour's conduct in his judicial capacity from the date of his present appointment ; in doing so, they will endeavour to refrain from any remarks foreign to the question which they wish to bring under Your Honor's consideration ; namely, whether Mr. Latour can be considered properly qualified for the performance of the duties of his position, and whether in justice to your petitioners he can be allowed any longer to retain his present appointment.

The charges which your petitioners prefer against Mr. Edward Latour, and which they will be prepared to establish are these :—

1st That in cases before this Judge, where a Zamindar or wealthy native is concerned, whether the proceedings are of a civil or criminal nature but more especially where the question in dispute involves considerations of the legal relations existing between the Zamindars and their tenants, he has repeatedly pronounced decisions against the landowners in violation of the law, and in direct opposition to facts clearly proved ; in many instances suppressing material facts, grossly mis-stating others, assuming that for which no evidence was adduced, and misapplying the law even to the facts admitted by himself.

2nd That Mr. Latour's treatment of his subordinate Courts, when they happen to entertain opinions differing from his own, in cases where landholders and their tenants are concerned, has been of such a nature as seriously to interfere with the independence of these Courts.

3rd That Mr. Latour's prejudices are so obstinate that he refuses obedience to, or neglects to carry out, the orders of the Sudder Court when they happen to be opposed to his preconceived views, and thus practically, as far as lies in his power, makes his own whims and caprices of the force of law within his district.

4th That in recording such decisions as are liable to appeal to the Sudder Court, Mr. Latour also suppresses or ignores facts proved in the Lower Courts, and thus has frequently misled the Sudder Court upon the hearing of an appeal from his decisions.

The vast amount of injustice which Mr. Latour's persistencies in this conduct has occasioned, could only be fully estimated by a review of all his decisions since his appointment to the Civil and Sessions judgeship of the 24 Parganas, and more specially of those cases decided on appeal from his subordinate Courts and in which no appeal lies to the Sudder Court ; even from the cases decided on special appeal, Your Honor will perceive that your petitioners have made no exaggerated statement.

Sometime in the year 1857, Mr. Latour was appointed to his present post. Seventeen cases from his Court were appealed to the Sudder Dewany in the following year, as reported in the Sudder Decisions. Of these, six were confirmed and eleven reversed or remanded. In the succeeding year (1859) no less than thirty-one cases were appealed, of which six were upheld and twenty-five reversed or remanded. In the past year the proportion continues about the same. If an analysis were made of these reversed or remanded cases, it would be found that the great majority of them were suits in which Zamindars or wealthy natives were concerned, and that the erroneous decision of the judge was uniformly against these classes ; his strong prejudices in such cases unfitting him for distinguishing truth from error, and leading him to disregard the law, which it his duty to interpret and administer, not to make or alter according to his own caprice.

There is not another so blameworthy a trait in the character of our nation, as carrying subserviency to the point of truckling against conviction, against truth, against interest. Hoping to curry favor, a body of sycophantic Muktears volunteered to submit the following counter-petition :—

To

THE HON'BLE J. P. GRANT,

LIEUTENANT-GOVERNOR OF BENGAL.

The humble petition of certain inhabitants and residents of the District of 24 Parganas as also of the Pleaders and Muktears attached to the judge's Court of the 24 Parganas.

Respectfully Sheweth,

That your Honor's petitioners have learnt with the deepest feelings of sorrow and regret, that a petition has been sent to Your Honor praying for the removal of Mr. Edward Latour the present able and impartial Judge of the 24 Parganas from his post.

That Your Honor's petitioners have so very high an opinion of the efficiency, impartiality, and honesty of purpose of Mr. E. Latour, that they cannot refrain themselves from approaching Your Honor with this counter-petition, which they do with sanguine hopes that Your Honor would graciously be pleased to take into Your Honor's consideration, whether the petition submitted against Mr. E. Latour has not emanated from malice as Your petitioners confidently suppose it to have been.

Many of Your Honor's petitioners are eye-witnesses of the manner in which Mr. Latour has conducted his duties since his accession to the judgeship of the 24-Parganas, and they have never had the least cause of complaint against him. He might have now and then differed with the able and efficient Judges of the Sudder Court, but that can in no way disqualify him for the post he holds or for promotion to a higher post, for it is the lot of every independent and conscientious Judge to differ with other Judges—and time alone can show whether Mr. Latour is not right in some of the opinions he maintains. The point on which Mr. Latour differs materially with the present learned Judges of the Sudder is the application of the Law of Limitation in cases of enhancement of rent, but as a similar opinion like Mr. Latour's was entertained by two of the late best Judges of the Sudder, Messrs. A. Dick and J. S. Torrens, your petitioners do not percieve why Mr. Latour is taxed for this his opinion when others are allowed to hold it unimpeached. As to the results of appeals as shewn by the Returns, it is not, Your Honor's petitioners humbly observe, a safe criterion to judge of an officer's merits, for a slight amendment in the decision as to the interests or cost places a decision in the returns as reversed, when even the Appellate Court concurs with the Lower Court in the decision of all other material points of the case, and so a decision is sometimes remanded when the Appellate Court thinks that proof has not been taken on any one point of the case, and it does not unfrequently happen that the same decision is arrived at by the Appellate Court on the merits afterwards, even by seeing the additional proofs which the Lower Court thought unnecessary.

A reference to the opinions accorded by the Sudder Court on the civil reports and returns of the 24-Parganas since 1857 will show that that Tribunal has recorded praise to Mr. Latour in terms of high approbation almost every year.

That Your Honor's petitioners will not follow the accusers of Mr. Latour in every thing they have advanced against him now, but will do so hereafter if necessary. They will now only state that there is no foundation whatever in the charge that Mr. Latour suppresses facts and misstates others ; and if any thing of the kind might appear on the record of any case, that is owing to inadvertance occasioned by the hurry of the moment, and not to any willing attempt on the part of Mr. Latour to pass any partial decision or to mislead the higher Court.

That Your Honor's petitioners will now conclude this relying on Your Honor's justice and impartiality.

And Your petitioners as in duty bound will ever pray.

The attempt at stultification did not succeed. Babu Digambar gained his object by Mr. Latour's elevation to the Bench of the High Court. At all events, his force of will, and spirit, and daring could not but have been the subject of his contemporaries' talk and admiration.

In June 1861, Babu Digambar's services were again in requisition on the occasion of the Income Tax Conference. For years past, the country was suffering from a "chronic deficit." The Mutiny, suppressed with a vast expenditure, left the State on the verge of bankruptcy. England sent out a veteran financier and political economist —James Wilson, to restore the Indian finances. Under stern necessity admitting of no delay, his genius had not time to hit upon a better re source than the Income Tax. It was therefore imposed as a temporary expedient for immediate relief. But the unsuitability of the tax to the circumstances of India soon made itself apparent on practical grounds. Unpopular from the beginning as a "war tax" and a "national mulct," the impost proved a vast engine for oppression and extortion, coupled with unproductiveness. It was bitterly denounced for its inquisitorial valuations of income. Lord Canning wanted to allay the outcry and put people into a good humour. His Lordship called a conference on the subject. It was a constitutional course which introduced a new era in the history of British rule and financial legislation. No Governor-General had thus acted before him. Lord Cornwallis is known to have called for Native opinion on the subject of the Permanent Settlement, but it was *apka-wastai* opinion of men in service. Lord William Bentinck also consulted with distinguished non-official Europeans and Native gentlemen like Rammohun Roy and Dwarkanath Tagore on occasions of important measures affecting their interests, but they tendered only private advice. Lord Canning's concession, for the first time, involved a constitutional principle. The Conference was appointed in the month of June, 1861. The Government invited the co-operation of the British Indian Association by delegating two members out of their body. None were thought so worthy to represent them as Babus Ramanath Tagore and Digambar Mitra. The recommendations of these delegates were largely accepted by Government. Of the work done by them, the following account was given by Babu Digambar at the monthly General Meeting of the Association held on 26th July, 1861:—

He begged permission on behalf of himself and his colleague Babu Rama Nath Tagore to lay before the meeting, as they had been asked by some of the members to do, an outline of what they urged at the Income Tax Conference as delegates from the Association. He said that he did not feel himself at liberty to communicate what Mr. Harington had said on several points mooted in the Conference. He need only say that the suggestions and recommendations which he and his colleague offered for the improvement of the Act were received and discussed with all the earnestness, which might be expected from an officer acting under the inspiration of a Ruler, who has never been slow in redressing a just grievance, and who has given an unmistakeable proof of his solicitude for the elevation of the millions subject to his rule by recognising for the first time their political existence. Leaving aside minor points, he would confine himself to the objections taken to the more important sections of the Act which had rendered the tax so odious in its practical working. The first in importance were those sections, *viz.*, sections 47,54, and 55, which gave to the assessors the power of surcharge in the first instance. By the restrictive provision in section 46 prohibiting them to summon or question the parties making the returns, they the assessors were scarcely in a position, except by drawing largely upon their imagination and caprice, to make correctly such surcharges. The consequence has been that the assessors, according to the measure of their zeal for the public revenue, have laid down fixed rates ranging from 50 to 500 per cent upon the return made for making the surcharge. The remedy provided against such arbitrary surcharge by section 55 proved entirely ineffectual, since both in Calcutta as well as in the Mofasil, instances were known, and they were not few in number, in which the provision of that section has been entirely disregarded, and parties have been called upon and made to pay under threat of attachment and sale of property. The tax was practically levied at such surcharged valuation without the parties being served even with a notice of surcharge. In the instances in which the parties were served with notices, the cases were so hurried through that they obtained little or no redress whatever. In fact by the plan adopted of surcharging almost every return, the cases were so largely multiplied that unless the number of officers charged with the disposal of them were considerably increased, it was impossible to ensure careful and patient investigation of the proofs (which were generally elaborate account books) offered against such arbitrary surcharges. The immoral tendency of such arbitrary and indiscriminate assessment had been also dwelt upon, shewing that if parties making an honest and faithful return of their income were subjected to all those annoyances and ultimately to an inevitable surcharge, without reason or justice, they would of course take very good care to mould their future returns after the known pre-possessions and whims of particular assessors, and the fixed rates of valuations to which they might be peculiarly partial.

The remedy proposed to meet the evil was to take away the power of surcharge from the assessors, rendering the offence of making false returns punishable by imprisonment and not simply by fine as provided in Section CCIV of the Act. A few examples made upon clear and sufficient evidence of persons making such false returns would it was contended deter all but the most desperate from making the attempt. At any rate it was better that the finance should suffer in the comparatively few instances in which the remedy proposed should fail to offer an effectual check. rather than that such a fertile source of injustice, annoyance, and oppression should be suffered to continue.

The next section, commented upon was section 97. In reference to rule 4 of that section it was proposed that some fixed rate should be laid down in the manner of the first rule of the Section for assuming the profits derivable from the permanently settled Estates in Bengal—and it was suggested that 100 per cent. upon the Government Revenue would be a fair approximate valuation of the profits ot such Estates except in respect of the properties in the Districts of Hooghly, Burdwan and Twenty-four Pargannas, where in consequence of the more accurate ascertainments of the rentals before the settlement (most of the Estates having been held in khas management prior thereto and the absence of waste land in them during the settlement), the Estates were less profitable than in the other districts. In respect of these it was proposed that 50 per cent. of the Government Revenue would be a fair rate at which to assume the profits, arising from them. The rule 8 of the same Section, which provided that owners of houses occupying the same be charged at rack rent at which the same were worth to be let, was also objected to, as opening a wide door to oppression, since in the Mofasil, except in the Sudder Station, not a single house was to be met with which was let out at rent. The owners there generally occupied their own houses. Under such circumstances there was nothing to show the tenantable value of a house. The over zealous assessors have made this a convenient means for bringing under assessment many who were not otherwise liable to it, by valuing the houses they occupied at a most unreasonable rate of rent, which after all they had no means of meeting by any satisfactory proof. It was proposed that in such places where the tax from such sources was likely to be inconsiderable, it should be abandoned or some definite rules laid down to guide the officers in valuing such houses.

The next point urged was as to the injustice of the loss shewn in the return under one schedule not being allowed to be set off against the returns under another. Thus, a man losing 50,000 rupees by a trade and deriving an income of 5,000 Rs. from his landed property, would still be taxed on the latter. This it was contended was a great hardship and directly trenched upon the principles of the Income Tax. The absence of any provision in the Act for the speedy refund of 4 per cent. deducted from the interest on Government Securities, owned by parties who may not be liable to the tax, or if liable, not to 4 per cent, was pointed out. The next point objected to was the minimum limitation of assessment to two hundred rupees. This it was contended brought within the purview of the tax a large number of persons scarcely in a position to bear the burden, and caused unnecessary trouble to the officers without bringing in a corresponding gain to the State. It was proposed to raise the minimum to 400 Rs. assessable at one uniform rate of 4 per cent. This it was argued would remove the anomaly of one man being taxed at double the rate for the other, though the difference in their respective incomes might not after all be more than a rupee. Why not relieve a very large portion of the population, and just that portion which is the least able to escape from the oppressions inseparable from such a mode of taxation ? Why not lighten the duties of the officers and allow them time for a more faithful and conscientious discharge of their trust ? The loss to the exchequer likely to result from it could not be much, since a portion of it would be made up by an additional rate of 2 per cent. upon income of Rs. 400 which at the present rate was assessable at 2 per cent, and the number of persons thus released from the burden of the Income Tax coming under the operation of the License Bill would very much make up the loss under notice.

Such were the principal objections and recommendations which he and his colleague Babu Ramanath Tagore offered towards the improvement of the Act, and he was happy to find that the Bill introduced into the Legislative Council, and which in all likelihood will pass into law tomorrow will remove, though for a year only, many of the causes of complaint against the existing Act. Sufficient for the day was the evil thereof. In this spirit of resignation the proposed measure with all its short comings, its disregard of the primary principle of a direct tax was to be hailed as a boon. It was at any rate a sure indication that the Government was alive to the general discontent which the working of the Act in its present form had caused, and though the apprehended deficiency in the opium revenue and the high favor which direct taxation found with many statesmen, did not warrant a hope that this obnoxious tax would be abolished, there was very little to fear that it would ever again be presented with the repulsive features with which it was first ushered into existence.

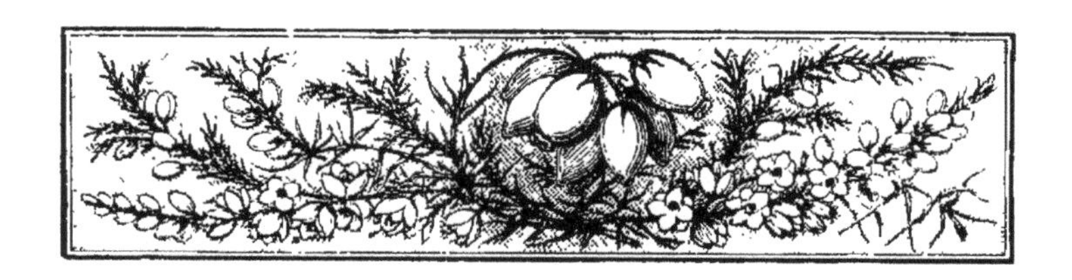

CHAPTER X.

THE HARISH MEMORIAL MEETING. THE MONSTER WELLS MEETING. THE SATI CASE.

THE Harish Memorial Meeting took place in the middle of July, 1861. Babu Digambar is found not to have taken an active part in that meeting. His name simply appears in the Committee. The Harish Memorial project is one of those many instances of much bruit and little fruit in the history of Bengali enterprises, which greatly discredits our nation in the opinion of foreigners. There were speeches in profusion, complimenting Harish to the length that "he was the greatest Hindu that had lived since the days of Raja Rammohan Roy," but no liberality in proportion to the grateful effusions. The Bengali eagerly takes to the imitation of European customs, but he seldom brings European spirit towards the fruition of the object. He fails to do even the justice that foreigners sometimes do. The Bengal Government honored the memory of Pandit Iswara Chandra Vidyasagara by giving half-holiday to its public offices. But our national appreciation did not go beyond the pupils of his schools taking off their shoes, and observing mourning for ten days. Those who expect their memory to be honored, should leave behind them examples of large-heartedness and open-handed charitv, which are needed to educate our nation in "loving money wisely, and not too well," which should teach us to be not merely sentimental, but also practical.

In August following, happened the famous monster Wells meeting. From the time of Sir Elijah Impey "by whose-hands Hastings murdered Nandakumar," down to Sir Morduant Wells vituperations, the Judges of the Supreme Court of Calcutta have many a time acted an extra judicial role travelling out of their sphere. In addition to their function-proper of administering justice, they undertook to discharge the duties of political leaders, who, in the words of Sir Charles Wood, made "the Legislative Council a Debating Society or Petty Parliament." From pride of race and conquest, Sir Morduant converted the Bench into a political platform. Presiding at the Criminal Sessions Courts, he often forgot himself into a Reformer of Crime. He never dealt with a case of perjury or forgery without inveighing against the Natives as "a nation of liars and forgers." The Natives resolved to catch the bull by its horns. They called a monster meeting at the house of Raja Radhakanta Deb, petitioned against the political Judge, and brought him to his sense. In this celebrated meeting, Digambar performed no other part than propose a vote of thanks to the chair.

The Sati case that next claims notice, occurred in December, 1863. A short rehearsal of certain foregoing facts is necessary to place the event in its proper light. The practice of Sati-ism, traced to the authority of a Vedic text said to be misinterpreted by priestcraft, had acquired the sanctity of a religious rite from observance for centuries, and become enshrined in Hindu opinion. In vain did Akbar try to put it down. The first instance of this barbarity noticed in Anglo-Indian history dates from the early times of Job Charnock, who rescued a Brahman widow from a funeral pile at Barrackpur, and took her as a quasi-wife. Ever since that day set in the current of an adverse opinion from which must be reckoned the beginning of the end. From the time of Warren Hastings the attention of every Governor-General—of every Englishman in authority, was drawn to the abolition of the rite. Lord Cornwallis and Lord Wellesley deplored the revolting practice, but shrunk from incurring popular resentment. A daring attempt was made during the administration of Lord Hastings, when a man was arrested for assisting at a Sati case, and tried for murder. In 1826, Lord Amherst made illegal the burning of a widow without the body of her deceased husband.* It was legislated also that all widows intending to perform the rite should procure permission by appearing in person before a Magistrate. The third rule disabled all families stained with Sati-ism from holding office or employment under Government. And it was further regulated that all property belonging to a Sati and her husband should become forfeited to the State. These indirect enactments gradually paved the way for the final death-blow dealt by Lord William Bentinck. Throwing out feelers on the subject, his Lordship elicited a variety of opinions. There is never a question before the public which meets with universal suffrage—it is welcome to one party and repugnant to another. The opponents were not only orthodox Hindus, but also Europeans with Hindu sympathies, conspicuous among whom was Dr. H. H. Wilson, the great Sanscrit scholar. On the other hand, the great advocate of reform was Raja Rammohun Roy, with whom at one were his Brahmo-Shava followers and Babus Dwarkanath Tagore and Kalinath Chowdhry. Thoroughly sifting the evidence on both sides, Lord William Bentinck made up his mind to deal with the matter from the humanitarian point of view. He rightly concluded that the deterrent bugbears existed more in timid apprehension than in reality. He rightly calculated that the Brahmans no longer enjoyed their ancient power

---

* "At Mulgher, a woman, 17 years of age, hearing of the death of her husband determined to burn herself with his *shoe* as the corpse had been previously consumed. Her relations resorted to every means to prevent her; but all was of no avail.—*The Chandrika, 1822.*

and popularity ; that the custom was mostly prevalent in Bengal where little resistance was likely to ensue from its pliant population ; that the Natives were rising superior to the influence of their prejudices ; that the fairer half of the community would accord their support and the widows hail the measure with loud paeans ; that the reward of his legislation would be the approval of all Christendom and the hearty gratitude of a nation. Upheld by a strong faith in eventual good, his Lordship issued his fiat against Sati-ism, on the 4th of December, 1829. His benevolent motive was at once acknowledged by all right-minded men. No emotion was manifested in Northern Hindustan. Rather thankful addresses were offered by certain Rajas in the course of his Lordship's tour through Behar. Only the members of the Calcutta Dharma Shava failed to read his edict in its true light, and got up a deprecatory petition to the Privy Council in England which was justly consigned to "the limbo of vanities." The diabolic practice fell into complete desuetude. It has been so entirely forgotten, that it is now a matter of memory and almost an incredible fact of history.

But after many years – after a generation had passed away, the repose of the public mind was disturbed by the occurrence of a case in an obscure village near Monghyr. The following letter, dated 4th December 1863, from the Secretary to the Government of Bengal to the British Indian Association thus dwells upon the facts :—

"I am desired by the Lieutenant-Governor to send for the information of the British Indian Association, a copy of the decision of the Sessions Court of Bhaugulpore in a case of Suttee, which recently occurred in the district of Monghyr, and of a letter this day addressed to the Commissioner of Bhaugulpore on the subject.

The case demands the earnest and the attentive consideration of the Association, and of every thinking member of the Hindu community, who has at heart the welfare of his country and desires to purge his religion from the reproach of affording countenance and encouragement to a most barbarous and cruel crime.

The law rigidly declares that the practice of Suttee is revolting to the feelings of human nature, and is nowhere enjoined by the Hindoo religion as an imperative duty. It may be added that in the older *Shastras* down to the institutes of Manu, the practice is not only not enjoined or permitted, it is not even spoken of, while in the later books it is only mentioned as an alternative to which a widow may resort though not in preference to marriage or to retirement and abstinence. And there is nothing in any book held sacred by Hindoos which justifies one in encouraging or persuading a woman to commit Suttee, much less in using physical force or moral compulsion to induce its commission. While, therefore, the religion of the Hindoos neither enjoins the commission of Suttee, nor justifies the abetment of it, the law of nature, in which all true religion, in the estimation of the Hindoos, as well as of others, is founded, absolutely forbids the crime, and the law of the country, which is the command of the sovereign, stigmatises it as a violation of the paramount dictates of justice and humanity, and punishes those who abet it with transportation, and, if the act be not voluntary on the part of the woman, with death.

4. Moreover, the law requires all land holders of every description and their under tenants, all farmers, and agents employed in the collection of rents, and all head men of villages, to give immediate information to the Police of any intended Suttee, and punishes them, if they willingly neglect or delay to furnish such information, with fine or imprisonment.

5. In the present case, it appears that the intention of the widow to commit Suttee was generally known in the neighbourhood early in the day on the morning of which her husband died, and that when she went forth, apparently at that time a voluntary victim, accompanied by her husband's relations, men of the Kaith caste, the chief abettors of intended suicide, preparations had been made for the horrid sacrifice, and upwards of a thousand people had assembled to witness the tragedy. Among these were several Zamindars and others, people holding a respectable position in life, whose bounden duty it was to give immediate information to the

Police, yet not one was found to show the least disapproval of the intended immolation. Not only did no one endeavour to put a stop to the proceedings, to dissuade the woman from the act of self-destruction, or to warn her abettors of the legal consequence of the crime, but all were eager participators in it, and when the unfortunate victim, tortured by the flames, repented of her resolution, threw herself from the pile and tried to escape, declaring that she would not complete her self-sacrifice, many of them called out to her and reproached her, saying that she would make herself and the village a laughing-stock, and it is stated by one witness that they surrounded her so that she could not run away. Thus she was eventually induced or compelled to remount the pile, from which, however, unable to bear the agony, she almost immediately again fled; on this the crowd dispersed, and the wretched woman, scorched and burned, was left to roll in agony on the ground till death put an end to her sufferings. It was not till the following day that information of the occurrence was given to the Police, and the person who gave the information was the chowkeedar.

6. To add to the horror of the scene, and to show how deliberate was the act of abetment on the part of the relatives of the deceased, the pile was lighted by a boy of tender years, the son of one of the chief abettors, and the *Purahit*, or family priest (a miscreant who has not yet been brought to justice), made him repeat the

Mantra, or invocation usual at a funeral, before he applied the fire.

7. The Lieutenant-Governor does not presume to dictate to the members of the Association the course which it may be incumbent upon them to take on this occasion as leaders of public opinion associated together for the purpose of promoting the efficiency of the Government by every legitimate means in their power. His Honor has no doubt that the highly intelligent and benevolent Native gentlemen who compose the Association, will be able to agree among themselves as to the best means of bringing their influence to bear upon the ignorant portion of their fellow-countrymen who are still so far the slaves of a corrupt superstition, as to defy the laws of God and of man, in obedience to the commands of their priests and to the dictates of a brutal and degrading, but still cherished, custom.

8. The law has been vindicated on this occasion by the infliction of severe penalties on some of the principal offenders, and it will be enforced with vigor in any future case of the same kind, if such should unhappily occur, but it is beyond the power of the Government to exercise much influence on the feelings of the people in respect to a rooted custom founded on a mistaken view of the obligation of their religion unless its endeavours are supported by some practical manifestation of opinion on the part of

the leading Hindoo gentlemen of these Provinces, evincing not only their abhorrence of a practice which is the standing reproach of Hindooism in all parts of the civilized world, but their determination by every possible means to suppress."

The Association took the above communication into consideration in a Special General Meeting held on the 4th January, 1864. It adopted a Resolution expressing deep regret and participation in the feeling of sorrow and indignation with which His Honor the Lieutenant-Governor of Bengal regarded the barbarous act. In seconding the said Resolution Babu Digambar thus spoke on the subject :—

The meeting had not been convened for the purpose of discussing the subject of Sutte as a religious question. The law had declared the commission of Suttee a most barbarous crime, and even if it had the sanction of religion which he denied, for nowhere was it enjoined in the Hindoo Shastras as an imperative duty, the time had now happily passed away for discussing the propriety of suppressing it with the strong hand of law. That the Suttee was a most degrading custom, opposed alike to the laws of God and man, and revolting in the highest degree to human nature, few would at this time of day deny, and it was the duty of every right-minded Hindu, which he owed to himself as well as to society at large, to exert his best for the suppression of this inhuman act. He was, however, glad to say that Suttee was now quite unknown in Bengal proper. He regretted deeply the circumstances which attended the Suttee case reported by the Commissioner of Bhagulpur, and particulars of which were now before the meeting. It was indeed painful to notice that so many men, and among them those occupying the position of zamindars, were present on the occasion as spectators, and that instead of taking steps to repress this cruel immolation countenanced it by their presence and apparent sympathy. But at the same time he derived some satisfaction from the fact that this was one of the rare cases, which had occurred within the district of Bengal since the humane measure of Lord William Bentinck had become law. The resolutions which will follow lay down the course which the Association should adopt in giving the utmost publicity to this painful case, and in their urging upon the zamindars and others in the Mofasil to exert their individual influence towards rooting out this revolting custom, the remnant of which still *appeared to linger in some distant and dark spots in the country*. By this he meant not simply the suppression of this practice with a high hand, but also the promotion of this humane object by infusing in the minds of the ignorant a proper sense of the degrading nature of this practice, and awakening in them a just abhorrence for it. He could not, however, conclude, without tendering his best thanks to His Honor the Lieutenant-Governor for his laudable desire to consummate, so far as his Government was concerned, the reform with which the memory of India's best Governor-General was identified. At the same time he believed the meeting would go with him in feeling grateful to His Honor for making the Association the medium of co-operation, for while it was complimentary to the Association, it was also unquestionably true that in questions of social reform the action of Government, unless seconded by the advanced portion of the community, must in the end prove fruitless in producing the desired change in moral sentiments and feelings of the people. He had no doubt that the call of His Honor would be responded to in the same spirit in which it had been made, for the practical disuse of the custom in Bengal proper showed that it had lost the hold upon the religious feeling of the Hindoo which it once had.

How marked is the contrast between the sentiments prevailing in 1830, and those entertained in 1863. Culture had worked a revolution in conviction. If a plebiscitum were taken now, there would be a universal execration of the rite, and an overwhelming consensus in favor of the abolition. The Government came to the protection of widows, and Sati-ism has ceased. They came to the protection of infants, and

Infanticide is no more.* They came to the protection of the traveller, and Thugi-ism has disappeared. They came to the protection of the slave, and not a bondman breathes in India. They came to the protection of Meriah-boys, and cruel human sacrifices have come to an end. They came to the protection of the outcast, and civil or moral transgression incurs not the for feiture of ancestral property. They recently came to the protection of girl-wives, and these have been saved from brutality. It now remains for them to come to the rescue of the unhappy Hindu girl-widows, who wait for a benevolent enactment in their favor. There is nothing like the co-action of law to quicken the sluggish operation of enlightenment. Many of our countrymen have a knack of opposition to every liberal measure. But they take to it as a wanton *tamasha*—a game in apish imitation of Hyde Park demonstrations and Parliamentary party-Opposition. After all, they have no compactness in their organization, no persistency in their efforts, no edge in their discontent. No sooner the effervescence subsides, than they come to justifiy the measure and acknowledge the law to operate to their benefit and not to their detriment.

* It is not altogether a groundless apprehension that under the daily increasing difficulty of marrying their girls, Hindu parents may resort again to female infanticide. It is a crime only one degree higher than abortion, which is committed in hundreds of instances.

CHAPTER XI.

The Epidemic Fever in Bengal. The Epidemic Commission.

WE are now about to dwell on that historic act by which Digambar has left the deepest trace of his name in the memories of men. It refers to those important services in the cause of suffering humanity which stand forth as his noblest deed, and furnish the episode of greatest interest in his life-story.

The history of human afflictions abounds with many instances of malignant outbreaks. In ancient Athens, there broke out a type of eruptive typhoid fever which Thucydides feelingly describes from personal suffering. Procopius dwells on the pestilence in Justinian's reign which raged for fifty years. The Decameron of Boccaccio opens with a plague-story the scene of which was Florence. De Foe has left the best account of the plague in London. The pestilences spoken of in ancient India were the Visuchika and Pushkara. In modern times, the Cholera is its great scourge.

But though Cholera is

"Fierce as ten Furies. terrible as hell,"

the great killer in Lower Bengal is Fever. More or less a constant enemy, it is properly an annual visitant. Each season it comes as an Endemic with "the first falls of rain in May," when "severe cases have been noticed, but they are too few in number to cause much alarm."* Increasing with the increase of the wet weather, the disease reaches its height in the steamy months of August and September, causing heavy mortality. The period is termed *Yamashtaka* in the popular calendar, when "the eight portals of Yama's (Pluto's) mansion are open to receive the dead." It is when other influences aggravate the usual conditions, that the disease assumes the potency of an Epidemic, killing "numbers without number."

Such aggravations have taken place from time to time in the present century, and they are traced as far back as 1804 at Berhampur. The second instance, dated 1824-25, occurred in the district of Jessor, where the outbreak was "very fatal at the village of Mahmudpur on the banks of the large river Ellenkhali,

* The Epidemic Fever Commission Report, dated 31st March 1864.

and along the Chitrá river, and at Nuldanga." In 1840, a fever depopulated Gudkhali, "a large and populous village on the swampy banks of a nullah, and surrounded by low marshy ground. From Gudkhali the fever travelled and diffused itself over a wide track, till it reached Ula at the commencement of the rainy season of 1856." Next year it visited Chagda, whence it "extended along the east bank of the river in a southerly direction down to Kanchrapara, Halisahar, Nayihati, and other places."

The Epidemic under notice, if not identical with, was of the same class as, the remittent fever of Bengal. Everywhere it was spoken of by the Natives as a "Nutan Jwar," and became popularly known under the name of "Bardwan Fever." It made its appearance towards the end of the rains, between the months of July and August, in the year 1860. The place of its first out-breaking is not accurately known. They called it the Bardwan Fever, not from its first appearing, but from its most virulently raging there. No clear statement on this head has been made in the Epidemic Commission report. The starting-point indicated there, is the neighbourhood of Triveni, where, according to Dr. Elliot, "intermittent fever of a severe type seems to have been prevalent, still the disease did not appear there as an epidemic until the commencement of the rains of 1860. From Triveni, the epidemic spread along the western bank of the river to Kalna in the Bardwan district."

In the accounts of all old writers, the plague is described to have been characterised by contagion, entire prostration of the strength, local eruptions, with livid spots peculiar to the disease. The epidemic fever of Bengal bore not the character of a plague. It did not spread by contagion. "Our enquiries," says the Epidemic Commissioners, "have not established the contagious nature of this fever. On the contrary, a remarkable circumstance related to us at Gram-Kalna seems to bear evidence to its absolutely non-contagious character. We were informed that a considerable number of people, residents of a village named Karuna, situated at some little distance, attended a 'Shrad' at Gram-Kalna; that while there they all fell sick; some died there, others returned to their village, and they also subsequently died. But the disease did not spread at Karuna. No inhabitant of that village who had not gone to Gram-Kalna caught it. * * * The disease was not transferred by contagion from the one village to the other. * * Viewing contagion in the widest meaning usually attached to the term, we have no sufficient grounds for stating that it is characteristic of the present fever. Still it is highly probable that the disease may be directly communicated by the effluvia of numerous sick persons congregated together in small ill-ventilated houses."

The Bengal, or more properly, the Bardwan epidemic fever is described "as essentially a congestive remittent fever, for the reason that the local organic congestions appear to be more marked and more formidable than are usually observed in the ordinary and less dangerous remittents of the country. During a first attack, the head is the seat of congestion. The eyes are bloodshot and aching, the face is suffused, delirium early ensues, and collapse, terminating fatally in from 36 hours to 4 or 5 days, closes the scene. Next in urgency to the cerebral symptoms we have to deal with a highly congested state of the thoracic viscera, and with great difficulty of breathing, the air tubes being loaded with mucus, and death finally resulting from asphyxia. The abdominal viscera do not appear to be so frequently implicated during the earlier stages, but they are almost invariably affected during the later period. The premonitory symptoms appear to be not well marked, but there is little doubt that for some time previous to the actual attack the patient is indisposed, though he seldom pays much attention to this warning. The first stage is ushered in by an accession of febrile heat, preceded by only slight shivering, frequently by no sensation of coldness whatever. This heat rapidly increases, and the disease runs the fatal course we have described. Should the patient, however, escape this deadly and urgent attack, the fever clings to him with unabated violence from 15 to 25 days from the commencement of the attack. During this period many succumb and die from exhaustion. After the fifteenth day, however, remission or intermission takes place, and the heat of skin and more urgent symptoms disappear, leaving the sufferer in a dangerous state of weakness and exhaustion. This freedom from febrile excitement continues for some ten days, when the enemy again assaults him, and though this takes place generally in a less violent and deadly manner than at first, yet from previous suffering and exhaustion the enervated frame is less able than before to withstand the attack, and the result is often fatal. This second attack, as just stated, is in itself less violent than the first, and it is of far shorter duration. The fever now assumes a well marked intermittent type; it returns usually after an interval of fourteen days, at new and full moon, and clings with great obstinacy to its victim. Still, though the well-marked intermittent type has set in, with its three distinct stages of cold and shivering, hot dry febrile skin, and perspiration, yet it is not by any means unusual for the fever again to relapse into a well-defined remittent. Again, all types of intermittent are met with from the true tertian and quartan to fevers recurring at intervals of five and fifteen days; and, as a rule, few who have been seriously attacked completely shake off the disease until change of season has fairly set in, or until they remove from the locality. When the disease has become chronic, and has assumed the intermittent type, enlarged spleens are the general rule. With this the liver also is frequently enlarged and congested, and the intestines are more or less implicated, chronic diarrhœa and even dysentry being no infrequent sequelæ. Anasarca and a general anœmic and emaciated condition are more or less seen in all these chronic cases, and the fatal result is, in the case of the majority of these debilitated wrecks, a mere question of time."

The first few cases here and there passed unheeded—the symptoms having no novelty to attract notice, and the people taking it for their usual endemic with a little more malignity. But when in the muggy days of September, between wet and heat, the disease began to rage violently and extend its progress from one, two, and three, into a group of villages, when not a hut or household in them was left unattacked, when none—Hindu or Mahomedan, rich or poor, men, women or children—was spared, the formidable visitant drawing every body's attention excited a deep alarm, and caused the utmost solicitude. All the resources at hand—the country Vaidyas, quacks, and empiric drugs were tried. But it soon became evident that the art of man was not able to overcome the disorder. The appalled villagers then looked for aid to charms and incantations, and supplicated Heaven with pujas. But nothing availed. The fever raged most violently, without any body being able to ascertain its mysterious cause. Filled with gloom and despondency, the demoralised people either resigned themselves to their fate, or removed to a better locality. Hundreds fell victims in the affected villages. Those that withstood the first acute virulence, were left subject to periodic attacks terminating in a late summons of death. Not till the approach of the cold weather was there any abatement, when the disease went into a lull from the absence of exciting causes.

This is the tale of the year 1860. Those of 1861 and 1862 are still more harrowing. In 1861, the epidemic broke out with redoubled force. The extent of its attack was widened westerly from Dwarbashini on the south to Bardwan on the north, and easterly as far as the villages in and about Barasat. The places most affected were Triveni, Halishahar, Kanchrapara, and Goulpara. It largely multiplied the number of its victims, and swept away whole families. The public noticed the serious mortality with great pain. The District officials became actively engaged in adopting measures of relief. Towards the end of the year, the British Indian Association memorialized the Government of Bengal for a proper system of medical relief as well as for timely steps to prevent the recurrence of the calamity. In the country, the people rendered the private aid lying in their power. The Government organized for a supply of medicines and the assistance of medical practitioners. But the fiend, laughing a hyena-laughter, renewed its attack the following year with the utmost fierceness. In 1862, the fever-stricken area extended northwards between Katwa on the west and Meherpur on the east, and southwards between Dwarbashini on the one hand and Goverdanga on the other. Further south, it reached down to Khurda and Belgharia, leaving out

Barrackpur and Dum Dum. Within this large tract every place suffered more or less, and in certain villages the ravages were terrible. One of these was Kalna-gram, where "a great number of homesteads had been deserted, and there was scarcely a house in which several inmates had not been carried off. Numbers of sick were to be seen lying in the verandas of the houses in the most emaciated and deplorable condition." In Bardwan, hundreds dying daily were carried away in dead-carts. The old and populous village of Dwarba shini, in Thanna Pandua, was nearly depopulated. The dead there lying without funeral became prey to the dogs and jackals. Santipur and Ula suffered most severly. Kanchrapara lost 1,354 out of 3,326 inhabitants. Halishahar, a town six square miles in area, was left with 1,727 families making a population of 6,687 persons. Describing the condition and appearance of some of the affected places within his jurisdiction, the Commissioner of Nadiya then wrote* :—" Every village has its homesteads, which have been emptied by death, or deserted by the occupants, in order to escape the scourge. Almost every man I met had a story to tell of his own sufferings, which his appearance confirmed, and a list to give of parents, wife, children, or relations carried off In some villages above a third of the population must have died in the last three years, and I have been assured by two respectable inhabtants of Halishahar that the state of debility to which the adults of this village

* Letter from the Commissioner of Nadiya to the Government of Bengal, dated the 4th July 1864.

have been reduced is so universal and so extreme that accessions to the population from the most natural source have almost ceased."

The cause of the inscrutable malady that had become an annual visitant defying all human skill and committing wide-spread ravages, now aroused a keen scientific enquiry. In Dr. Elliot's opinion, "it was as bad as, if not worse than, Cholera, and from its being of a new type it is not well understood, but this much seems established that it lies comparatively dormant during the cold weather, and begins to rage and extend itself further during and towards the end of the rains." It was at first supposed that the epidemic commenced in the crowded and unhealthy villages on the bank of the Hughli from some cause unknown as to the state of the river ; but this surmise proved to be altogether incorrect, as it made its appearance inland, commencing in the north east corner of Zillah Hughli and down the right bank of the Hughli river, working gradually on to the south and south-west corner. Next it was thought that the sickness proceeded from the insanitary condition of the villages—from the jungly brushwood and clumps of bamboos in the midst of habitation, from close fruit trees overhanging the roads and obstructing passage for sun and air, from decomposing offensive matters in the ditches during the rains, from innumerable holes and small tanks containing filthy water, from using and drinking the almost putrid water of *panah*-covered tanks, from an utter disregard to the simplest conservancy arrangements, and from poor living and clothing. All these made the *primafacie* evidence that could not fail to strike even the most superficial enquirer ; and no doubt to some extent they were aggravating accessories. Sanitary operations were therefore entered upon by cutting down the dense jungle, filling up the receptacles of impurities, improving the roadways, and cleansing the drinking-water tanks. But like the leg of mutton that Dr. Johnson pronounced to be "as bad as bad could be, ill-fed, ill-killed, ill-kept, and ill-dressed," a Bengali village is ill-located ; ill-built ; ill-ventilated ; and ill-conditioned from generation to generation. Jungle and tanks have existed from many ages, and yet no such visitation occurred in former days. Dwarbashini was to all appearance a healthy place, but it was worst up there. There was no jungle or underwood on a *Chur*, and yet the village upon it suffered severely. The existence of vegetation was not the sole or principal cause of the epidemic.

Owing to the jungle-clearances, less rain-fall, and a thinned population, there was a slight abatement of the virulence in 1863. But the large number of deaths still fully kept up public anxiety. The return made by the Pandua Police Station showed a mortality of 25 per cent in six months. One official wrote "nothing has been done to stop it, and whether any human means can do is still a question to be decided." A second remarked "no one that I have seen can account for its rise or spread." A third one returned "I cannot conceal from myself the fact that we have not arrived at the real causes of the pestilence that is extending year by year, and I consider that the subject demands a closer enquiry. I would therefore beg to suggest, for the consideration of His Honor the Lieutenant-Governor, whether it would not be advisable to appoint a Commission, consisting not only of Medical Officers, but European and Native gentlemen combined, who have had an insight into Mofasil habits, and can sift the matter more thoroughly, and that no further outlay be made excepting in medical aid and the dispensing of medicines until the real cause of the epidemic has been arrived at." The British Indian Association also made a similar representation.

In pursuance of these suggestions the Government of Bengal, early in January 1864, decided upon appointing a Commission to enquire into the causes of the epidemic, and to report on the best remedial measures for the prevention of its recurrence. Besides three medical officers and one officer of the Civil Service, the Government wanted to have a Native gentleman "whose local interests and intimate acquaintance with the habits and customs of the people may be likely to render his aid of especial use in furthering the object of the enquiry." Writing for such a competent individual to the British Indian Association, the Committee of that body submitted the name of Babu Digambar Mitra. The nomination meeting with approval, he was appointed a member of the Commission on 9th January 1864.

The British Indian Association possessed several eminent men, but beyond dispute Digambar was one of the ablest and worthiest of them. In the beginning, he gave little promise of the abilities or of the character which he afterwards displayed. But the Association was a training ground where he ripened in a few years, and began to attract notice. Digambar had a mind to make himself useful to his nation, and a will earnestly bent upon that object. With this aim, he was waiting for a favourable juncture to issue from the shade into the broad day of public life. The Epidemic Commission turned out to give the desired opportunity to push into that life. Shortly afterwards, on the 23rd February 1864, there followed a second opportunity by Government further nominating him along with Mr. H. Fraser to conduct the investigation and trial of claims to Waste Lands, in the Twenty-four Parga nas. There was not another man more qualified and willing to undertake the two duties required of him. In the first place, he had spent many years out of home, during which, withdrawn from every eye, he acquired those stores of the knowledge of Mofasil life and that practical experience which the Government urgently needed, and which no body else possessed in the same degree excepting Babu Jaikissen Mukerjea. Next, he was a man of acute common sense. The peculiar faculty of his mind was that quickness of perception in new situations and sudden contingencies which penetrated into remote causes and consequences. He pursued objects with a steady resolution, undiverted by trifles, unembarrassed by scruples, and undeterred by difficulties. Such were the qualifications with which he was prepared to go through the two sacred trusts reposed in him by his associates and the Government. To the execution of his task in the Epidemic Commission he brought all his thoughts and energies. His strenuous exertion in the interests of his suffering countrymen was his great life-work, which he accomplished with the approbation of his conscience, the esteem of his nation, and the honor with which his name shall be long remembered by posterity.

Holding a preliminary meeting in which it was settled that the members "should personally, and as far as possible in concert, visit the fever-stricken villages," the Epidemic Commission proceeded with their work. From the 19th January until the end of February 1864, they were engaged in visiting the villages reported to have suffered most severely during the past three years. They entered upon their tour of investigation through the Districts of Hugli, Bardwan, Nadiya, and the Twenty-four Parganas, visiting Triveni, Pandua, Dwarbashini, Balagar, Guptipara, Kalna, Krishnagar, Ula, Chagda, Kanchrapara, Halishahar, Majergram, Jaguli, Rajhat, and Barasat, and many other minor villages affected by the epidemic fever.

Babu Digambar kept company, and proceeded through all the above places in which the brunt of questioning the inhabitants fell on him for being the Native member, who was best fitted to elicit satisfactory answers. The enquiry of the Commission consisted of two parts: the first and most pressing one was to relieve the present distress of the patients ; the next and more difficult part of the task was to trace the evil to its source and provide measures against its recurrence. We cannot here attempt to give anything more than a very general account of the result of their labors. Abstaining from all matters connected with the nature of the soil and the condition of the villages, we shall confine ourselves simply to the statements made with reference to the first part of their business, namely, the suggestion of remedial measures for immediate relief, or in other words, of curative treatment, regarding which the Commission, in their Report, submitted on 31st March 1864, remarked :—"It can hardly be said that every mode of treatment hitherto adopted has proved altogether successful, probably because few of those who recover from the first attacks of fever are able to remove from the localities in which they were first taken ill, and in which the exciting causes of disease continue to exist in full force, and so all who have once suffered are liable to constant relapses, which debilitate and eventually wear out the system. It must be borne in mind that, do what we may, the disease must run a certain course, which is neither to be accelerated, nor retarded by any means within our reach.

. . . The greatest tendency in its course is to congestion of the liver or spleen, or of both, to obviate which all remedies seem to have failed. With each relapse of fever there appears to be a fresh tendency to sub-inflamation and consequent enlargement of the spleen, until at last a sort of local inflamatory action of low-grade seems to be established, to which, perhaps, the successive attacks of fever are in some measure to be attributed." The treatment suggested by them is what is commonly followed in fever cases, *viz.*, "the regulation of the bowels; cold douche and application of ice or leeches or a blister to the shaven head; sponging the body; placing the feet in hot water once or twice daily; and cooling or effervescent draughts to relieve nausea and abate thirst. In the absence of actual fever bitter tonics with iron, quinine, and mineral acids should be prescribed. If the type be intermittent, then after the bowels are regulated, quinine is the only anti-periodic which is of any service whatever, and even its effects seem to be only temporary, for, notwithstanding the steady use of it for days, fresh attacks of fever occur at intervals of ten to fifteen days, attended with further congestion, and enlargement of the liver or spleen, or both, till at last the system is worn out and dropsy, diarrhœa, dysentry, or some of the other sequelæ terminate an existence of protracted misery. After placing the sick in a condition as favourable to recovery as circumstances admit, it appears that we must proceed to a great extent on the expectant system, save the strength as much as possible by avoiding the use of unnecessary medicines, such as strong or drastic purgatives, which debilitate and depress the system; and guard, if possible, the functions necessary to life from sustaining serious injury."

With reference to the other part of their business—that of tracing the malady to its cause or causes, the Commission reported :—"We have been led to ascribe the prevailing sickness to (1) Miasm, (2) Polluted drinking water, (3) Vitiated air and deficient ventilation, (4) The excessive use of farinaceous food, and (5) Contagion to a slight extent" Out of these diverse causes, they recommended that "our first object must be to reduce, as much as possible, the generation of miasm, or malarious exhalations rising principally from moisture in the soil during the drying process after the rains; and any means by which this drying process can be accelerated and shortened will produce a *pro tanto* diminishing effect on the total amount of miasm generated. To effect this object the obvious course is to improve the drainage of the country obstructed by the silting up of rivers and khals, and the general assimilation of levels which have gradually taken place of late years. Remembering that the direction of the natural drainage of the villages situated along the river banks is inland, we have no difficulty in believing that it is impeded by the Railway embankments on both sides. . . . With a view to improve the internal drainage of the villages, we would strongly recommend the construction of open water-ways to carry off the surface water directly to any neighbouring river, khal, or beel that may be available, or failing such to some one or more low pools or tanks outside the village." In justice to the Commission, it should be said that in laying stress upon miasm and suggesting the improvement of drainage, they made an approximate hit upon the primary cause of the disease, and upon the most effectual means of checking its repetition. But, as will be shown hereafter, they made a close approach to, and then went off in a tangent from, the mark. A water-logged subsoil arising from defective drainage was indeed mentioned as the chief exciting cause, but they did not definitely trace the abnormal humidity to the right source, and only incidentally attributed it to the silting up of rivers and khals. This left the question open to future enquiries and opinions which seriously interfered with the good results expected from the Commission.

With regard to the removal of the collateral causes, the suggestions refer to those endeavours of sanitary improvements—to jungle-cutting, and tank clearing, and subsoil-draining, and village building, and burial removing, and to the use of stamina-improving food, to dwell on which would be to tell a tale twice over.

The Report was duly subscribed with the other members by Babu Digambar. But as he had to tell something more about the drainage, he appended the two following papers under his own individual name.

STATEMENT RELATIVE TO THE EPIDEMIC FEVER AT COSSIM BAZAR AND THE NEIGHBOURING VILLAGES.

* * * * * *

Choonakhally, Bhautpara, Cossim Bazar, Kalkapore, Bamunghatta, and Furreshdanga were situated on a curve of the River Hooghly, until a straight cut was made some sixty years since forming the chord of the curve, thus changing the course of the river and throwing those places inland. This engineering operation was closely followed by the breaking out of an epidemic in all those places which, in its virulence and mortality, is unparalleled by any pestilential visitation in Bengal, saving perhaps that which depopulated Gour.* During its rage cremation or burial in due form was found impracticable, and the dead are said to have been carried in cart loads to be disposed of any how; and thus the city of Cossim Bazar, once noted for its commercial importance, the extent and magnitude of which is said to have called into existence upwards of a hundred shroffs or banking firms to meet the monetary requirements of the same, was reduced, within the short space of five years, to almost a deserted waste.

This fever continues there to the present time, shewing that its causes are still in active operation. In other respects Cossim Bazar does not at all differ from any healthy town in Bengal. Its waters, vegetation, houses, and the mode of life of its inhabitants are exactly alike; but no man sojourning there even for a day can help being struck with the extreme dampness which is felt even during the hottest months of the year. This dampness can only arise from excessive moisture in the sub-soil, owing to the disturbance in the drainage of the place, occasioned, most probably, by the diversion in the course of the river, aided perhaps by a number of roads running transeversely to the direction of the drainage. How caused it is not easy at this

* It is highly probable that the long continued pestilence which necessitated the removal of the seat of Government from Gour to Tanda was caused by interruption in the drainage of the city. The heavy embankment on the margin of the lake or bheel on its eastern extremity, while guarding the city from inundation, must have effectually shut out the drainage in its flow into the lake.

distance of time correctly to trace, and perhaps immaterial to our present enquiry. Enough that the place is extremely damp. This is undeniable, and I think it is likewise undeniable that this extreme dampness is owing to an excess of moisture in the soil.

* * * * *

MEMORANDUM RELATIVE TO CERTAIN OBSTRUCTIONS TO THE DRAINAGE OF THE EPIDEMIC DISTRICTS.

The drainage of all the villages in the Epidemic Districts, as elsewhere in Lower Bengal, is effected by water first running into the nearest *paddy fields* lying in the direction of their slope, thence it collects in the *bheels* from which it rushes through *khals* into larger streams, which again communicate with navigable rivers. An obstruction occurring in any one of these conduits must interfere with the drainage, and its effects are felt more or less according to the proximity or remoteness of the obstruction from the scene of its influence. Accordingly it has been found, as will be noticed more particularly hereafter, that the stoppage of the mouths of the different streams has not been productive of such serious consequences to the villages lying within their influence as when the same occurred more in the vicinity of those villages.

The obstructions appear to have arisen chiefly from roads and partly from embankments thrown up across khals for purposes of fisheries. I had neither time nor opportunities at command to trace in every instance how, and when, the stoppage had taken place, enough however, has been discovered to satisfy me of the correctness of my general conclusions.

The banks of large rivers as a rule being always high, the slope of the village situated on either side of the Hoogly runs inland. Accordingly the drainage of all the villages from Trebeni to Nasurye, as also of those lying more inland, at one time passed over the adjoining paddy fields to the west into the River Koontee through the Jhenook Khalee Khal. On either side of this khal are beds of sand of a superior quality, which is extensively used for building purposes. In the process of excavating this sand a large quantity of surface earth is thrown up and deposited close to the bed of the khal, and being gradually washed into it has caused some obstruction in that channel. The mouth of the

Koontee again, called Nasurye Khal, has since several years considerably silted up, closing its navigation soon after the rains. These stoppages, though interfering to a certain extent with the drainage of the country, did not produce any serious consequences. About five years since, however, a road was run by Baboo Mudoosudun Nundy (unprovided with a single bridge) from Mugra to Nasurye, crossing the watercourse and thereby completely intercepting the drainage of all the villages noticed above in its flow into the Koontee. This resulted in the breaking out of the epidemic a year or two after almost simultaneously in all those villages. In the same manner Joypore, Bagaty, and the other adjacent villages were attacked soon after the village road from Trebeni to Mugra was raised and metalled without any outlet being kept across it, thus stopping the drainage of those places, which when the road was kutcha and on a level with the country, flowed over into the Koontee.

A road from Rajhat to Dwarbashini crossing a bheel where the drainage of the latter place used to collect, has stopped its passage into the Kadermuttee. There is an apology for a bridge constructed, the ryots said, about two years since, but I was satisfied by personal observation that it was quite insufficient to afford free passage to the drainage of the place, as large collections of water in the bheel itself at a time of the year when even large tanks begin to dry up otherwise fully proved. The result is that a violent epidemic has been raging in Dwarbashini since August last. Again, the Unjona, which was at one time a navigable stream during the rains, carrying in its fall into the Matabhanga the drainage of a number of villages in the vicinity of Kishnaghur, has silted up at both the ends since fourteen years, yet none of the villages of which it was the main sewer suffered therefrom. A kutcha road, however, running from the Barobazar of Kishnaghur to Lollbagaun, crossing the water-courses of Baroepara, has been raised within the last two or three years, completely intercepting the drainage of that village. which had hitherto flowed over it into the paddy fields; and it has been followed by the breaking out of a fearful epidemic in Baroepara since August last.

In like manner the Eastern Bengal Railway and its feeders, when the same have crossed the water-courses of villages lying on the eastern bank of the River Hooghly, and of others more inland, but situated to the west of the line, have obstructed the drainage of those places; the fall of the villages lying on the eastern bank of the Hooghly, as I have before observed, being towards the east, and consequently Chagda, Kanchrapara, Halisahar, and many others similarly situated have suffered.

I may here remark that the face of the country being perfectly flat, the drainage runs over the whole surface towards the direction of its slope, and consequently roads running transversely to it must of necessity intercept the drainage. Both the East Indian and the Eastern Bengal Railways are provided with capacious viaducts whenever they have crossed what appeared to the eye as water-courses; but these are in reality khals and other large streams, which as I have already observed, received the drainage in its flow from the villages over *paddy-fields* and *bheels*. The latter exhibit no visible signs of their being water-ways, and could not be known as such unless narrowly watched during the rains, though a road crossing them would more effectually shut out the drainage, and the evil consequences resulting therefrom would be much sooner felt than when it crossed distant channels. Taking into consideration the number of roads which have sprung up of late as also others in course of construction, and bearing in mind likewise the manner in which the drainage of the country is effected, and the difficulty thereby entailed of providing those roads with a sufficient number of outlets, it is not improbable that in the cases of those villages which have not yet been examined, obstructions to their drainage would, upon enquiry, appear to have proceeded chiefly from roads having been made without reference to the water-shed of the country, and without being provided with a sufficient number of water-courses.

The foregoing papers contain the germs of that theory for which Babu Digambar stoutly contended in the Epidemic controversy. He enunciated it more fully in a series of articles in the *Hindoo Patriot* at a subsequent date, when, in order of time, we shall advert to the subject in its proper place.

CHAPTER XII.

THE FIRST CAREER IN THE BENGAL COUNCIL. THE GREAT RENT CASE.

BABU Digambar's labours in the Epidemic Fever Commission, with his shrewd remarks on the subject principally involved in its enquiry, became the foundation of his fame. Henceforth "his talents and abilities became known to Government." Henceforth he occupied a space in the public eye, and rose in public opinion. We shall see him now influencing Legislative measures for the good of his countrymen. In consideration of his various valuable services and in justice to his merits, the Government, towards the end of 1864., honored him with elevation to the Legislative Council of Bengal. After making a solemn declaration of allegiance to Her Majesty, and that he would faithfully fulfil the duties of his office, he took his seat in the Council on Saturday,

November 12th, 1864. The only Hindu gentlemen who had preceded him in this honourable appointment, were Babu Prasana Coomar Tagore, Raja Protap Chandra Singh, Babu Ramaprosad Roy, Babu Ramgopal Ghosh, and Raja Satya Sharan Ghosal.

In offering seats in the Council to Native gentlemen, the Government must be understood to have made an opening for training them in statesmanship. The individual lifted there ascends the political stage, and begins a political career. He becomes the recognised representative of his country on whom all eyes are fixed with hopeful expectations. A sacred trust is committed to him in which he has to act in a dual capacity, holding in his own hand his reputation. The office is not for the mere patrician Maharaja, or millionaire, or Zamindar, or merchant, or pleader, or attorney, or doctor. It is not for the dummy, with silence, and not Sarasvati, on his tongue. It is not for the toady, with whom "to hear is to obey." It is not for the *apkawastai*, who sells "his soul for a mess of pottage." The man must have versatile experience, with qualities both of the head and heart. The Government have been chary enough in conferring the appointment, but have in some instances favored the weakness of parvenues coveting the distinction. The selection of Babu Digamber must be acknowledged to have been a happy one. He was not born, but rose to the station of a wealthy man. He possessed experience with an active inquiring intellect.

He could as well "give an understanding" as "tongue" to the matters on the tapis,—"was inured to public speaking and public writing. He mastered points with a grasp of mind that enabled him to give speedy and unembarrassed judgments. He had an enlargement of mind, with moral courage. His loyalty was combined with manly independent sentiments and principles of honor. He was recommended by the proofs he had shown of intelligence, activity, prudence, and humanity. Hence, he rendered important services during the tenure of his legislative office, and did not disappoint his nation.

It was hardly a month after taking his seat in the Council when an opportunity occurred to give a proof of the stuff he was made of. There were two Bills, one on Protection against Fire in Ports, and another on The Storage of inflammable oils in the Town and Suburbs of Calcutta, on which he at first sat in Select Committee without any difference of opinion. They were followed on the 17th December following by the Bill for the Regulation of Jails, introduced by Mr. Cockerell. In consequence of "the insecurity of many Jails, the use of irons, although not strictly legal," had been adopted in this Bill. Babu Digambar took objection to this point, and said :—

Before the motion was affirmed, he craved leave to say a few words in reference to the principle of the Bill. It struck him that the principal aim of this Bill was to provide means for the conduct of the Jails with the least possible expense to the State. The object certainly was very desirable, if it could only be attained without disregarding the calls of justice and humanity. The Hindu rulers of old dispensed altogether with the necessity of maintaining such costly institutions, by punishing the criminals with the deprivation of the different members of their body according to the different degrees of criminality. The 4th Section of the Bill in question looked like an attempt to ignore the modern necessity of secure and commodious buildings for the reception of prisoners, by providing that, for the purpose of safe custody, the inmates of the Jails should be put in irons. This, he respectfully submitted, was a retrograde move in legislation and Jail discipline, and he did not see in the Statement of Objects and Reasons that any necessity had been made out for so flagrant a departure from the only true principle which would justify the infliction of pains and penalties upon humanity, namely, the prevention of crime. It must be presumed that the laws of the land were sufficiently vindicated by any punishment prisoners might have been sentenced to. The infliction of any additional suffering, not for any offence committed afresh, but simply by way of security against their escape, even if it were infinitely less galling and degrading than the measure proposed, would be an outrage against humanity, as it would be subversive of the just principles of legislation. But whence arose this anxiety? It should be borne in mind that the prisoners confined in these insecure divisional kutcha Jails were mostly those who were sentenced to short periods of imprisonment, because those who were undergoing long periods of imprisonment could be easily removed to District Jails, which were pucka, and, for purposes of safe custody, secure enough. Was it for a moment to be supposed that these short term prisoners were insane enough to run out of the frying pan into the fire? That they should exchange their sufferings of two or three months for rigorous imprisonment for two years? They must know full well, that sooner or later they must be recaptured, unless they preferred the worse alternative of roaming among wild beasts—perpetual exiles from home. But even if it were otherwise, he respectfully contended that it were infinitely better that a prisoner or two occasionally escaped, until proper places were ready for their safe custody, than that this Council should commit itself to a doctrine so far behind the age. He had grave objections to some other Sections of the Bill, but those Sections, however, might, and no doubt would, be remedied in Committee. He felt it his duty to press upon the Council that the Bill might not, at any rate, be referred to a Select Committee with the Section he objected to. He would conclude by moving that the fourth Section of the Bill be expunged before it be read in Council.

In reply to him the Honourable Ashley Eden said that "the Honourable Member had totally mistaken the scope and object of the Bill. The Section to which he had objected contained no new principle. The practice had been in force ever since this country had been under British rule. If 'humanity was outraged' by the imposition of fetters, it had been outraged without murmur for a century." Mr. Cockerell followed him by observing that "he hoped the Bill would be read in Council as it stood. The Honourable Member who spoke last had pointed out how mistaken the Honourable Member (Babu Digambar) who had preceded him had been with regard to the objects of the measure, and it was unnecessary for him to say more. It was simply a temporary measure, and one of expediency, on account of the insecurity of the existing Jails." Mr. Jennings thought that "the first consideration was, the security of honest people. He had no sympathy with that morbid consideration for criminals which was too common in India, and if Jails were at present insecure, a measure like the one now proposed was absolutely necessary." To all these, Babu Digambar replied "that notwithstanding what had been said he adhered to his original opinion. It was no argument that the principle of using fetters was an old one. What should be considered was,

was it a good one." The reader needs no comment to form his opinion on the matter—to decide between expediency and humanity.

We come next to narrate an interesting event in the annals of our country. Ever since the Grant of the Dewani to the East India Company in 1765, the laws relating to land formed the most important part of British legislation in India. At first the revenue was collected according to the existing Mogul system. "The zamindars, or Government farmers, whose office always tended to become hereditary, were recognised as having a right to collect the revenue from the actual cultivators. But no principle of assessment existed, and the amount actually realized varied greatly from year to year. Hastings tried to obtain experience, from a succession of five years' settlements, so as to furnish a standard rate for the future. Francis, the great rival of Hastings, advocated, on the other hand, a limitation of the State demand in perpetuity. The same view recommended itself to the authorities at Home, partly because it would place their finances on a more stable basis, partly because it seemed to identify the zamindar with the landlord of the English system of property. Accordingly, Cornwallis took out with him in 1787 instructions to introduce a Permanent Settlement." The Regulations of 1793, the most important of all Indian enactments, because affecting more closely than any others the daily life of the people, became the great Land Law of Bengal.

"The framers of that Land Code found a vast number of ill-defined and sometimes conflicting rights in the soil. They selected the most conspicuous class of these rights, namely, those of the superior holder, and defined them with a fair amount of precision. The subordinate rights were acknowledged to exist in a general way and reserved, but they were not defined. While, therefore, the landholder or superior tenure-holder entered the courts with clearly ascertained rights and a legislative sanction for getting them enforced, the vast multitude of under-tenants and cultivators could point to no ascertained rights nor to any legislative definition of them. A uniform enforcement of so amorphous and incomplete a measure was impossible. Practically, the District Officer cut the knot by settling in his executive capacity such cases as threatened the tranquility of his people, and trusted to his personal influence to get his decisions accepted and carried out. The cases which came before him in his judicial capacity produced a mass of conflicting decisions, which, when the subject was seriously taken up by the Legislature at the commencement of the Queen's rule, the best lawyers in India, after years of labour, failed to unravel. Even after the Land Law (Act X) of 1859 had supplemented the Regulations of 1793 by defining the rights of the cultivators and subordinate tenure-holders, the subject was so involved that no class of the agriculturists knew precisely what its rights were. The Land Act of 1859 threw Bengal into a paroxysm of litigation."

In all the Mofasil Lower Courts, the files swarmed with innumerable cases. The High Court, recently come into existence by the amalgamation of the Supreme and Sadar Courts, was flooded with incessant appeals. Towards the end of 1864, after five years' experience of the operation of the new law, the Judges felt it their imperative duty to come to a final decision of the question of Rent pending between the landlord and the tenant. The whole staff of fifteen Judges representing the highest legal talent, with Sir Barnes Peacock, the acutest lawyer that ever came to India, at the head, and Justice Sambhunath Pandit at hand, met together to definitively interpret the provisions. They sat at the long hall of the Town Hall, making an imposing scene. The Counsel on the side of the Zamindars and Landholders, was Mr. Doyne, the first Barrister of his day, with a host of the most noted Native Pleaders. The Rayats relied upon the efforts of only one individual—Babu Dwarkanath Mitra, who was but just pushing his way. But just as the genius of one single man—Babu Harish Chandra Mukerjea, carried them successfully through the Indigo Crisis, did the genius of Babu Dwarkanath Mitra alone carry them through the great Rent Case trial. He fought single-handed with a cleverness and adroitness that earned him in a little time a seat on the Bench. Protracted through a number of days, the big trial came to its end with the judgment of the majority of the Judges in favour of the Rayats. But "in order to decide a simple claim for rent, they travelled out of the statute-book into the domain of unascertained history, and made their decisions antiquarian discussions rather than declarations of the written law," making "confusion worse confounded."

In a little time, opinion became pretty unanimous that their judgment had failed to offer a satisfactory solution of the difficulties experienced in the adjustment of rent since the passing of Act X of 1859. It was criticised by Babu Jaikissen Mukerjea in a pamphlet called *The Permanent Settlement Imperilled.* Babu Digambar Mitra also came out in 1865 with a little brochure styled *Observations on the Judgments of the High Court in the Rent Case.* He thus alludes in it to their entering into questions of recondite history:— "Instead of wandering in the mystic regions of the Vedas and of Manu, if the learned Judges had only confined themselves to the Act itself which they were expounding, they would have avoided commiting themselves to the dangerous dictum into which they have evidently been betrayed. Touching "the Pargana rates for the time being" on which the Judges had laid particular stress, and "a certain share of the Rayats in the produce of the soil" Babu Digambar says:—

I fully admit the force of the truth that the land belonged to him who first reclaimed it from its virgin state, just as much as I admit that the whole human race is one brotherhood, and that the heritage derived from one common Father should be shared and enjoyed by all alike. I only regret that the degeneracy of man should have so fast set in, as to necessitate even in the days of Menu (Satya yoge) the maintenance of institutions, which deprived the proprietors of the soil of one-sixth of their hard-earned produce. There is no knowing what mutations this rate gradually underwent until during Akbar's reign it swelled up to ½ the produce as the sovereign's share, with cesses innumerable. It would be a mere waste of time to hunt for materials whereupon to rest any general principle of right, when the will of the sovereign was its only measure, and might the only arbiter. I only wonder that the learned Judges should have considered it safe to draw judicial conclusions from opinions expressed in historical works, in matters which they must of their own experience, know well enough, are not easy of solution, even upon an enquiry conducted with all the precision of a judicial investigation. Whatever may be the value of the authorities quoted, or the logical sequence of the facts recited in the judgment, one thing is certain that the invariable customary rate, which is alleged to have governed the sovereigu's share from time immemorial in the produce of the soil, had varied from one-sixth in the time of Menu to ½ in the reign of Akbar with cesses limited only by the ryot's capacity to bear. Let us see how this customary or Pergunnah rate and the right of occupancy have been recognized and respected under the British rule.

The brochure, dwelling minutely on the salient points, makes a critical exposition worth the research of the student of Revenue Law. Though written principally from the Zamindar's point of view, the author vindicates himself from an one-sided argumentation by the following remarks :—

In conclusion I owe a word to the reader in explanation of the motive which has impelled me to these hasty remarks. Living in a country almost exclusively agricultural, I feel that a clear and precise understanding of the relative rights of the landlord and tenant in the soil, is of the most vital importance to the peace and harmony of its teeming millions. The question, notwithstanding numberless legislative enactments and judicial decisions, yet remains on a most unsatisfactory footing, and the amount of misery, litigation and heart-burning caused by it, can be adequately conceived by those only, who, like myself, have constant opportunities of experiencing them in their stern reality. Any attempt, however humble and insignificant, to aid in the solution of this all-important, though much vexed question, I regard, therefore, as a contribution to the cause of humanity. Class interest I most emphatically disavow; it is the furthest from my view. That even handed justice—justice without fear or favor—may be done to all who are interested in the matter, is my only and most solemn desire; and if in the heat of argument I have said aught that might savour of partizanship, I beg that it may be attributed to the disadvantage I unhappily labour under, of writing principally on a side of the question, the justice due to which, I am afraid, has been very much overlooked by too generous and sympathetic a leaning to the other and indeed the more popular side.

CHAPTER XIII.

THE GANGA-JATRA CASE. THE ORISSA FAMINE. THE HOOK-SWINGING BILL. THE INOCULATION PROHIBITION BILL.

IN the latter half of 1865, an old man was taken to the river-side at Dacca to die. He had been carried there in an early stage of his sickness, and not quite in a moribund state. Shortly after his removal his relations made him undergo the *Antarjali* ceremony, or the immersion of his nether limbs in the river. He survived this performance for many days, during which they laid him exposed to a fierce sun in the day, and to night dews in the evening, without a cover over him. Death, either purposely hastened or happening in due time, at last relieved him. The atrocity of the case—his Antarjali long before the proper time and subsequent neglectful exposure, kindled public indignation. The *Dacca Prokash*, then the only vernacular local paper, published an account drawing the attention of Government.

The Missionaries on the spot also raised their voice by demanding an official enquiry into the matter, and adequate punishment upon the delinquents. The Government of Bengal, promptly attending to the call and finding no over-statement in the report, became minded for a measure repressive of the barbarity.

Like the Sati and Infanticide, the barbarous *Gangajatra* custom of the Hindus is "ghat-murder" in the European eye. Many outrageous instances had come to notice from time to time. In 1818, Mr. Corrie (a chaplain), during his journey up the Ganges to Benares, entered in his Diary :—" During the 19th and 20th, we had an opportunity of witnessing two distressing instances of the unfeeling conduct of the Hindus towards the sick and dying. On one occasion, two women were employed at the river side, filling the mouth of a child with mud. Miss B. asked them, if the child were ill? One of them answered 'yes;' Miss B. :—'you are going to kill it outright? On which they began to laugh, and talk with each other; and prosecuted their work of death. Further on, a sick man was laid, with several people sitting round. A young and handsome Brahman was attempting to bind a weight round his neck, in order to sink him in the river, which the sick man was resisting, with marks of much remaining strength. Abdullah called out :—'Take him into some warm place, and he will recover,' to which the Brahman answered with a significant nod :

'Aye, aye, we will put him into a warm place; on which the persons around laughed aloud."

Actuated by Christian humanity, a Missionary gentleman made an able representation on the subject many years ago in an old number of the *Calcutta Review*. The Government had long perceived the necessity and meditated a measure against the evil. The Dacca case gave a plea for interference. It engaged the attention of the Bengal Government at nearlv the same time with the removal of the Burning Ghat from Calcutta, on which Babu Ramgopal Ghosh made his famous sensational speech with success. Under the Lieutenant-Governor's instructions, the Hon'ble Ashley Eden circulated a confidential unofficial communication to several gentlemen—to "Officers of Government whose experience was likely to give weight to their opinions, as well as intelligent Natives, both orthodox and those not so strict in the obser vance of national usages,"—requesting an expres sion of their views upon the points noticed therein. Raja Satya Sharan Ghosal and Babus Prasana Coomar Tagore and Digambar Mitra, were the Native gentlemen who were addressed on the occasion. The views expressed by Babu Digambar Mitra are contained in the following letter.

To THE

HON'BLE A. EDEN, SECRETARY TO THE GOVERNMENT OF BENGAL

(*Dated the 25th October 1865.*)

MY DEAR SIR,

I am in receipt of your letter of the 11th ultimo, and in reply beg to submit the following remarks :—

The subject you refer to may be considered under the *heads, first,* that of *Gunga Jattra,* or the practice of taking sick people to the river side to die ; and *second,* that of *Antarjali,* or the ceremony of immersing the nether limbs of dying persons in water at the moment of death. The first is but the prelude to the second, but taken by itself, there is nothing in it revolting or pernicious. As a general rule it is resorted to only in the case of people advanced in years who have been given up by their physicians, and whose dissolution is hourly expected. Men and women under 40 years of age are seldom taken, and children never. If allowance be made for these as also for sudden deaths, want of means and other causes which interfere with the practice, bearing in mind at the same time that 50 per cent of children die before the seventh year of their age, and that three-eighths of the remaining 50 per cent, die before they grow up to the fortieth year, it will be found that but a very small number of sick people are taken to the river before their death. Nor are the majority of those who are so taken subjected to any avoidable hardship or suffering. The time selected for the purpose is generally the dawn or the night, and every precaution is taken, that the means of the dying and their nearest relatives can afford, to avoid exposure to the weather on the way and during their stay near the river. Medical treatment is never intermitted. This I state from extensive personal experience, and I have no hesitation in saying that the assertion of the Editor of the *Dacca Prokash* about *uncovered* exposure to the fierce rays of the sun, and to the violence of storms and rains, is as unfounded as the rest of his remarks are high-colored and exaggerated. Such exposure might take place by accident, but never by design or culpable neglect.

What the physical effect of a transition from the close atmosphere of a sick chamber to the river side may be on a dying person who has been given up by his medical attendant, it is needless to enquire; for admitting the medical men to be inefficient in many cases, they are the best the patients can command, and their chance of life must therefore depend upon their treatment whether at home or by the river.

It is not to be denied that the mental effect of announcing to a sick man that he was about to die, and of taking him to the place which is most intimately associated in his mind with immediate death must be generally very depressing, but as they are not resorted to until the attending physicians pronounce the patient to be past all hope of recovery,.

their evil consequences cannot be great, nor can they over-balance the great good they otherwise effect by soothing the mind of the faithful at a time when, with eternity before him, he most needs the succour of a higher power than that of man. The anxiety which dying natives often evince to be taken to the river at their last moment ; the supplications they put forth to impel their relatives not to lose time in affording them their last solace of religion, clearly shew that the practice is not so repulsive to those who are most concerned in it as it may at first sight appear to a foreigner. Certain it is that the announcement of the near approach of death to the dying cannot be avoided, for it is at that time that religion steps in, and, whether it be in the form of religious consolation, the last mass or the ceremony of crossing the Styx (Voitarani) invariably does long before what the "procession to the Ganges" but supplements in the case of the Hindoos. It might offend our feelings of delicacy, but there is nothing in it that would amount to criminal neglect or render any party morally culpable. The Hindoos believe that it is unfortunate to die within a room, and therefore in places where the river Bhagirathi is not easily accessible, the dying are taken out of the house and placed in an open spot surrounded by tulsi shrubs with the body touching the bare ground. This, as regards exposure, is worse than the procession to the Ganges, for in the one case the patient is kept in a room, and in the other under the canopy of the sky ; and for the sake of consistency, the one ought to be as soon suppressed as the other. The concern of the dying, however, at such a time is with his Maker, and Government cannot, without doing great violence to the religious belief of the people, interfere and legislate as to how and where a man should die.

As regards *Antarjali,* it is no doubt a very offensive ceremony. As a religious observance it is not enjoined by the Hindoo Shastras as absolutely indispensable, nor is any penalty attached to its neglect. From its very nature it cannot be observed except along the banks of Bhagirathi otherwise called the Ganges, for it is there alone the ceremony is enjoined ; and consequently it is confined to but a few districts of Bengal. But it nevertheless exercises a potent influence on the minds of the community, and as a means of spiritual consolation to the dying, it is most intimately connected with the religious fabric of Hindooism. The twenty-eight

Digests of Raghunandan, which govern the religious observances of the Hindoos in Bengal, hold death in the waters of the Ganges as the most important for salvation. The digest on purification (*Sudhitatto*) quotes several verses on the subject, one of which, from Karmapurana, lays down that "in the Ganges salvation (Moksha) is secured in water; at Benaras it is secured both in water and on land, but at Gungasagara (Sagore Island) it is obtained in land and in water as in mid-air," death in mid-air being, under ordinary circumstances, reckoned highly unfornate. Elsewhere the Karmapurana adds that "the man who dies conscientiously in the Ganges obtains salvation (Mukti), but he who dies unconsciously goes to the Brahmaloka." According to the Skando Purana, Siva addressing his wife Doorga, says, "I shall now relate to you. O thou of a beautiful face, the merit of dying in the river Ganges. I pour into the ears of such dying people the *Mantra* of the great Brahma and assign to him my own rank." The Agni Purana quoted in the "Digest or exposition" by Rughunandan (Prayschittatatta) says—"he who departs this life half immersed (up to the navel) in the water of the Jahnobhi (Bhagirathi) is never born again, and obtains the rank of an equal of Brahma." As long as Hinduism will last so long will those verses continue to govern the Hindoo mind, hallowed as they have been by the custom of ages in a country where custom exercises a much more powerful influence than even the precepts of its scripture. The ceremony, barbarous as it is, has been in practice from time immemorial, and to suppress it, a case ought to be made only sufficiently strong to justify legislative interference. This I believe has not yet been done. The mere fact of a particular custom being barbarous is not enough, it must be proved likewise to be criminal before legislation can be brought to bear upon it. I am aware that the European mind has been from a long time inflamed by exaggerated stories of enormities committed during the ceremony of *Antarjali.* It is generally believed that the mouth, nostrils, and the ears of the dying are stuffed with clay, and death is hastened by immersion of the head into water. These are, however, not facts. The nether limbs are all that are immersed, the body being supported on the lap of a relative, and nothing is put in the mouth but drops of water. Further, the immersion is never thought of until the death-rattle has set in, and the dying is in his last gasp. It is a mistake to suppose that those who have to get rid of troublesome and obnoxions relations would wait till that moment and then commit a gratuitous murder. There are ample opportunities during sickness and at other times to effect their purpose, without the least apprehension of detection. The anxiety to get rid of a relation must be mild indeed which would patiently wait till that relation has the death-rattle set in his throat. It is possible that criminal neglect should take place in the cases of old prostitutes in populous towns, who sometimes bequeath their property to their priests or gooroos on condition of their taking them to the river at the time of their death and performing their funeral rites, for in such cases the persons employed in attending the sick at the river-side are the veriest mercenaries, whose interest and that of their employers would be to get rid of such patients as soon as possible. But they are quite exceptional, and however much official interference may be desirable in such cases, it cannot be brought to bear against the general practice of *Antarjali*; unprotected persons left under similar circumstances in their own homes would be equally liable to the same neglect.

It has been said "that persons who are taken to the river-side to die, but who recover and return, are looked upon with disgust and excluded from caste." This, however, is not the case. I can, as a Hindoo living in that part of the country where the practice in question is in every day observance, most positively declare that no person suffers any social inconvenience on that account. Such return entails no stigma and no disgrace, much less any loss of caste; indeed I had never heard of such a thing until I read of it in your letter. Perhaps the impression of loss of caste has originated from the visit paid to goddess Kali, and from certain other ceremonials observed on such occasions before returning home. They are, however, thanks-offering and precautionary measures, and not expiations.

Such being the case, you will perceive that what has been supposed to be "a powerful inducement to the commission of murder" does not exist at all. I do not deny that the practice is a very repulsive one, and I would hail the suppression of it as a blessing to the country. But I do not think that the time has come when it could be put down by Government interference without giving serious offence to the religious feelings of the great bulk of the Hindoo community of Bengal. Such interference, while it would prove intolerant and highly vexatious, will do little in favor of humanity and civilization. The evil is one of those which should be removed by education and enlightenment, and not by the hand of law. It has alreay begun to die out, and, if left to itself, will soon disappear, while legislation on the subject is sure to give it an adventitious importance and evoke the most serious discontent.

Notwithstanding the confidential character of the communication, the matter oozed out to the public. The question was publicly discussed both in the English and in the Native newspapers. By the former, the practice was termed Ghat Murder, condemned, and its absolute prohibition called for. By the Native papers, the worst features were denied, and the interference of Government was deprecated. Looking, however, at the thing as "opposed to public decency, and common humanity," and expecting "the assent and acquiescence of the intelligent portion of the Hindu community," the Local Government thought it expedient to "adopt a measure tending to the discouragement and gradual suppression of the practice." It solicited the opinion of the Government of India on the subject. Reading the several interesting papers accompanying the Lieutenant-Governor's letter, the Governor-General in Council thought the question to have been "discussed with much candour and impartiality" by Babu Digambar. Quoting his letter from the beginning to the end as "essentially a correct account of the custom and of the mode in which it is carried out," His Excellency replied that he was "not prepared to say that it was desirable to have recourse to special legislation for the repression of the practice, and particularly by recourse to what, in India, would be the highly preventive measure of a compulsory notice to the Police." *

Indeed, the reply of Babu Digambar forms a most temperate and cautious discussion of the question. The evil, seated deeply, required a remedy which was to be found best in a new spirit—in an enlightened aversion to the practice. Men's minds were to be brought into a frame for the reception of the change before taking any premature steps. But sometimes it becomes the duty of Government to still superstitious ears, and abolish barbarous usages hallowed by long prescription, by the interposition of authority. Many changes are gently taking place in spite of us, and all those which we ought to make should be hailed, and not fill us with a thoughtless and preposterous alarm and excite murmurs of discontent. Not that we deny the equity of Babu Digambar's sentiments, but we wish that the evil had not been left to stand over in all its integrity without a limitation. Had Sati-ism been left to be got over by time and enlightenment, it would have lingered to this day.

The year 1866 is memorable in the annals of Bengal for the Famine in Orissa. This province was always known to produce more grain than it consumed. It was reputed as an exporting, not an importing country, which sent away its surplus paddy by sea in native sloops. But in the year 1865 the autumnal rains ceased prematurely, and a

* See Appendix A.

general failure of the December harvest was followed by a partial failure of the next spring crops. Orissa suffered more from deficiency than any other district. In addition, it had "allowed a million and half pounds of the precious commodity to leave its shores" on the eve of the famine. It stood in perfect isolation for want of means of inter-communication. There were no trading or planting Europeans, who are always followed by roads, railways, or canals into the interior. The previous grain-stock was below the average. During the earlier months, the scarcity was felt as elsewhere. The native merchants, relying on the stores in the country and curtailing their export transactions, saw no necessity for importing. But towards the middle of February Orissa was found to be nearly destitute of rice. In March it began to suffer from starvation. "Grain poured into the other affected districts from all parts—railways, canals, and roads vigorously doing their duty." But importation to Orissa was impossible. "The south-west monsoon had set in. The harbours there, never open more than a part of the year, had become impracticable. The only landward route was wholly unfit for the transport of sufficient food for the country, and the doomed population found themselves utterly isolated in the condition of passengers in a ship without provisions." A gentleman, belonging to the Public Instruction Department, wrote:—"The subordinate Native officers, about eight hundred in number, behaved with a steadiness, and, when called upon, with a self-abnegation beyond praise.

Many of them ruined their health. One died while on circuit, almost in his palanquin. The touching scenes of self-sacrifice and humble heroism which I witnessed among the poor villagers on my tours of inspection will remain in my memory till my latest day." Another gentleman has recorded:—"The people endured silently to the end, with a fortitude that casual observers of a different temperament and widely dissimilar race may easily mistake for apathy, but which those who lived among the sufferers are unable to distinguish from qualities that generally pass under a more honourable name." The loss of population in Orissa was about two-thirds of three-quarters of a million in all Bengal.

Babu Digambar very much distinguished himself in the Orissa Famine. His natural kindliness, coupled with personal motives, disposed him to render the duties expected of him as landlord on the critical occasion. In an early stage of the famine, he went over to his Zamindari in Katak to learn the true state of facts, and exercise his personal agency in directing ameliorative measures. "The general idea, both among the best informed officials and non-officials, was, that large private stores existed in the hands of speculators. 'The populace held it very decidedly;' and the Commissioner thought there was 'enough to supply the market for a couple of years.' In the total absence of a system of rural statistics, there was no evidence to controvert these views." * But from personal

* The Famine Report.

enquiry on the spot Babu Digambar ascertained the facts, and, communicating them through the *Hindoo Patriot*, first disabused the mind of Government, and opened its eye to the urgent measures for relief. In the words of Kristodas Pal:—"he zealously co-operated with Government in devising measures of relief in the Orissa Famine of 1866. He possessed estates in Katak, and was thus in a position to obtain accurate information regarding the condition of the people in the famine-stricken districts. And his first-hand information seemed to embarrass Government sometimes. In order to utilize him the Government appointed him a member of the Executive Committee of the Orissa Famine, to which he rendered invaluable services."

The Improvement of the Port of Calcutta came on in 1866. It required a Committee. The Municipal Justices being asked to send in some members, Babu Digambar was one of the returned. He was also appointed a Visitor of the Wards Institution this year. Towards its end, his first career in the Bengal Council closed.

In the sessions of 1865 and 1866 there were many Bills, such as the Slaughter Houses in the suburbs of Calcutta, Regulation of Contracts for Labor, Sale of Under-Tenures, Suburban Police, Calcutta Police, and other Bills, on which he sat in Committee and suggested many amendments. But we select for notice the Hook-Swinging Bill, which is remarkable for having been introduced by

Raja Satya Shurn Ghosal, who, considering the inhuman practice to have arisen from a misapprehension of the purport and meaning of the Shastras, and quoting the following prohibitory *sloka* for its continuance in the Kali Yuga,

অশ্বমেধং গবালম্ভং সন্ন্যাসং পলপৈতৃকং।
দেবরেন সুতোৎপত্তি কলৌ পঞ্চ বিবর্জ্জয়েত্‌॥

"The sacrifice of a horse or bull, the practice of *Sunyasa Dharma*, the offering of meat to a parent at the time of annual oblation (*Sradha*), and the marriage of a woman with her deceased husband's younger brother, are prohibited in the *Kali Yoga*."

moved for leave to bring in a Bill to declare the practice of Hook-Swinging illegal. Babu Digambar agreed with him in considering the practice to be extremely barbarous, but thought it should be left to die out under the influence of enlightened public opinion and under the remedy provided in the Penal Code. The other Bill which calls for notice is the Prevention of Inoculation, on which Babu Digambar made the following amusing speech.

He thought that perhaps it would not be uninteresting to the Council if he were to state his belief as to how this measure was likely to be received by the Hindoo Community of Calcutta. He had no hesitation in saying that it would be received with great favour, inasmuch as he knew it to be a fact that, ever since a quarter of a century, vaccination had been quietly and gradually introducing itself into the most orthodox and respectable families in Calcutta, and that even that venerable and scrupulously conscientious townsman, Raja Radhakanta, had not been able to disregard its superior claims to preference. To the credit of his countrymen, it must be admitted that, in this particular instance at any rate, they had shown a greater freedom from religious and national prejudices in the consideration of a purely scientific question, than their more advanced brethren of the West. Strange as it might appear, yet it was nevertheless true, that so late as in the early part of the present century it was gravely discussed amongst scientific men in the civilized countries of Europe, whether the introduction of the cow-pox into the human system did not effect a change in humanity itself. Stories were freely circulated and readily believed, of vaccined children having manifested bovine sympathies, and even abscesses on their foreheads were dreaded as an indication of the sprouting of horns. Such visions never haunted his countrymen. Whatever doubts they might have as to the cow-pox being a better prophylactic than small-pox, they had never denied to the former the merit of not being attended with those immediate dangerous consequences which followed Inoculation. They were strongly impressed with the infectious character of small-pox, whether brought on naturally, or induced by Inoculation; and they also felt that the injurious expedients which their forefathers had devised to prevent the spread of the infection, however well they might have succeeded among small communities, could not be enforced in large cities. Such being the state of the public mind in respect of the two systems, he could confidently assure the Council that the proposed measure, when it had passed into law, would be received with great satisfaction, as removing, at any rate, one of the potent causes in the propagation of that terrible disease which was at the present moment raging in Calcutta and its neighbourhood with frightful virulence and mortality. In his opinion, in one respect, it was rather too limited, for it only provided for the enforcement of the Law in the Town and Suburbs of Calcutta and certain other places, and he felt sure that there were many populous villages where the inhabitants would be glad for an extension of the Act to them.

CHAPTER XIV.

EXEMPTION FROM ATTENDANCE IN CIVIL COURTS.
THE ORISSA REVENUE SETTLEMENT.
THE MELA QUESTION.

BY a notification in the *Calcutta Gazette* in February 1867, the Lieutenant-Governor of Bengal was pleased to exempt Babu Digambar, with six other Native gentlemen, from personal attendance in the Civil Courts. This privilege calls for a remark or two. It is granted by Government out of deference to the feelings of natives of rank, who, conceiving that they are entitled to superior rights and privileges, think themselves disgraced and reduced to a level with servants, coolies, and labourers, by being called into Court on any occasion and examined publicly as witnesses. But it must be acknowledged to be a remnant of the feelings belonging to the times of *no law* in the country. It was said by Napoleon Bonaparte that "scratch a Russian, and he will be found a *Tartar* beneath his skin." Equally, scratch a Young Bengal, and you will find him an *Oriental* beneath his skin. We wish that Babu Digambar had set an example of the apprecia- tion of the glorious beauty of British Law consisting in its impartiality and non-respect for persons.

In June 1867, shortly after "gaunt Famine had stalked abroad in the land," the renewal of the revenue settlement of Orissa fell due. The system followed there was neither the permanent nor the ryatwar, but something between the two. It recognised between the crown and the cultivator middlemen-farmers without a permanent title to the soil, and re-let on fresh terms after every thirty years instead of every year.

Babu Digambar was a staunch advocate of the Permanent Settlement. His richest Zamindari lay in the district of Katak. Just before the occurrence of the famine, he had persuaded his native brother landholders to join him in a representation to the Government on the dis- couragement to cultivation which the postpone- ment of a permanent settlement caused in Orissa. Far from listening to this proposal, the Govern- ment was minded to renew the settlement with an increase of the assessment. Babu Digambar en- tered an energetic protest. He dwelt on the exhausted resources of the country, and "showed by irrefragible facts and logic that if any measure could resuscitate the miserable people of Orissa, it was the continuance of the settlement on the original basis" The Government accepted his recommendation, and Orissa recoverd in a little time.

There had been held at Constantinople, in 1866, a Medical Conference of European savants, in which it was given out that Cholera emanates from India, where its large periodical *melas* and pilgrimages give rise to the disease and become the most ready means for its propagation. This opinion drew the notice of the Indian Government, and set it upon enquiry into the matter. Regarded as an authority on the subject by his best opportunities of study, Babu Digambar was addressed for his opinion, which was given in the following letter.

To

R. B. CHAPMAN ESQR,

OFFICIATING COMMISSIONER, PRESIDENCY DIVISION.

13, January, 1868.

SIR,

I have the honor to acknowledge the receipt of your letter No. 202 of date the 16th November last, enclosing copies of correspondence as per memorandum in the margin, on the subject of epidemic disease arising from pilgrimages in India, and requesting my opinion on the questions therein raised.

2. These questions owe their origin to an opinion, enunciated by the Medical Conference which assembled in 1866 at Constantinople, to the effect that "Cholera emanated from India only, and that the large periodical assemblies at fairs and pilgrimages is one of the most probable sources of its origin and the most ready means of its propagation: and they are intended to elicit the opinion of the people of this country as to how far certain remedial measures, suggested in Mr. Secretary Bayley's letter, are desirable.

3. The measures proposed are *(1st.)* that "if possible the people of the country should be made aware of the risk which they run, and should be dissuaded and discouraged as far as practicable from making pilgrimages, on the ground that they entail largely exposure, disease, and death, and lead often to demoralization ;" and (2nd) "at any rate some system should be devised under the orders of the Local Government whereby, at all places of pilgrimages and at all large fairs, sanitary arrangements should be invariably made and carefully supervised, and the cost thereof should be made up by levying a small tax or toll upon pilgrims."

4. It does not appear that any enquiry has been made in this country, as to how far the theory of the Medical Conference is correct, although there seems to be considerable difference of opinion on the subject, and many eminent physicians both in India and Europe, are still of opinion that cholera is neither infectious nor contagious. Under these circumstances I am humbly of opinion that the first thing to be done is to appoint an Indian Commission of medical men from the different Presidencies to enquire and report on the nature and character of cholera, how it is generated and propagated, whether it is really infectious or contagious, or is due to atmospheric and other causes independent of emanantions from the disease itself. Such an enquiry carried out here by competent persons would draw the attention of the natives of the country to the subject, and its results would command much greater respect and confidence, and would prove more effectual in suppressing pilgrimages than the opinion of a conference held in a far away foreign country by persons, the majority of whom had no personal knowledge of India, can possibly be.

5. Assuming the theory of the Medical Conference to be correct, it is necessary to enquire to what public gatherings the remedies suggested are likely to apply.

6. In India, as elsewhere, people collect in large numbers on occasions (A) of festivals, (B) to visit holy places or temples to discharge particular religious obligations, and (C) at public fairs ; and as the physical conditions of such gatherings must always be alike and disease is liable to be generated on all such occasions, it must follow that the people of this country should not only be dissuaded and prevented from per-

forming pilgrimages; but also from attending and holding large fairs and festivals.

7. (A) Now, the festivals held in this country are sometimes got up by public subscriptions and sometimes at the expense of private individuals, but in either case they are thrown open to the public gratis. They are common in almost every District of Bengal, and in the North-west are the centres of some of the largest gatherings. They generally last for a day and not uncommonly for two, three, or four days. On such occasions people from different Districts assemble together, and for their accomodation booths, stalls, and shops are established in great numbers. In some of the noted festivals of this description collections of 30 to 50 thousand persons are not uncommon. But these gatherings take place on private property and often by private or public invitations, and they, although in a sanitary point of view quite as obnoxious as pilgrmiages, cannot be subjected to taxation, without grave injustice to the rights of private hospitality, and serious injury to the social customs and usuages, of the people.

8. (B) Of pilgrimages there are two kinds: 1st, those that are undertaken at all times of the year: and 2nd, those that are held most meritorious at particular seasons. Of the first kind are visits to the temples of Benares, Mathura and Brindaban, the pilgrimages to Gya for the performance of the Shradhs, and to Allahabad to cast the hair of the head in the holy confluence of the Jamuna and the Ganges. For these all times are propitious, but for the sake of convenient travelling in the cold weather, from October to February, is generally preferred. Many thousands proceed on these pilgrimages, from Bengal, every year, and cause considerable crowding in the towns and cities they visit; but under no circumstance, can they be said to originate or propagate disease. The experience of centuries is adverse to such an opinion. On the contrary, it is universally believed in this country that such pilgrimages are peculiarly beneficial to health. Old and infirm people often resort to them with the express object of reviving their failing energies, and they are rarely weak and emaciated, returning to their homes hale, hearty, and completely restored to their wonted health in the course of a short pilgrimage to Gya or Benares. In many instances, recovery no doubt is attributed to religious merit and the benign grace

of the divinities visited, but the people are not aware that the good they derive is due in a great measure to change, and the effect of travelling in a climate which to the majority of them is peculiarly salubrious. Under any circumstance it is impossible to persuade them that such pilgrimages are injurious to their health, and should therefore be avoided.

9. The 2nd class of pilgrimages, or those which require the devotees to be present at particular places on stated days, are not often found to be quite as beneficial as those mentioned in the preceding paragraph. It is a common practice in Bengal for people suffering from long standing chronic complaint, or who have recently recovered from them, to proceed, in fulfilment of vows, to Tarkeswar in the Hoogly District, on the occasion of the Sivartri holiday in February or to other noted temples, and they return home generally with marked benefit to their health, and the number of radical cures effected by these pilgrimages is by no means insignificant. The crowd that assembles round the temple at Tarkeswar on the Sivaratri night, it is believed, includes 20 to 30 thousand persons, but rarely causes the outbreak of any epidemic disease. The same may be said of the pilgrimages to Baidyanath in Beerbhoom, to Poreshnath near Sherghatty, and to the inunmerable other temples and shrines to which people repair on paticular occasions. In fact, however, the bulk of the people who assemble at those places come from the neighbouring villages and return home after a day's sojourn, in many cases persons come in the morning and return to their homes in the evening, repeating their visits on successive days, till the close of the ceremony, which rarely takes more than two or three days for its performance.

10. There are some pilgrimages, however, to which the abov remarks would not apply. They are performed at very unfavourable seasons of the year, and under circumstances which entail considerable hardship and suffering, and may lead to the generation of virulent disease. The pilgrimage to Juggernath on the occasion of the Rath festival in the month of June is particularly open to this objection. Forty to fifty thousand persons generally assemble at Pooree at that time, and they are mostly in a condition peculiarly subject to disease. The way to Pooree is by land, and pilgrims have to travel from 150 to 500 miles to reach their destination. These have to submit to

long and tedious marches over roads of the most primitive description, exposed to the most inclement weather, scorched for days in the burning Indian sun of June, and then drenched by heavy monsoon showers of many hours continuance. The serais in which they have to put up, either on the way or at Pooree, are miserable in the extreme, and the food supplied them is unwholesome. Of medical aid they can have none besides what they carry with them. Under such circumstances great suffering and often disease and death are the necessary consequences. Nor are the people of this country unaware of this, but so strong is the religious fervour by which they are impelled to undertake the pilgrimage, that they undergo all the sufferings attendant on it with cheerfulness, and repeat their visits as often as they can afford the means and the leisure to do so. Privation on such occasions they look upon as a sort of penance calculated to enhance their religious merit, and it is hopeless to expect that persuasion alone will suffice to keep them away from such undertakings to any perceptible extent. They must be convinced by irrefragable evidence, either that they propagate disease, or that such pilgrimages are of no religious merit, before they will give them up, and this cannot now be afforded. Certain it is, however, that of the many thousands who annually return from Pooree to Calcutta in July, few can be said to have brought cholera with them. The disease, to the best of my knowledge, has never broken out epidemically in Calcutta in that month, and I have no doubt that my experience will be fully borne out by all who have studied the subject.

11. (C) The fairs of the Bengal Presidency may be classed under three heads : first, fairs purely commercial and owned by private individuals : *second*, national or public fairs of a quasi-religious character ; *third*, State fairs or those held under the auspices of Government. Most of these fairs are held two or three times a week, others are held weekly, and others at longer intervals. All fairs of the first class are village institutions, held to supply the ordinary every day wants of small communities, who cannot support the existence of shops in their villages and for such small trade as they can carry on. The quarterly, half-yearly, and annual village fairs, in the same way, are intended to bring to villages, supplies of such articles

as are not required at shorter intervals, and for purposes of more extensive commerce. Many of these are associated with religion simply with a view to secure a larger gathering and thereby ensure more extensive traffic than would otherwise be the case. Indeed, if a Zamindar wanted to set up a new fair, he would place the celebration of some one of the many festivals of which the Hindoo calender is so full in the foreground, and thereby at once appeal to the religious, the social, and the utilitarian sentiments of the people, and his fair is sure to be encouraged by all classes.

12. Most of the fairs are over by the close of the day. But even in those that are held for successive days, the large gatherings are composed, as in the case of festivals, chiefly of men living within a radius of five to six miles from the centre, who all disperse and return to their own homes by dusk, leaving the fairs for the night in the occupation of the shop-keepers and a few strangers.

13. These fairs, I hardly think, can come under the category of those which are described by the Medical Conference as centres for the generation and propagation of Cholera or any other epidemic disease, and therefore they may be altogether left out of consideration. They are generally held on open and well ventilated spots, interspersed with shady trees or topes and where an abundant supply of wholesome water is always available, so that sanitary consideration in connection with them are not entirely lost sight of. Much, however, may still be done to their conservancy arrangements with a little additional care and expense, and the subject ought to engage the attention of the local Municipal Authorities.

14. Some of the quasi-religious fairs have no doubt attained to gigantic proportions. The Sonepur and the Pokhar fairs are visited by thousands, the amount of trade carried on there is vast, and the extent of crowding is necessarily very great, but even in this case a pilgrim tax does not appear to be at all commendable. The people who assemble at these fairs are generally traders intent on buying and selling, and men bent on pleasure, the number of persons among them desirous of performing particular religious ceremonies being comparitively very small. The same may be said of persons who go to Hurdwar

at the ordinary annual fairs, though very different is the case at the duo-decennial fairs at which vast numbers collect for purposes of religious ablution. To distinguish the religious pilgrim from the trader and the pleasure hunter in these fairs is simply impossible, and were it possible it would be highly impolitic to tax the former alone and let off the latter. The measure would not be justified on the ground of sanitation, and it is sure to cause much ill-feeling and irritation. It is true that such a pilgrim tax was formerly levied at Allahabad, Gaya, and Juggernath from all persons who performed certain ceremonies at particular spots there; but it is also true that it was given up owing to its extreme unpopularity and as a relic of Mahomedan bigotry and intolerance. The British Government cannot possibly in this time of day revive such a tax; and to make it general on all classes of persons who come to fairs, whether for trade, racing, sight, seeing, or religious ablution, would be so injurious to trade and so universally obnoxious that the Government should not for a moment entertain such an idea. If sanitary reasons be allowed to override all other considerations, they will apply equally to the Palampore, the Cachar, the Titalayah, and other fairs held under the auspices of Government as also to the agricultural and other exhibitions, as to the national fairs of the country. But they are, for social, commercial, and even political purposes, of such great importance that it would be most injudicious to interfere with their success by taxing every body alike who frequented them.

15. In a country so full of temples, shrines, and sanctuaries as India is, where almost every river has more than one holy spot, and every lump of stone under a big tree is an emblem of some God or other, and all of them draw pilgrims more or less from distant places, it would be a positive nuisance to have a general pilgrim tax, and if the example set by the British Government be taken up by the Native States, the amount of mischief that will be done in the name of sanitation will be incalculable.

16. If it be urged that questions involving life and death ought to outweigh all others, it must, in my humble opinion, follow that Government cannot fully discharge its duty to humanity by simply raising a small tax for conservancy purposes. If it be certain that Indian pilgrimages and fairs propagate cholera and lead to untimely death of thousands, if not millions, they should be at once put down with a high hand.

But such certainty is wanting, and even the question of the contagious character of Cholera is still an open one, and under these circumstances the proposed pilgrim tax cannot be held to be reasonable by the community at large while it is sure to be a most frightful source of widespread harassment, extortion, and oppression, which the Government cannot possibly prevent or check. It may be said that even in the case of a much more frightful and most positively contagious disease, the plague, no Government has yet thought proper to forbid all commercial intercourse with its birth-place and permanent stronghold, Egypt, except when the disease is actually prevailing, and the British Government cannot adopt such a stringent measure in the case of cholera, as the total stoppage of all fairs and pilgrimages. Cholera, however, being epidemic in many places in India, and more frequent and more fatal than plague, if the theory of the Medical Conference be correct, such active and universal a remedy appears but a natural *sequiture.*

17. When an epidemic is already raging in any place of pilgrimages or if it should have been overtaken by any other calamity from which the pilgrims arriving at their destination are likely to suffer, it is the clear duty of Government to put a *cordon sanitaire* around it, and authoritatively to cut off all communications with it, and the people of the country will fully appreciate its motive and fully act up to it. They have only to learn the fact to postpone their intended pilgrimages, as has already been seen in the case of Baidyanath in 1865, when small-pox had broken out epidemically there, and during the last two years of famine in Juggernath. But it will be impossible to convince them of the necessity of desisting from such pilgrimages on the strength of what is yet a mere theory. They know full well that cholera is a new disease, that it was not known before 1815, and that it first broke out in Jessore, which was far from being a thickly propulated village at the time. They also see continually around them that cholera and other diseases rage epidemically in places and at seasons to which the above theory cannot have the remotest application, either as regards their generation or propagation. Any attempt, therefore, to dissuade them from undertaking these pilgrimages, on the ground of the risk to human lives not being confined to their own but extending to others, is sure to be received by them in the light of an insidious attempt to interfere with their religion and therefore cannot possibly be effective.

18. I most readily admit that travelling in large numbers must lead to some demoralization, but it remains yet to be shown that on this side of India, of which alone I can speak confidently, it is of a character that calls for State interference in the interests of public morals. According to the customs of the country the female pilgrims, except in rare cases of very poor people, are accompanied by male members of their family, and every possible care is taken to lodge them so as to prevent their being intruded upon by strangers. The zenana system, though originally introduced by foreigners has, it is well known, taken deep root in the country, and far greater sacrifices are made for its sake, than for health, comfort, or convenience, or even for the barest necessaries of life. The females are never allowed the opportunity of exchanging words with strangers, and therefore beyond the demoralization which might arise from occasional side glances between the two sexes, I do not see how these periodical gatherings are more likely to provoke their evil passions, than many social usages and institutions which are encouraged by the most civilized nations in other lands.

19. While however I am clearly of opinion that persuasion is not at all likely to deter the Hindoos as long as they maintain their belief in the present system of religion, and a pilgrim tax is calculated to do more harm than good, I entirely concur in the opinion of H. E. the Governor-General in Council that some system should be devised whereby sanitary arrangements should be invariably made and carefully supervised at all places of pilgrimages and fairs. Such a system is most urgently wanted, and it can be, I believe, easily carried out. In the case of small private fairs such arrangements could be readily enforced by obliging the proprietors, either through the agency of local Municipal or the Police authorities, to do the needful, as is done in the case of bazars under the Municipal Act. No tax or toll will be necessary for such a purpose, and no interference on the part of Government Officers in their management than occasional inspection.

20. In the case of such fairs as are held on commons, where no particular individual or individuals derive any pecuniary benefit, the expenses of the necessary sanitary arrangements should under ordinary circumstances, be borne by the local Municipal authorities. But under extraordinary circumstances, as in the case of duo-decennial Hurdwar

fair, where the expenses are likely to be heavy, a small toll may be levied upon the traders and shop-keepers through whom it would fall upon the pilgrims at large, without causing any great amount of oppression or opening a wide door to extortion.

Hardly could a statement be more lucid, exhaustive, and sensible. His suggestions, commending themselves to Government, have since been acted upon, particularly on the occasion of the *Kumbha*, or twelfth year, *mela* at Haridwar, in 1879, and in the *mela* held there in the present year.

CHAPTER XV.

THE BRITISH INDIAN ASSOCIATION CLIQUE. THE AGE OF BRANDY AND THE AGE OF BRAG. THE SECOND CAREER IN THE BENGAL COUNCIL, AND THE IRRIGATION AND DRAINAGE BILL.

IN February 1869, seniority lifted Babu Digambar to the Vice-Presidentship of the British Indian Association. In time, this body had grown in organization, in energy, in authority. It had evinced a most intelligent interest in several matters of public moment. To its suggestions we owe the reconstruction of the Legislative Councils on a broader basis, and the amalgamation of the Supreme and Sadar Courts of Judicature. But unfortunately age tells as soon on a Bengali institution, as on the Bengalis themselves.* Hardly had

* We had the Theo-philanthropic Society, the Society for the Acquisition of General Knowledge, the Landholders' Association, the British Indian Society, the Indian League, the Indian Union—but where are they. The British Indian Association still "drags its lengthening chain along," but hardly will a successor be found to the two or three principal men that are keeping it up on its legs. The Congress has inflicted a deep gash on itself.

the Association approached its twentieth year and thriven to the fulness of its grandeur and power, when its features underwent a change. By 1869, death had taken away some of its best men—Babu Harish Chandra Mukerjea, Raja Radhacanta Deb, Babu Prasanna Coomar Tagore, and Babu Ramgopal Ghosh. Really born with talents, but denied the opportunities of turning out a full-blown statesman, Babu Jaikissen Mukerjea laboured under a physical disadvantage. In the course of discharging their duties the remaining prominent members of the Managing Committee drifted themselves into a clique of monopolists, who had the game in their hands. The four conspicuous members of this clique, were Babus Romanath Tagore, Digambar Mitra, Rajendra Lala Mitra, and Krista Das Pal.

Romanath Tagore belonged to one of those families in Calcutta, who are noted most for their intelligence, their taste, their polish, and their public spirit. He was brother to Babu Dwarka Nath Tagore, whose munificence was a proverb in his generation. Romanath Tagore picked up his English when the Hindu College was in the womb of time. The failure of the Union Bank put an end to his busy life, and the death of an only son happening shortly afterwards, the arena of the British Indian Association became his refuge from domestic affliction. He passed there the remainder of his life devoted to the public cause. Of all the members, he was the oldest. Manu inculcates respect for age, and his colleagues made way for him with unanimous deference. In politics, he was a conciliator, who, after the Mutiny, made himself remarkable by his steady efforts to effect a reconciliation between the rulers and the ruled. He had in his latter years become almost the first Native gentleman of Calcutta, from which consideration Mr. Hogg, the then Chairman of the Municipality, chose to come upon him first of all with his new Municipal Assessment for setting that scheme agoing. Indeed, he at last appeared so conspicuous in the public eye that when Mr. James Wilson, of the *Indian Daily News*, had once published that "the English were going to walk out of the country," we thought he was going to step into the shoes of the Viceroy. His public life called for recognition, and his hoary head was adorned with titles and dignities.

Of Digambar, we shall have our say towards the end of our sketch.

The third noted member was Rajendra Lala Mitra. He had a strong head filled with a stronger ambition—a "vaulting ambition that o'erleapt itself." His weight was derived from his scholarship, not from influence, or substance, or experience. He imposed upon the public with a factitious versatility and *subjantaism* which secured him a number of admirers. That he was an able writer and speaker is beyond dispute. But he was most clever in putting on imposing colors. The possible quantity of dust that he threw up, blinded the eyes of all men to the fact that he was a Sanscrit scholar without the *Mugdhabodha* and *Panini.* The only sure ground which did not slip away from beneath his feet, was his *English.* His real power lay in combativeness. Opposition was his forte. His dearest wish was to cudgel his opponents into a respect for his opinions, and his life was one long ostentatious display of literary pugilism. If this spirit could have been nursed in independance, he would have figured as one of the Gracchi of ancient Rome—or Rienzi of mediæval Italy.

The most illustrious member of all—the soul of the Association and a phenomenon, was Krista Das Pal. He was born so poor as to "be bent to the most abject servitude, or ready for the most desperate adventure." Finally, he had the benefit of D. L. R's instruction, under whom in reading Shakespeare he seems to have felt most the force of, and taken to heart to act upon, Iago's repeated advice to Roderigo to "put money in his purse." From his youth his thoughts were turned to money-making. He keenly looked out for windfalls, and very wisely attached himself to Pandit Iswara Chandra Vidyasagara "like barnacles to the hull of a great ship." The bequeathment of the *Hindoo Patriot* by Babu Kaliprasana Singh to the British Indian Association took place. It cleared away the gloom from Krista Das's prospects. He succeeded to its editorship. Krista Das commenced his editorial career with the usual effervescing spirit of a raw beginner, who went on with his knock-on-the-head principle, until brought down on his knees by the Europeans resenting an offensive leader, and dropping their subscription to his paper with John Bull unanimity. From this time he steered a middle course between authority and affinity,—between respect for "the powers that be" and the good-will of his nation. Young Bengal commenced an ill-starred existence—he was baptised in brandy. The youthful Krishna Mohan Banerjea introduced the era of Brandy. Krista Das Pal introduced the era of Brag. Brandy scores a limited number of victims. But under the intoxication of Brag, the whole nation has become demoralized. Kristadas, made Talleyrand's maxim (language has been invented for the concealment of thoughts) the pivot of his politics, and governed native opinion by his pen and tongue. To his necromantic politicalism, or the art of holding up matters in a glare, may be traced the breaking out in a malignant type of the moral epidemic which has muddled the brain of Young Bengal with an abnormal development of self-esteem. He taught his countrymen to run before they could stand alone. He made them forget that we were in a begging, and not in an extorting, position—that agitation without the necessary qualifications and state of genuine fitness has the appearance of beggary on horse-back. Indeed, he became a mighty dexterous puffer—a wizard who worked miracles in favour of his benefactors and friends. A man of the people by birth, he disappointed his nation by spending his energies in Zamindari harness. But one thing must be said to his honor. It was formally proposed to make him a Raja. His reply was, "it seems the natural way, but that cannot be. I have an oath in Heaven against it; I will not close my career in that foolish way, as so many have done before me."*

Here, for the present, we leave the foregoing subject to return to our main narrative. After an interval of four years from November 1866 to November 1870, Babu Digambar was raised a second time to the Bengal Legislative Council for reaping the benefit of "his practical common sense and intimate knowledge of the country." On the 10th December following, the Hon'ble Ashley Eden moved to read his Drainage and Irrigation Bill. Since the year 1861 the attention of the Government of Bengal had been directed to the virulent Epidemic Fever prevailing in several districts. Subsequent to the Epidemic Fever Commission, the subject had been investigated by "Special Committees, Sanitary Commissions, Engineers, and others." They had all made their reports from time to time, but "although there were differences of opinion as to the real causes of the fever, there seemed to be a very general unanimity of opinion that at least one of the chief causes was the miasma arising from insufficient drainage consequent on the silting up of water-courses and khals in the districts." Upon the strength of this opinion, the Bengal Government deputed a Civil Engineer to report on the possibility of draining the Hugli district. He first of all investigated the Dankuni Julla, or the swamp west of Serampur and between

* This was Fox's reply to the proposal to raise him to the peerage.

Bali and Baddibati. It appearing from his report that "the khals or natural drainage channels which once led from the swamp to the Hugli, and were formerly navigable for small craft throughout the year, had so silted up as to be only capable of carrying off the marginal overflow during the monsoon, and that the want of drainage was the probable cause of the prevalence of the type of fever in that particular locality," the Lieutenant-Governor, taken up with the idea of combining improved agriculture with drainage, issued orders for the preparation of plans and estimates to remove the swamp, and to bring the land covered by it under cultivation. The Zamindars who had an interest in the land were strongly in favor of the measure. Babu Jaikissen Mukerjea signified his hearty approval. The Government of India promised to advance the outlay of three lacs of rupees on the condition of its repayment. It was with the view of securing this repayment that the Bill was introduced as a tentative measure, the subject being an entirely novel one. In the course of his introductory remarks, Sir Ashley Eden alluded to the two theories with regard to the cause of the obstruction to the drainage—the one, the theory of the minority, that it was the Railway, and the roads in connection with them, which had stopped up the drainage; the other, maintained by a large majority of experienced and scientific men, that it was the silting up of khals and other water-courses which, by blocking up the drainage of large *beels*, had spread dampness and miasma into all the villages. Babu Digambar was of the first opinion, and fought hard against the Irrigation and Drainage Bill founded upon the second opinion. He made on the occasion one of his celebrated speeches by which he succeeded in getting his theory accepted and acted upon. We present it entire, because a few extracts would not make the matter sufficiently intelligible.

The primary object of the proposed measure appeared to be the removal of the cause of the epidemic fever which had been raging in some parts of Lower Bengal since a few years. The chief cause of that type of fever was said to be "defective drainage," and hence the necessity of encouraging and bringing into existence drainage works, the costs of which were to be borne by the holders of land, inasmuch as such works, it was held, while subserving the purposes of sanitation, must of necessity, at the same time, prove beneficial to agriculture. The question for consideration therefore was whether there was any connection between the defective drainage of the culturable lands and the epidemic, and whether those lands generally were likely to derive any benefit from drainage. With due deference to the professional experience of Mr. Adley, on whose report the proposed measure seemed to be entirely based, he must admit that he felt considerable difficulty in subscribing to the opinions expressed by Mr. Adley in that report as to the cause of this epidemic. Mr. Adley assigned some thirty causes to account for it, and it was difficult to make out which of them he considered to be the proximate and the exciting cause. But as the hon'ble mover had made his choice of defective drainage as the existing cause, and had framed the proposed Bill under that conviction, he must necessarily confine his remarks to it. Now, referring to the report, he found that Mr. Adley had made mention of nearly a dozen conditions under which miasm, whatever that might be, but which was said to be the germ of the epidemic fever, was generated, and none of them was removable except by complete drainage, both surface and subsoil, which the geological formation of the country could not possibly admit of at any expenditure of money, even if the same were forthcoming. First in Mr. Adley's catalogue of causes was the "marshes of jheels and jullahs, whether of fresh or salt water ; the last are most pernicious ; where salt and fresh water intermingle, putrefaction is more rapid."

Now, the whole country—he meant Lower Bengal—was full of these bheels or depressions, which were the natural receptacles of the drainage of their surrounding lands. At the lowest estimate he would take a hundred of these bheels to every district. In the eastern districts most of these hollows or bheels communicated directly with navigable streams during the monsoons, when they were from twelve to fifteen feet under water. These, he sincerely trusted, it was not pretended should be drained.

But suppose some of the inland bheels, in the district of Hooghly, were capable of being drained, how were the hollows to be filled up, except by a gradual process of silting up by the sewage of the surrounding country finding its way into them ? And when, after a series of years, they did silt up, they could not present a more elevated surface than the adjoining lands. But unfortunately for Mr. Adley's scheme of drainage, and the removal thereby of the cause of the epidemic, the adjoining lands happened to be paddy lands, over which water lodged to the depth of two to three feet, and which continued in that state for at least four months in the year, and these lands, according to him, were equally productive of miasm. In this list of causes were found "moist lands and meadows, or a water-lodged subsoil when dried up under the sun ;" again, "rice grounds, especially in jullahs, where the ears of the crops only are cut off, and the stalks left to rot in the water,—thus adding fuel to the fire." Now, was Mr. Adley prepared to drain these rice lands, which constituted nine-tenths of the culturable lands of Lower Bengal, and deprive the people, if possible, of the only food crop the lands were capable of bearing ? But what made Mr. Adley so sure that these *bheels* and "rice grounds" were the causes of the epidemic fever ? Was not Calcutta within a mile of an extensive salt-water lake, which, according to him, was still more generative of malaria than a fresh water one, and had it notwithstanding, within the memory of the present generation, ever suffered from a type of fever which was met with only since a few years in some of the most healthy localities of Bengal, and which decimated in the short space of a year and a half the population of a village where it broke out? On the contrary, was not Calcutta particularly healthy of late, and its death-rate reduced to that of some of the English towns, and yet was not the salt-water lake in existence in all its glory? But even as regards the villages surrounding the Dankoonee bheel or jullah, the drainage of which was considered so imperative in the cause of the epidemic that an estimate had been already made, and the drainage operations of which would perhaps be commenced upon immediately on the proposed measure becoming law, did we find anything like an epidemic there? In appendix B, subjoined to Mr. Adley's report, it was stated that in 26 villages surrounding that *bheel* the mortality in three years was only 2,145 amongst a population of 10,949 souls, or about 6½ per cent. per annum; whereas, in an epidemic village, one-third, and even half, the population was carried off in one year. But the idea that the *bheels*, which had existed since the formation of the country itself, and the rice lands which meant the surface of the whole country, were the generating causes of the epidemic, and that they must be drained if the epidemic was to be checked, was so preposterous, that he would not detain the Council with further remarks on that head. Nothing was so natural as that those ugly and offensive sights—the stagnant bheels, rank vegetation, and paddy-fields immersed in water—would suggest themselves to a European, unaccustomed to those sights, as the most probable causes to account for a terrible epidemic; but he was really surprised to find that local conditions of soil and climate, which were as inseparable from us as our very skin, or perhaps more so, should be deliberately and professionally pronounced as causes adequate to account for a phenomenon of recent or casual occurrence, and the same gravely proposed to be adopted as the basis for action. If we were incompetent to grapple with this fell epidemic, as we had evidently proved ourselves to be, let us in all humility admit our inability · but he protested against the adoption of any crude, ill-digested, and baphazard measure, which without eliminating the cause of this epidemic, or in the least degree mitigating its virulence, only served to constitute an additional source of calamity to the people. It was not long since that, in the name of sanitation, and in the cause of this epidemic, a fierce crusade was waged against the vegetable kingdom, with what wisdom he would quote a most able and conscientious officer of Government (he meant Mr. Dampier) to show. In his letter to Government, dated 4th January 1864 in paragraph 24, he says :

"It has been said, that as their own neglect of sanitary precautions is the cause of the sickness under which they suffer, the villagers have no claim to assistance from without; but I do not believe that the inbabitants of the tracts which have suffered have been greater delinquents in this respect than those of other parts of Bengal, or of this division, who have hitherto escaped. I have seen jungle as thick, and habitations as unclean, in the suburbs behind Alipore, as I have met with in the worst of the fever-stricken villages which I have visited; and it is by no means clearly established that the neglect of precautions which were within the means of the villagers is the primary cause of the epidemic, although doubtless that neglect has intensified the visitation."

With what success such measures could be carried out, even if initiated, would best appear from a letter from the Government of Bengal to that of India, dated 16th January 1868 :—

"It must specially be borne in mind that, under the conditions of Lower Bengal, any clearance of spontaneous vegetation, however thorough, is of the most transient effect only. To cut down the jungle and underwood is worse than useless; to root it up is extremely laborious and costly; and even when uprooted it is replaced by a no less luxuriant growth in the course of one or two rainy seasons, so that the question is not one of thoroughly clearing the villages once for all. To be effectual, active and organized measures must be continuous."

But, notwithstanding these sensible protests and wise deductions, the crusade was vigorously continued, in obedience, as he supposed, to professional opinion, and thousands of bamboo and mango topes were ruthlessly destroyed, aud many a fever-stricken sufferer, whilst yet prostrated by sickness, was dragged from his sick bed to assist in this work of demolition of perhaps his only means of support. Such was the kind of measures which, in the name of humanity, had been hitherto tried for the removal of this epidemic—with what success the experience of a decade had amply testified.

However reluctant he might be to express himself dogmatically on questions like the present, he had however no hesitation in saying that the proposed measure, so far as it aimed at eradicating the cause of the epidemic, or even mitigating its severity, by draining the *bheels* and paddy lands, would meet with equal failure ; though, if the experiment were tried, it would be attended with still greater calamity to the people.

But while he deprecated in the strongest terms the drainage of bheels and rice-lands, with a view to the removal of the epidemic, he was fully sensible of the absolute necessity of drainage, so far as the villages were concerned. In fact, he had always held, and still held, that fever, wherever and whenever it had epidemically broken out in this country, was wholly and solely traceable to impeded village drainage, caused in many instances by railway feeders, which of late had sprung up in large numbers, wherever the same have crossed the drainage course of a village or villages. The same might be said of railways and other kinds of obstructions, whether they were offered in the passage of the rain water from a village to the adjoining paddy-field, or from the paddy-field into the bheel, or from the bheel into a navigable stream. To place before the Council in a clear light the manner in which the drainage of the Bengal villages was effected during the rains, he would, with permission, read some passages from a memorandum written by himself which would be found in the appendix to the report of the Epidemic Commission, of which he had the honor to be a member :—

"The drainage of all the villages in the epidemic districts, as elsewhere in Lower Bengal, is effected by the water first running into the nearest *paddy-fields* lying in the direction of their slope, thence it collects in the *bheels*, from which it rushes through khals into larger streams, which again communicate with navigable rivers. An obstruction occurring in any one of these conduits must interfere with the drainage, and its effects are felt more or less according to the proximity or remoteness of the obstruction from the scene of its influence. Accordingly, it has been found, as will be noticed more particularly hereafter, that the stoppage of the mouths of the different streams has not been productive of such serious consequences to the villages lying within their influence, as when the same occurred more in the vicinity of those villages.

The obstructions appear to have arisen chiefly from roads, and partly from embankments thrown up across khais for purposes of fisheries. I had neither time nor opportunities at command to trace in every instance, how and when the stoppage had taken place ; enough, however, has been discovered to satisfy me of the correctness of my general conclusions.

In like manner, the Eastern Bengal Railway and its feeders, when the same have crossed the water-courses of villages lying on the eastern bank of the river Hooghly, and of others more inland, but situated to the west of the line, have obstructed the drainage of those places ; the fall of the villages lying on the eastern bank of the Hooghly, as I have before observed, being towards the east, and consequently Chagdah, Kanchraparra, Halisahur, and many similarly situated, have suffered.

I may here remark that the face of the country being perfectly flat, the drainage runs over the whole surface towards the direction of its slope, and consequently roads running transversely to it must of necessity intercept the drainage. Both the East Indian and the Eastern Bengal Railways are provided with capacious viaducts, whenever they have crossed what appeared to the eye as water-courses ; but these are in reality khals and other large streams, which, as I have already observed, received the drainage in its flow from the villages over paddy-fields and bheels. The latter exhibit no visible signs of their being water-ways, and could not be known as such unless narrowly watched during the rains, though a road crossing them would more effectually shut out the drainage and the evil consequences resulting therefrom would be much sooner felt, than when it crossed distant channels. Taking into consideration the number of roads which have sprung up of late, as also others in course of construction, and bearing in mind likewise the manner in which the drainage of the country is effected, and the difficulty thereby entailed of providing those roads with a sufficient number of outlets, it is not improbable that in the cases of those villages which have not yet been examined obstructions to their drainage would, upon inquiry appear to have proceeded chiefly from roads having been made without reference to the drainage level of the country, and without being provided with a sufficient number of water-courses."

He had no hesitation in saying that many villages in Lower Bengal, especially in the districts of Hooghly and Burdwan, were at this moment, and since some years, suffering from defective drainage, caused in some one or other of the various ways indicated in the passages he had quoted: and wherever the same had occurred, it had been invariably followed by the breaking out of this epidemic fever, the intensity of the attack being regulated by the complete or partial nature of the impediment offered to drainage. But the proposed measure, while it provided for the drainage of the bheels and paddy-fields, made no provision for the removal of the obstructions to the free drainage of the villages. Perhaps this was not quite an oversight, but the necessary result of the reluctance expressed by the Government of India to contribute funds for the purpose, as it would appear from the letter of the Government of India to that of Bengal, dated the 21st January 1870, which, with permission, he would read:—

3. "The Governor-General in Council concurs fully in the remarks made in the commencement of the 6th paragraph of your letter under reply, and looks with the greatest interest on the further prosecution of these inquiries, which he trusts, will lead to the early adoption of measures that may effectually alleviate the dreadful scourge that has affected these parts of Bengal during the last few years.

4. The Government of India will do all in its power to facilitate the prosecution of works required for improving the drainage of districts of Bengal subject to these dreadful epidemics; but it must impress upon His Honor the Lieutenant-Governor that it will be essentially necessary, in granting pecuniary aid towards carrying out any projects having this end in view, to provide that the general revenues of the country shall not be permanently burdened with charges arising from their construction.

5. The Government of India will be prepared, when suitable arrangements have been entered into to secure the State against any future risk, to give all help in its power, by lending money at the lowest rate of interest possible without actual loss to itself; and the Governor-General in Coun-

cil would leave it to His Honor the Lieutenant-Governor to suggest how an arrangement of this sort may best be effected, whether by a voluntary association of landholders, or by a cess to be levied under a special law."

Whatever the cause might be, there was no question that the framer of the Bill under consideration, in a vain endeavour to combine sanitation by means of drainage with land improvement, which in this country were perfectly incompatible, had entirely omitted to make any provision for the drainage of the villages where the same might happen to be defective. As for land improvement, he hoped it was not pretended that drainage, *per se*, was beneficial to agriculture in a country where nine-tenths of the culturable lands were only fit for the cultivation of paddy, which required for its growth and maturity a continuous supply of water for four months. The only tracts of country where drainage works could be introduced with advantage were those which were covered by *bheels*. Some of these, he admitted, might be drained at a cost which might prove remunerative; but who was the proper person to decide upon such undertakings but the owner or owners of the *bheel* themselves? Suppose, for instance, the drainage of the Dankoonee jullah, which had been estimated at three lakhs of rupees, was to cost three times that amount, which was not at all improbable, would the work prove remunerative? Again, was it not probable, at any rate possible, that the undertaking, after all, might turn out a failure, as many such projects often turned out to be? Was it in either case fair and equitable that the owner or owners of the *bheel* who had no choice in the matter, and on whom the undertaking was forced by a paternal Government in the name of sanitation and land improvement, should bear the loss? The only condition, he submitted, under which the State should lend its aid in such undertakings, was when the owners could agree amongst themselves to bear all the costs, whatever they might turn out to be, and furnish sufficient security for repayment of the same if advanced by Government. But a matter of this sort was best disposed of by means of private Bills, as was done for keeping open the navigation of the Kurrotia river, at the instance of the late Hon'ble Prosunno Coomar Tagore, and not by a Bill like the one sought to be introduced. So that from whatever point of view the poposed measure might be looked at, it failed entirely in its scope and object.

He, therefore, respectfully moved that the Bill be not read in Council.

The determined opposition and thorough exposure of the fallacy of the scheme produced the desired effect. The Lieutenant-Governor (Sir William Grey) was convinced of the logic that agricultural improvement always required the supply of water, but the contemplated sanitary improvement required the draining out of water. He abandoned the general scheme, and confined the experiment only to the reclamation of the Dankuni Beel, by which a "considerable amount of public money and much private suffering were saved."

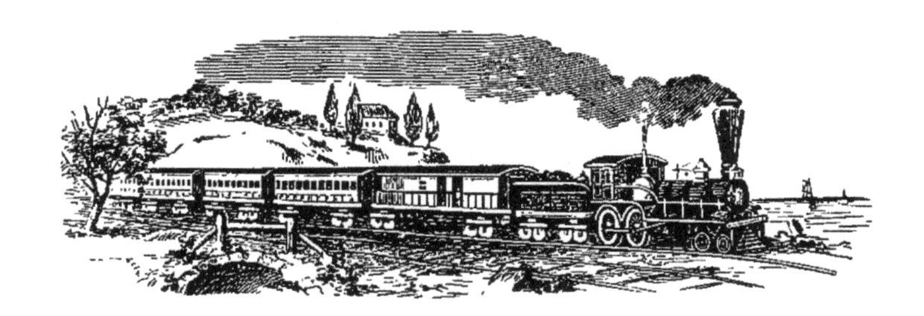

CHAPTER XVI.

MEETING IN HONOR OF SIR WILLIAM GREY. THE ANTI-CESS MEETING. THE ROAD CESS BILL.

EARLY in 1871, came on the retirement of Sir William Grey, who was a conscientious and sympathetic Governor. In commendation of his general policy, and in grateful acknow ledgment of the vigorous stand he made in support of the Permanent Settlement, the zamindars of the British Indian Association held a public meeting in his honor, at their Hall, on the 11th of February, 1871. Babu Digambar pronounced on the occasion the following eulogium :—

Gentlemen :—It has been said, and no doubt with some show of reason, that our retiring Lieutenant-Governor's knowledge of the country and the people was limited, inasmuch as his period of service in such offices as would alone have brought him into actual contact with the people did not extend beyond three years. True, but it should be borne in mind that the best history yet written of British India was the production of one who had no personal knowledge of the country, nor would it be for a moment contended that Lord Lawrence, by reason of his intimate knowledge of the people, a knowledge which as a settlement officer in the North-West for a long time he had had more than ordinary opportunities of acquiring, proved a more successful ruler than those noblemen, who fresh from England had successively ruled over India from 1790 downwards. It is no wonder therefore nor quite so anomalous that in spite of his alleged shortcomings, Mr. Grey should have achieved such signal success in his administration of the country. But I deny, Gentlemen, that his means of studying the people closed with his removal to the Secretariat. On the contrary, I maintain that such removal opened to him a more varied and extensive field for the exercise of his wide and strong sympathies, and offered greater opportunities for acquiring an accurate knowledge of the condition and wants of those whom he was destined to rule. How he had profited by those opportunities, and the rare combination of high, rational and the equitable principles which he had brought to bear on the administration of the country are sufficiently evidenced by his educational policy, his consistent opposition to the income or any form of direct tax as unsuited to the condition and the genius of the people, and the manly stand he had taken to preserve inviolate the solemn compact of the British nation with the Zamindars of Bengal. Gentlemen, it is not my wish to detain you with a lengthy statement of what Sir William Grey has done for the country. Many of his measures have already attained an historic interest and I presume are sufficiently and widely known. I would therefore conclude by observing that if a continuous and distinguished service of thirty years should entitle a man to the gratitude of those for whom he had laboured. and whose material and moral progress he had earnestly and unceasingly endeavoured to promote, Mr. Grey has unquestionably established his claim to it, and I trust, Gentlemen, that you will agree with me, when I say that by coming forward so readily, as we have done, to do him honor we are only honouring ourselves.

On the 25th of March 1871, the motion for the introduction of the long contemplated Bill for Local Rates for Local Purposes, was formally made in the Bengal Council. As far back as 1861, Mr. Laing, the Financial Member of the Governor General's Council, had urged "the policy of easing the Central Exchequer by Local Rates." His advice to the Provincial Governments was "Take what we are able to give you, and for the residue take certain powers of Local Taxation and raise it yourselves," at the same time that he enumerated several sources of revenue "which could be dealt with far better by Local than Imperial Taxation." His successor, Sir Charles Trevelyan, in his budget speech of 7th April 1864, observed:—"It is impossible that all the wants of this great continent, according to the continually rising standard of the public requirements, can be provided for out of the Imperial Revenue. Local agency and local revenues must be increasingly drawn upon; and the Imperial expenditure must be gradually confined to such objects as are of common interest to the whole of India. It is time that the people of this country should learn to raise and spend their own money in maintaining roads, improving the sanitary state of the towns, assisting education, and promoting every other object of local interest." The next Financial Minister, Mr. Massey, insisted on Local Taxation "as the chief resource in case of a financial crisis." Agreeably to these views, the Government of Lord Lawrence, in 1868, requested that the Local Governments should provide means for education and the construction of roads and other works from Local Cesses. Considerable discussion took place about the measure, in which the Local Government of Bengal under Sir William Grey strongly expressed the view for the maintenance of good faith in the preservation of the Permanent Settlement. The matter was referred to the Secretary of State for India, who, entering fully into the question and going into long explanatory arguments, decided the question in favor of the proposed Local Cesses by a despatch dated the 12th May, 1870. Preceded by the financial collapse of 1869, this final decision gave an impetus to the introduction of the system of Provincial Finance. In July 1870, the Government of Bengal proceeded to the constitution of the Cess Committee. It wrote to the Committee of the British Indian Association to nominate a member of their body to act on the Committee. They deputed Babu Digambar.

Few questions have been so hotly contested as that of Indian Finance. There have been the State party, the zamindar party, and the rayat party, all battling in the arena of fiscal politics over the question—who is the real landlord? The result of their gladiatorial combats has been, that a mass of information has been culled and gathered together; that an ill-fated experiment has been made; and that eventually there is an effort to rectify the mistake by the adoption of an intelligent policy. The levy of Cesses involving in it a breach of the Permanent Settlement, the zamindar party stood in defence of their rights and interests on the Bill coming into the Legislature.

The Committee of the British Indian Association convened a Public Meeting at their Hall, on the 3rd April, 1871, of most of the Zamindars, Talukdars, Patnidars, Darpatnidars, and Mukraridars of Bengal. They mustered strong for the purpose of adopting a petition to the Imperial Parliament against the imposition of the Land Cess. The juncture was favourable because the House of Commons then had appointed a Select Committee on Indian Finance. In this meeting Babu Digambar moved the first Resolution and delivered the following speech :—

Judging from the controversy which is now going on on this subject of the Permanent Settlement, it appears to me that the real question at issue is not so much whether the terms or the mutual understanding on which that settlement was made precluded, as a question of strict justice or of law, the imposition of an additional cess on land, as whether, even if they did, it was politic and expedient in the cause of good Government that such a settlement should be respected and maintained in all its integrity. It seems to be almost a settled conviction with our rulers that the Permanent Settlement was a great political blunder, that but for that settlement, Government would have at its command a source of revenue sufficiently elastic to meet the growing necessities of the State—and taking shelter under that convenient maxim "the greatest good of the greatest number," our rulers do not seem to feel much compunction in breaking through a barrier, which is supposed to circumscribe their efforts towards progressive administration. That this is not a mere idle surmise or a misrepresentation of the views of our rulers would appear sufficiently clear from a passage in a letter of the Government of India to the Secretary of State published in the blue-book, along with other correspondence on the subject of this proposed cess, which, with your permission, I will read. "Considering moreover," the Government of India writes, "that nothing can be done in this matter without legislation, the Government of India is placed in a difficult position. We cannot force the Bengal Council to legislate, and it would be hardly expedient to legislate on such a purely local matter in the Council of the Governor-General, and in opposition to the views of the local administration. This last difficulty, however, will be greatly diminished, if not altogether removed, after the local Council has passed a measure imposing a cess on the land for the construction of roads. When this has been done, a more addition to the rate of the cess will possibly give every thing that is required for educational purposes." So that a cess on land is simply a precursor to other cesses which are to follow in quick succession. This policy of partial injustice, that universal good may result therefrom, is the natural consequence of an erroneous belief which has unhappily taken hold of the public mind, and which, as I have already observed, is largly shared by Government, *viz.*, that the Zamindars of Bengal obtained the settlement of their properties on easy terms, and secondly, that the State has been thereby deprived of an elastic source of revenue. Both these propositions are, in my opinion, utterly untenable. I deny that Lord Cornwallis made the settlement with the Zamindars of Bengal on easy terms, and I deny also that the land is rich enough to bear the growing demands of the State. With regard to the first I need only observe that while the land settlement in the North-West was made on the basis of 70 per cent. of the gross rental for the State, and 30 per cent. for the Zamindar, Lord Cornwallis had made the settlement with the Zamindars of Bengal by reserving out of the total rental 90 per cent. for the State, giving up only 10 per cent. to the Zamindars, which was hardly sufficient to meet their collection charges. The only compensation made to the Zamiadars for so exorbitant a revenue charge was the surrender of all the waste lands comprised within their respective estates, free of rent. But the cultivation of these waste lands was a work of time, and as there were very few Zamindars, who had sufficent command of capital to bring these lands into cultivation, and at the same time to meet the deficiency in the collections from their estates, and thus preserve them from sale for arrears of revenue, the consequence was that within the first decade of the settlement, with the exception of small estates or farms which were mostly cultivated by the proprietors themselves, about 80 per cent. of large Zamindaries passed by revenue sales from the hands of those with whom the settlement had been made. It was not until by a large expenditure of capital the waste lands had been brought into cultivation that such of the estates as contained these lands yielded any profits to the proprietors, while the assets of such estates as had no waste land in them shewed very little or no change except within the last 14 or 15 years. And the reason is not far to seek. If you refer to old records, you will find that there had been very little or no variation in the price of produce or wages of labour in Bengal since 1780 to almost 1854; consequently the rent of land remained very much the same during that long period. It is only since 14 or 15 years that a great demand having sprung up in foreign countries for the several staple productions of Bengal such as rice, seeds, and jute, that a corresponding rise has taken place in the value or rent of land, and hence it is we find that while suits for enhancement of rent were rarely instituted prior to 1853-54, our courts have been flooded with such suits since that period. It is on these grounds that I infer that the assets of the permanent settled estates underwent very little or no change until within the last 14 or 15 years, except what was obtained by the reclamation of the waste lands. It is not to be wondered at, therefore, that down to 1852-53, the average profits of the permanently settled estates in Bengal did not exceed 44 per cent. of the revenue payable upon them, as I stated not long ago in this very Hall, and as I shall now prove from the official report of the revenue administration of Bengal for 1852-53. In that report, I find a tabular statement shewing the result of the management of the estates of the disqualified proprietors under the Court of Wards. With your permission I will go over the figures of that statement. I find that in 1852-53 there were 199 estates under the management of the Court of Wards situated in some of the most fertile districts of Bengal, such as Jessore, Moorshedabad, Dacca, Patna, Bhaugalpore, and where, as every Zamindar must know, the proportion of profits to revenue is comparatively higher. The gross rental of those estates is put down at Rs. 11,16,728, balance of previous year at Rs. 8,06,058, and consequently the total demand for the year at Rs. 19,22,787, collection at Rs. 11,00,296, revenue charges at Rs. 7,46,244 and collection charges at Rs. 27,173. The sum total of the last two figures, Rs. 7,73 417, deducted from the gross collection, leaves Rs. 3,26, 879 as the net profit of the 199 Zamindaries under the management of the Court of Wards. The proportion of average profits to revenue therefore is at Rs. 3,26,879 'to Rs. 7,46,244 or little better than 44 per cent. I admit, as I have already done, that owing to a rise in the value of produce, there has been a considerable rise in the value or rent of land since 1853-54, and suppose for the sake of argument we assume that rise at cent. per cent., and also assume that in consequence thereof, the average profits of the Zamindars, which in 1852-53 were only 44 per cent. of revenue, are at the present moment 88 per cent. of the same, even then the profits of the Bengal Zamindars would be found to be less by 12 per cent. of what it has been wisely decided should constitute the proprietor's portion of the rental, and which it has been determined upon should be allowed to Zamindars of the North-West at the renewal of the existing settlement, *viz.*, half the gross rental, and yet it is contended that the Zamindars of Bengal obtained from Lord Cornwallis the settlement of their estates on easy terms. Again, suppose instead of a permanent settlement, Lord Cornwalls had made a 30 year's settlement, and on the same terms as were subsequently thought fair, on which land settlement of the North West should be made, what would have been the financial result of such a settlement ? Why just 70 lacs of rupees per annum less than what was obtained from the Permanent Settlement, as I shall prove to you by a few figures. The rental of the *mal* or revenue paying lands of Bengal at the date of the Permanent Settlement must have been in round numbers 4 crores of rupees, or 90 per sent. of the gross assets would not have given a revenue of 3 crores and fifty lacs. I give the figures in round numbers. Deduct from 4 crores the total rental, 1 crore and 26 lacs the Zamindar's share of it at 30 per cent., balance 2 crores and 8 lacs would represent the revenue of the State under a 30 years settlement ; or, in others words, just 70 lacs of rupees less than what was obtained under the settlement of Lord Cornwallis. Well, there must have been two renewals of this settlement up to date, *viz.*, one in 1822-23, and another in 1852-53. I have shown that there was hardly any variation in the rents of land since 1780 until after 1854, consequently it is not likely that the two renewals would have caused any sensible increase to the revenue. So that in all probability the land revenue of Bengal from 1792 downwards, instead of being 3 crores and 50 lacs, would have remained at 2 crores and 80 lacs, and would also have continued so till 1882-83. or, in other words, instead of making a permanent settlement on the terms he did, if Lord Cornwallis had made the mistake of introducing a 30 years settlement in Bengal, the State would have suffered a loss of 63 crores of rupees, besides being deprived of the vast resources which, the reclamation of the waste lands computed at the time of the Permanent Settlement at one-third of the lands then under cultivation, must have brought within its reach. As regards the second ground urged against the Permanent Settlement, *viz.*, the State being thereby deprived of an elastic source of revenue, I have already shown that there has been no sensible variation in the value of the staple productions of the country between 1780 and 1850; there could not, therefore, have been any change in the rent of land within that long interval. It is true that there has been a considerable rise in the value of produce within the last few years. But I question much that this increase of price will continue. Already a great fall has taken place in the price of rice which occupies for its growth 2-3rds of the culturable land of Bengal, and every Zamindar here present, must have experienced great difficulty in realizing his rent during the last and the current year. The price of one description of paddy, I mean *patna horra,* from which table rice is obtained, has gone down from Rs. 16 to Rs. 10 a *kahana*, and there has been a corresponding fall in the price of other descriptions of paddy also. And with the large export steadily going forward from Saigon and other ports, and with the heavy, I may almost say prohibitory, duty laid upon its export from this country, I should not be at all surprised if the price of rice relapsed in a couple of years more to what it was so lately as 1854-55. Such being the condition of the chief staple produce of the country, and which, as I have said, occupied for its growth 2-3rds of the culturable land of Bengal, and upon which the rent of land is principally dependent, the idea that land if kept unfettered was sufficient to meet the growing necessities of the State, must be visionary indeed. If the truth were fully known, an additional cess on land should be the last expedient, that a liberal and enlightened Government would think of resorting to for an augmentation of its revenues. It is only by a system of rack-renting handed down from the Mahomedan times, and possible only in a country like India where there is hardly any other occupation to engage its teeming millions save agriculture, and where the people would suffer any and every privation rather than seek for a more comfortable living elsewhere, that the Zamindars have been hitherto enabled to pay such a large revenue to Government, and obtain a moderate return for the capital invested in the purchase of their Zamindaries. Make the settlement with the tillers of the land at a rate of rent which would be considered fair on principles recognized in the European countries, and I venture to say that even the existing revenue derived from land would to a great extent be imperilled.

The above is one of his important oratorical efforts, abounding with his usual logical and practical facts in support of his arguments. He had to deliver it only a few months after his heaviest affliction—the death of his only and hopeful son Girish Chandar Mitra. But the question of Provincial Taxation was a decided thing with Government. Lord Mayo's Resolution of 14th December 1870, placed it beyond all future controversy. The Cess Bill, coming on shortly afterwards in the Council, called forth the following remarks from Digambar :—

He said, he had no wish on this occasion to make any remarks on the budget statement which our President has done us the honour to lay before us; in fact he was under the impression that there would be no discussion upon it to-day. But as some of the hon'ble members had already opened the question as to what would be the most suitable form in which additional taxes could be locally raised to meet the anticipated deficit in the local budget, he deemed it right to say a few words on the subject. It was rather hard that while the imperial Government had retained in its hands all the known and available sources from which revenue had been hitherto derived, the local Governments should be called upon, by a strange and rather questionable policy of financial decentralization, to supply the deficit caused by the transfer of certain services to those Governments. That deficit, though apparently only 33 lakhs, was in reality very nearly double that amount; the allotments for those services having been made on the basis of the budget grant of an exceptional year. It was not easy in this country, as the imperial Government must know well enough, to discover new sources for taxation; but if from imperious necessity a choice was to be made amongst the existing ones, he perfectly agreed with the two hon'ble members who had preceded him, that an additional duty on salt was the least objectionable mode in which an additional revenue could be raised, and he said this, to the best of his belief, more in the interest of the poor than that of the rich. No tax could be productive in this country which did not reach the poor, because they constituted unfortunately ninety per cent. of the population ; and unless it was meant to exempt them altogether from contributing to the additional necessities of the State, no other scheme of taxation that he was aware of would be more acceptable to them than the one contended for by the bou'ble members. And he ventured to say that if his countrymen were polled on the question, they would almost unanimously vote for it.

A tax on tobacco, to which allusion has been made by His Honor the President, was no doubt one which would reach the masses ; but considering the thrifty and provident habits of his countrymen, he certainly thought it would not be productive : at any rate not permanently so. It was an article which had come largely into use only since the last fifty or sixty years. It was hardly known in our country a hundred years ago, and if a heavy duty was put upon it to make the tax productive, beside the oppression in various ways which the imposition of a new tax must necessarily entail, and that principally upon the poor, by calling into existence a new machinery for the assessment and collection of the tax, the consumption, he left confident, would be sensibly reduced within a short period.

Both this and the cess on land proposed to be levied would fall on the poor, and he was not prepared to say that those taxes would be less burdensome or oppressive to them than if the sum contemplated to be levied upon them were raised by an additional duty on salt. He had already placed on record his views as to how this additional salt duty was to be supplemented by another tax which would fall exclusively on the rich, and he need not refer to it now. He reserved whether he might have to say on the principle of the proposed local road cess measure when leave was asked for the reading of the Bill in Council.

And again, during a subsequent debate, he spoke in the following terms :—

The statement of objects and reasons did not, to his thinking, sufficiently make out the necessity for the present measure. One could not avoid inferring from it that the imposition of a local cess had been deemed necessary not so much for the purpose of keeping intact the existing means of communication, whether by roads or water, as of effecting improvements upon them. He did not for a moment question the desirableness of some improvement in that direction, but he certainly did think that it was not a crying want—not such as should be met by the imposition of a new tax, at any rate in Lower Bengal, where we had a net-work of khalls and rivers affording every facility for locomotion and transport at a much cheaper cost than by roads. In fact, roads in Lower Bengal had in many instances been known to have caused more harm than good, by impeding the surface drainage of the country, and thereby contributing to the generation of miasmatic fevers which, it might not be unknown to His Honor, had been epidemically raging in different parts of the Hooghly and Burdwan districts ever since something like a *furor* had set in for roads, consequent upon the introduction of railways. He thought that in dealing with this matter of roads you might with good reason, and without retarding the material development of the country, adopt the same policy which you had so wisely adopted in respect of some of the provincial services, viz. cutting your coat according to your cloth. Improvements were very good in their way, but they were not more pressing in this department than in others, and he should be afraid to admit that as a sufficient plea for introducing novel and harrassing schemes of taxation. In fact, if such a plea were to hold good, there would be no limit to taxation, as there could be no limit to schemes of improvement in these days of railways and electricity, however contrary to expectation those so-called improvements might very often turn out in their actual results. With due deference to the hon'ble mover of the Bill, he must say that he could not admit as sufficient the grounds on which he sought to introduce this measure of taxation, though he felt quite confident, from His Honour's known repugnance to burden the country with additional taxes, that even if this Bill passed into law, it would not be enforced except upon absolute necessity.

As regards the main principle involved in the proposed measure, viz. liability or otherwise of the lands in the permanently settled estates in Bengal to additional taxation, the question having been already disposed of in the affirmative by the highest executive authority, this Council, he supposed, had no other alternative than to carry out that order in all its integrity. He would therefore refrain from making any observations on that point. But it appeared to him to be rather strange that almost the only ground on which the Secretary of State justified this additional imposition on land should have been entirely lost sight of in the framing of this Bill. On referring to His Grace's despatch on the subject, dated 12th May 1870, he found it repeatedly stated, that to justify an additional cess on land, the same must be imposed alike on all property accessible to the rate. The words of the despatch were (para. 11)—

"The best method of making this distinction, and of making it clear, is to provide that such cesses should be laid upon the owners of land only in common with other owners of property which is of a kind to be accessible to the rate."

Again (para. 17)—

"And that when such rates are levied at all, they ought, as far as may be possible, to be levied equally, without distinction and without exemption, upon all the holders of property accessible to the rate."

And yet, notwithstanding this indispensable condition attached to the levy of a cess on land, and insisted upon in the despatch, and notwithstanding the interpretation put upon this part of the despatch by His Excellency the Viceroy in Council, as meaning that the rate should be levied upon all property, both real and personal, the Bill in question had exempted all personal property from taxation, thus throwing an additional burden on land. The only explanation offered in the statement of objects and reasons for the exemption was the bare affirmation "that immovable property of all kinds had been generally considered as justly accessible to a road rate."

If, for purposes of a road cess, it should be deemed neccessary to impose an income tax, he did not see any reason why such a tax should be confined to land alone. It should be borne in mind that in the despatch he had just referred to, a cess on land for roads was justified precisely on the same ground as that for education; and if personality was entitled to exemption in the one case, it must be so in the other: and yet it was not to be for a moment contended that the landholders were more interested in the moral elevation of the country than the fund-holders or the merchants. Again, the despatch said (paragraph 20)—

"I observe that you contemplate the extension of the cess to towns and villages. There is indeed no reason why the burden either of roads or of education should be thrown exclusively upon the agricultural classes, when other classes are equally interested in the expenditure, and have property of a kind which can be made accessible to rates."

And yet the towns were exempted from local rating, because they contributed to municipal rates, though the townspeople were quite as equally interested in the district roads as any one living out of town could be.

His next and last objection to the Bill on grounds of principle was, that it had not kept clearly in view the purposes and objects of local taxation. On this point the words of the despatch were (paragraph 22).—

"For this purpose it is above all things requisite that the benefits to be derived from the rates should be brought home to their doors,—that these benefits should be palpable, direct, immediate."

Now, was it to be for a moment supposed that an agency working at a distance of it might be from 40 to 50 miles from many parts of the district, would be able to bring home to the doors of the rate-payers the benefits to be derived from the rates, and make those benefits palpable. direct, and immediate? The requirements of the different parts of a district might be totally different. What was to ensure that the different requirements of the distant parts would be attended to and satisfied unless the parties directly interested in those benefits had a share in the management of the funds? The appointment of sub-divisional committees provided in the Bill, with power to offer suggestions, would for all practical purposes go a little way, he was afraid, to supply this want. Again, it was not to be denied that there were various parts in a district, and embracing, too, large tracts of country where roads were not wanted, and where water communication might not require any improvement, and yet, under the scheme of taxation recommended in the Bill, those parts would go to contributing to the road cess without ever reaping any benefits from it. This surely was not bringing home to the doors of the rate-payers the benefits to be derived from the rates, nor were any benefits conferred upon them which were palpable, direct, and immediate, for the sums they had been punctually and, it may be, monthly contributing. The fact of the matter was, that a district in Bengal was much too large to be adopted as a unit for purpose of local rating, and you would scarcely be carrying out the instructions of the Secretary of State, or your own doctrine of local taxation, by adopting the scheme contained in the Bill. It might be said that the scheme in question was precisely the same that had been recommended by the Cess Committee of which he was a member. His reply to that was that neither himself nor any member of the committee clearly apprehended at the time the distinction to be observed between a local, provincial, and an imperial tax, as the same had been brought home to us of late by the repeated discussions on the subject and by His Honor's own exposition of the principles which should govern each. On these grounds he would move that the Bill in its present frcm should not be permitted to be read in Council.

The question of Local Cess met with a serious obstacle interposed by the Permanent Settlement, because the main principle on which the Bill was to be framed involved in it the imposition of a tax upon land. As a zamindar, Digambar was strongly opposed to this principle. But when he found that legislation on the subject was inevitable, he gave his loyal adhesion to it and worked heartily in the Select Committee, "rendering every assistance in his power to the easy collection of the cess." On the motion in Council to take the report of that Committee into consideration, the President (Sir George Camp bell) "tendered his best thanks to the Select Committee for their labours in regard to the Bill. He believed that the Bill had emerged from the

Committee very vastly improved, and he might say, without any disparagement to the eminently able and useful labours of the official members of the Committee, that we were also most especially indebted to the non-official members of the Council who sat upon the Committee, and who had been good enough to afford their assistance in this matter. We feel the more under obligations to those Hon'ble members, inasmuch as he believed they were originally not wholly prepared to accept the principle upon which the Bill was founded. Nevertheless that principle having been asserted and accepted by this Council, those Hon'ble members (Babu Digambar Mitra and Mr. T. H. Wordie) had been good enough to give us most loyal and able assistance in carrying out the details of this Bill. And he (His Honor) had no hesitation in saying that from all that he had learned and seen, he believed we may congratulate ourselves upon this, that owing to the labours of those Hon'ble members the Bill had been put into a very much more practical and workable form ; that was to say, that owing to the labours of those members of the Committee, it had emerged from the hands of the Committee in a shape in which he hoped the Council and the public may be able to accept it with very little further amendment." His Honor's compliments refer to Babu Digambar's labors in the Cess Committee at first appointed by his predecessor to decide how best the cesses might be practically levied, as well as in the Select Committee that afterwards sat on the Bill.

The work done by him in the first Committee is attested by two able Minutes.* In the other Committee, he suggested those valuable amendments which materially shaped the Road Cess Bill. "If the Road Cess scheme is a self-acting one," says Kristadas Pal, "the merit and credit of devising it belonged to Digambar Mitra. It was somewhat modified in details by Mr. Schalch, but the main design was his—he was the *de facto* author of the scheme."

* Appendices B and C.

CHAPTER XVII.

THE MAYO MEMORIAL SPEECH. THE FAWCETT MEMORIAL MEETING. THE THIRD CAREER IN THE BENGAL COUNCIL. THE EPIDEMIC THEORY. THE EMBANKMENT BILL. THE ABKARI ACTS.

THE year 1872 had dawned fairly, but all on a sudden it became overcast with a deep gloom. Lord Mayo, who in January had left his capital in high health and spirits on a mission to Port Blair in the Andamans, made his re-entry into that capital by the middle of next February only to have his remains laid out in state. The slain Viceroy was received with a universal outburst of grief. They paid him the last sad homage, after which the mourning ship sailed away on her voyage to lay his remains in his Irish home. In next March, the Mayo Memorial meeting came on. Babu Digambar, in seconding the first Resolution moved by Mr. Justice Phear, thus gave utterance to his sentiments :—

I beg to second the Resolution, and in doing so, would refrain from addressing the meeting at length, lest I should mar the effect of the very able and eloquent speech which we have just listened to with such thrilling emotion. I will simply content myself by saying that my countrymen, one and all, deeply mourn the loss which the country has sustained by the late calamitous event. They regard with the greatest horror and abhorrence the diabolical act by which they have been deprived of such a wise and kind ruler. They cherish his memory with the utmost love and veneration—sentiments naturally evoked by the widely—diffused sympathy by which the late lamented nobleman brought himself in rapport with the highest as well as the lowest of the land. While the pages of history will chronicle many instances of sagacity and wisdom by which he nobly endeavoured to establish on solid foundations peace abroad and tranquility at home, tradition will not fail to hand down to generations yet unborn many incidents which though insignificant in themselves are yet most potent in endearing a ruler to the hearts of the people. I may recall to your mind one touching instance—I mean the gracious and chivalrous manner in which he responded to the welcome with which the unsophisticated young ladies and matrons of Ranaghat greeted their noble and beloved ruler to their native village a short time before his departure from these shores, alas! never to return. Few can forget the sunshine of Lord Mayo's face, always beaming with kindness and generosity, and his example ought to teach rulers of men that though duty may require them to be stern in the application of laws and measures, still there is nothing in the nature of that duty which need make the heart impervious to the generous impulse of our common nature.

Modern ethnology has traced the brotherhood of the Hindus and Europeans to one common Aryan parentage. But between the two, there is a wide gulf of foreignness in blood and language, in religion and manners, in taste and feeling. Hence the slowness of assimilation between the rulers and the ruled in a century and a half—the rareness of interchange of sympathy between them. No doubt, there have been amongst us several Englishmen the depths of whose good-nature were stirred by "compassion for suffering and hatred of injustice and tyranny". But the historic friends and benefactors of India are David Hare, Edmund Burke, and Professor Henry Fawcett. To David Hare, who dedicated his fortune with his labours to our cause, we "owe a debt immense of endless gratitude." Edmund Burke is entitled to the great praise of having devoted years of intense labour to the service of an alien people from whom he expected, "no requital, no thanks, no applause" He was a philanthropist to whom "oppression in Bengal was the same thing as oppression in the streets of London." Out of the same pure motives did Mr. Fawcett devote his talents and knowledge to the reform of abuses in India. Session after session *in* Parliament as well as *out* of it, he pleaded for retrenchment and reduction of taxation in her favor, and laid her sons under obligation. In grateful acknowledgment of his disinterested services, the Native inhabitants of Bengal held a public meeting in the British Indian Association Hall, on the 26th November, 1872, to vote him an address, and also another to the electors of Brighton for directing their attention to Indian affairs through Mr. Fawcett as their representative in Parliament. Babu Digambar Mitra in moving the first Resolution spoke as follows :—

The Resolution speaks for itself, and I should not take up your time nor offend your good sense by what I can say to commend it to you for adoption. To appreciate fully and thoroughly the man whom we have this day met to honor, we have only to examine closely the sources from which human actions generally proceed, and then contrast them with the guiding springs of his actions. I dare say such an examination will show that however sweetly the poets may sing, and however eloquently the philosophers may descant on the dignity of man and the divine attributes he is endowed with, he has in reality as a rule in no part of the world yet outgrown that stage of his development in which his actions are governed by motive power, other than that of self-love, which of course includes love for our offspring, developed in a still stronger degree in lower animals. Religious teachers and moral philosophers have in all ages and climes, sought to give a nobler and more refined direction to our impulses; but as yet self-love rules supreme, and the only victory their teachings have yet obtained, is simply the recognition of the truth, that there are other and nobler springs to human action than that of self-love. There is another sentiment which, fostered by poets and orators, and influenced most probably by external circumstances and surroundings, has had an early and extraordinary devolpment in certain climes—I mean patriotism or love for one's country. But patriotism is only developed clanship, and if properly analysed would appear to be another expression of self-love, although more intelligent and enlightened, which leads a man even to face the cannon's mouth for the defence of his own home and hearth and for the glory of his country, with which his own well-being is indissolubly bound up. But, gentlemen, a man may be very patriotic without being inspired with much of that universal and active sympathy which would impel him to do that for his brother man of whatever clime or creed, which he unceasingly strives to secure for himself, and which he thinks to be so essential to his own happiness. It is in the absence of this sympathy that you are to look for a solution of the apathy and indifference so generally and habitually exhibited by our rulers in England to the affairs of this country. But while we must accept the fact, that as a rule in no part of the world has humanity made such progress as to be swayed by a higher impulse than that of self-love, it is nevertheless equally true that like every other rule it is not without exception. It is undeniable that there are men, however few, whose wide sympathies for their fellow creatures are not to be circumscribed by creed, nationality or geographical boundaries, and who are unresistingly led to identify themselves with their brethren of every clime, creed or colour; and whether owing to the influence of a purer religion or any other cause such exceptions, it must be admitted, are more numerously met with in European countries than elsewhere, and amongst them perhaps nowhere else more so than in that land to which we owe our allegiance (Hear, hear,). It is superfluous for me to name the great philanthropists of England, who have dedicated their time, talents, energy and means to the good of mankind, for their names must be familiar to you as household words. Of this band of philanthropists, the sightless champion of India, as Mr. Fawcett has been happily described, is entitled to our warmest gratitude (Applause). In his case we see that where this noble sympathy of man for man, irrespective of country, color or creed, is strongly developed, even the gravest natural defects or disabilities, cannot check its active exercise. For though deprived ot the most valuable aid to human usefulness, Mr. Fawcett has nevertheless succeeded in watching over the millions of India, as if he were gifted with the eyes of an Argus. or Indra, if you please. I will not dilate on the services which he has rendered by his bold, intelligent, disinterested, and zealous advocacy ot our cause in Parliament. They have been well, though briefly, described in the address which I have read.

The Fawcett Testimonial Committee had raised a fund for the purpose of paying his election expenses. But hearing that they had been paid in England, the money was diverted to the purchase of some oriental jewellery for presentation to Mrs. Fawcett as a mark of respect for her husband.

During his second legislative career from 1870 to 1872, Digambar made a well-marked figure. He was a regular attendant and partaker in the deliberations of all important measures. Turning over the pages of the proceedings of the Legislative Council of Bengal, we find him frequently taking a prominent part in the chief local questions before that legislature. The Bengal Statute-book contains considerable traces of his legislative exertions and achievements. When ever the occasion arose, he did not fail to enter his protest by setting forth the true principles involved in the issue. His knowledge of the country associated with his keen insight gave weight to his utterances, and enhanced the value of his public usefulness. On the expiry of his time in November 1872, the Lieutenant-Governor was pleased to retain him in his Council for a fresh period, with a view to the benefit of his sound advice in matters of prospective legislation. He was thus honored for the third time.

In the course of his third career, the Embank ment Bill principally engaged his attention and was ripened by him into maturity. It is time now to resume the narrative of the Epidemic Fever left off in a previous page. The hopes with which the Fever Commission had been set on foot came to nothing. Year after year the epidemic broke out and committed its ravages, baffling all treatment and the ascertainment of its cause. But the Government persisted in its continuance of effort to probe into the mystery. From time to time it deputed doctors, sanitary commissioners, civil engineers, and scientific authorities who carefully went through the investigation. They all started different theories of their own, but agreed in the common opinion of its occurring from subsoil humidity. But they all went on a wrong track to arrive at the source of that humidity. They attributed the saturation of the soil to water-loggedness arising from defective drainage consequent upon impeded khals and rivers. But in fact it did not proceed from the absorption of the overflow of paddy-fields, beels, and obstructed water-courses. The right cause was hit by Babu Digambar. During his residence at Kasimbazar, he had marked the desolation of that once flourishing town and also its neighbouring places. He had heard that desolation ascribed to an epidemic which broke out on the excavation of a cut, that, straightening the course of the Bhagirathi, threw those places inland, and increased their dampness from confined moisture. He had found that epidemic prevalent up to his time. These facts made him very reasonably conclude that the Bardwan Fever was not a new fever, but identical with the old endemic of the country, bearing the same malarial type and character from which they suffered in Gaur and Kasimbazar, and originating from the same cause that had produced the disease in those towns. In his opinion, the Epidemic Fever was caused by "dampness arising from excessive moisture in the subsoil owing to the disturbance in the drainage of the place, occasioned, most probably, by the diversion in the course of the river, aided perhaps by a number of roads running transversely to the direction of the drainage." He showed very clearly that "the drainage of all the villages in the Epidemic Districts, as elsewhere in Lower Bengal, is effected by water first running into the nearest *paddy fields* lying in the direction of their slope, thence it collected in the *beels* from which it rushes through *khals* into larger streams, which again communicate with navigable rivers. An obstruction occurring in any one of these conduits must interfere with the drainage, and its effects are felt more or less according to the proximity or remoteness of the obstruction from the scene of its influence. * * The face of the country being perfectly flat, the drainage runs over the whole surface towards the direction of the slope, and consequently roads running transversely to it must of necessity intercept the drainage. * * Both the East Indian and the Eastern Bengal Railways and their feeders have crossed the water-courses of villages and obstructed the drainage of these places." From the verv beginning had Babu Digambar put forth this theory in the appendices tacked to the Epidemic Fever Commission Report. But, coming from a Native and layman, it was not heeded. Professional pride always snubs an outsider. The doctors and others floundered in the paddy-fields and beels, while the Epidemic annually made its appearance and carried on its devastations. Babu Digambar keenly watched the proceedings of Government, deploring the waste of public money upon wrong premises and programmes. His faith in his own theory increased with the failure upon failure happening to the measures pursued by Government. He therefore returned to the important subject with unquenched zeal, and "spared neither trouble nor money to commend it to the public. He deputed men at his own expense to the afflicted villages to report on their drainage outlets, to prepare survey plans, and to compile histories of their sanitarv condition past and present." The *Bengalee* says "something of the spirit of the apostle of a new faith animated him." Still his endeavours were fruitless. But again and again did he return to the advocacy of the only sure preventive of the disease. He sedulously sought every occasion to dwell upon it with prominence. He wrote on the subject, in 1872 and 1873, a series of articles in the *Hindoo Patriot*, which he reprinted in a pamphlet form called—*The Origin of the Epidemic Fever in Bengal*. "Off and on he discussed the question with officials and non-officials, Europeans and Natives alike, till by iterations and perseverence he succeeded in extorting the acceptance of his theory," and carried away the palm. Lord Lawrence first of all did him justice by observing "the only new cause suggested by the Native member of the Commission, Babu Digambar Mitra, as probably increasing the dampness, which the Commission considered to be the main source of the disease, was the obstruction to drainage by railways and roads and the shutting up of outlets into rivers."Next, the Lieutenant-Governor (Sir George Campbell) acquitted the rice-fields and jullas of participation in the generation of the epidemic by emphathically asserting that "in the reeking swamps of Bengal the human race seems to have multiplied to a greater extent than anywhere in India—perhaps in the world." Dr. Pettenkoffer of Munich fully endorsed his views by stating that "the dwelling ground of the people has much more to do with the origin of the disease than the surrounding district or the

the rice-fields and marshes." Duly noticing his statements, the *Indian Medical Gazette* of June 1872, concluded with the following observation :—"In all this we entirely concur, and we subscribe a general adherence to the theory which the pamphlet expounds." Very recently, in the Conference held at Belvedere on the 28th July 1892, they unanimously admitted the correctness of his theory.* Thus, after ten years' hard combating, "he had the satisfaction to see his theory embraced with open arms by the doctors, who had hitherto shown a cold shoulder The Government accepted his theory and recognized it in the enactment of the Embankment Act." †

The motion for leave to bring in the Embankment Bill was made in December 1870. The Bill originated from the circumstance of an innundation in the Twenty-four Parganas in 1868, caused by the breakage of certain dams which the neighbouring zamindars had refused to repair. At the same time that a stringent law in emergencies was thought to be necessary, it was proposed to proceed with caution in the matter of interfering with established rights. In this original state, the Bill was approved by Babu Digambar thus :—

* Dr. Sircar remarked that "the drainage theory has been ascribed to the late Raja Digambar Mitra. but I have shown that it originated with Dr. Dempster in 1845, when he was a member of a Committee then appointed." Certainly, Raja Digambar did not originate the theory that the prevalence of fever in Bengal was owing to humidity of soil. His especial contention was that dampness arose from impeded drainage caused, not by silted up khals and rivers but the Railways and their feeders which did not exist in 1845.—See Appendix D.

† The *Hindoo Patriot's* obitnary.

He said that this was unquestionably a well-considered and a very desirable measure, and he subscribed to every word that had fallen from the hon'ble mover while applying for leave to bring in the Bill; and he readily bore testimony to the fact of many drainage channels having been closed by zamindars, either wantonly or for their own selfish purposes. The Bill, as far as he had been able to judge, had scrupulously respected private rights, while at the same time it had taken every precaution to protect public interest from being jeopardized by the acts of individuals pursuing their own selfish aims. And he entertained great hopes that with certain modifications, which no doubt the Bill would undergo in Committee, the present measure, if carried out properly, besides furthering its immediate objects, would in a much greater degree contribute to check the ravages of epidemics, than the one which was avowedly intended for the purpose—he meant the Drainage Bill.

The Bill was referred to a Select Committee in January 1871. But the Decentralization policy of Lord Mayo having come into operation in the interim the original principle of the Bill was abandoned, and it was recast without any notice of the liability of Government to maintain certain embankments at State-expense. The question of this liability had been settled as far back as 1837, since which specified lines of embankments had all along been kept up at the cost of Government. They had ignored this important fact in the Select Committee. Backed by Maharaja Jotindra Mohan Tagore who was then in the Council, Babu Digambar undertook a united onslaught against the unconstitutional course of silent nullification. He brought the fact to notice in the Council. There in black and white was the decision of the Revenue Board in 1837, and there the Embankment Act of 1855. They could not be repudiated. He gave notice of certain amendments and delayed the progress of the Bill. Not only did he contest in the debate of the Council, but he penned also a number of articles headed *The Embankment Bill*, which appeared in the *Hindoo Patriot.* * The result of his fight was that the Government was obliged to make many substantial concessions. With reference to his success, the *Hindoo Patriot* of Monday, April 21, 1873 observed:—"We cannot withhold our meed of praise to the Hon'ble Digambar Mitra for the ability and perseverence with which he represented in Council the landed interests affected by this Bill. Indeed, we doubt whether the Government would have taken the trouble to go into the subject so carefully if he had not with his sledge-hammer logic exposed the serious defects of this measure. The Bill as it was framed involved a direct infringement of the Permanent Settlement, and a gross breach of faith. At every stage of the Bill fresh concessions were made, which showed the soundness of the position he had assumed. The great bone of contention was the distinction made between public and private embankments; this distinction was recognised in theory, but not unfrequently disregard ed in practice. The steady opposition, which Babu Digambar and his colleague Maharaja Jotindra Mohan Tagore offered, extorted from Mr. Schalch, the member in charge of the Bill, the schedule of public embankments maintained at the expense of the State, which has once for all settled the dif-

* See the Bengal Council proccedings of February and March 1873. We have every reason to attribute the articles in the *Hindoo Patriot* to Digambar.

ficulty." Indeed, the Embankment Bill stands to the credit of Digambar as his most important legislative achievement.

The one other Bill, considered in the session of 1873, to which we feel tempted to draw the reader's attention, is the amendment of the Abkari Acts, on which Digambar gave utterance to very pertinent remarks in the neat little speech reproduced here :—

So far as the proposed amendments aim at preventing jobbery in the disposal of licenses, I think they are calculated to do so most effectually, and they have therefore my hearty support. But there are other and very important questions raised in the speech delivered by your Honor at the last sitting of the Council, upon which I wish to be permitted to address a few words. Your Honor is reported to have said—for I was unavoidably absent on the occasion—that the primary object of the proposed amendments in the Abkaree Acts, was to put down the growing consumption of spirituous and fermented liquors—a necessity which has also been seriously felt by, and has since some years engaged the earnest attention of, some of the best men of our community.

There can be no question, Sir, that the Hindoos, especially the higher classes of them, were at one time noted for their abstemiousness, due entirely to restraints imposed by our religion against the use of intoxicating drinks. But from various causes, of which the spread of English education and ideas are perhaps the principal, the strong hold which religion had on the minds of the people is gradually but steadily weakenning, especially amongst the higher classes. It is, therefore, a matter of the highest gratulation to all well-wishers of the country that our rulers are determined, even at the sacrifice of revenue, to supplement the efforts of religion, by means of legislation, in checking the spread of drunkenness. But, Sir, however much we may deplore, we cannot shut our eyes to the fact that in this hot and enervating climate a great yearning has, from the earliest ages, been manifested for some kind of stimulating drinks, and hence it is that, as a concession to this national craving, our legislators of old were compelled to modify the total abstinence ordinance of our religion by sanctioning the use of spirituous liquors at certain stated days of the month, and in strictly regulated doses, in the case of those who manifested a strong desire for drink, and in whom the religious injunction of total abstinence was found to be inoperative. But the maxim that it was easier to abstain altogether from, than to be moderate in, the use of intoxicating drinks was soon exemplified, and the excesses committed by the Bramacharees may be said to have accelerated the advent of Choitunno, who again preached and enjoined total abstinence, and succeeded in a remarkable degree in checking the growth of drunkenness. But however greatly Choitunno and other religious chieftains who had preceded him might have contributed to stop the consumption of spirituous liquors, they do not seem to have ever taken heed that the popular craving was being satisfied in another way, that is, by the use of *subjee* and *ganja*. In fact, they seem to have encouraged their use, in order more effectually to check the use of intoxicating drinks; and there is no denying the fact that both *ganja* and *subjee* as well as opium are much more extensively used in this as well as the North-Western Provinces than intoxicating drinks. I have not had statistics at command to satisfy myself from figures what effect the increased duty on liquors has had on the consumption of *bhang*, *ganja*, and opium, but I can say of my own personal knowledge that the use of opium is fast spreading amongst the respectable classes of my countrymen, and in the majority of cases as a cheap substitute for spirituous drink both in Calcutta and other populous towns in Bengal. The injurious effect of opium and *ganja* both upon the *physique* and intellect is, I believe, never questioned. One may however satisfy himself on that point by a visit paid to the Dullunda Lunatic Asylum, and some of the many opium-smoking public houses in Calcutta. The former will show that more than half the number of such cases treated therein owes their origin to *ganja*, and the latter will present the sad spectacle of some of the best specimens of humanity reduced to a state of utter helplessness, both bodily and mentally, by a few months of opium smoking. I do not wish to express myself dogmatically on this difficult problem one way or the other. If possible,

I would put down the use both of intoxicating drugs and drinks. But I would in all humility submit for the serious consideration of our rulers whether, in our attempt to check the consumption of intoxicating drinks by making it an expensive luxury, we may not be encouraging the spread of a cheaper substitute for it, and one perhaps more deleterious to the healthy development of our species and less conducive to longevity.

CHAPTER XVIII.

THE PRESIDENTSHIP OF THE B. I. ASSOCIATION. THE AGRARIAN RIOT IN PABNA. THE FAMINE OF 1874. THE ADVENT OF THE PRINCE OF WALES THE STAR OF INDIA CHAPTER. THE NORTH-BROOK MEETING. THE DISTRICT APPELLATE BENCHES QUESTION. THE EPIDEMIC COMMISSION.

TOWARDS the end of 1872, Raja Romanath Tagore was raised to the Imperial Council of the Viceroy. The many important matters before that Legislature requiring much of his time and attention, he temporarily vacated the Presidentship of the British Indian Association. Babu Digambar was elected to officiate in his stead. His first presidential address was made at the half-yearly meeting held on the 20th September 1873:—

GENTLEMEN.—In opening the business of the Meeting I cannot help expressing my sense of unworthiness to occupy a chair, which within the last 20 years had been successively filled by such distinguished men as Raja Sir Radhakant, the Hon'ble Prasanna Coomar Tagore, and last though not the least by my Hon'ble friend Raja Romanath Tagore. Relying, however, upon the wise saying *kurmanang vadatha budhi,* I will endeavour to do whatever justice I can to your choice.

In taking into consideration the next six-monthly report of the Committee's proceedings, he did the following justice to the memory of one of his valuable colleagues :—

It is my painful duty to announce to you the untimely death of our lamented friend and colleague Babu Kissory Chand Mitter. He was associated with us as a Member of this Association for many years, took an active part in its proceedings, and rendered valuable aid in its deliberations. You will I dare say approve of the Resolution, which your Committee have recorded on this melancholy event.

Many important points were noticed in his speech, among which was the Agrarian rising in Pabna. In June 1873, the rayats of that District broke out in a serious riot. Moving in hundreds and thousands from place to place, headed by three ring-leaders, they not only looted, but sometimes murdered, and committed outrages upon females. The young widowed sister of a Zamindar was carried away. No one in the District felt himself safe. Those who could afford, sent away their ladies and children to Calcutta and other places. Ostensibly the movement was against the Zamindars, but none of the well-to-do was spared. The disturbance continued till the issue of a Proclamation by the Lieutenant-Governor, who warned all offenders of the severe punishments they incurred, and promised redress on a peaceable representation of their grievances. On the subject of this agitation Digambar made the following comments :—

The next question upon which I should like to offer a few remarks is that which is now agitating the district of Pubna. There is no doubt that the zamindar is much to blame for the state of things which has arisen there. He should have had the common sense to know, that he could not legally enforce any dues from his ryot which were not incorporated in his jumma, and which did not appear in the Jumma Wasil Bakee or rent-roll of the estate. I admit that a ryot would much more readily pay 4 annas in that shape, than 2 annas, if the same were to be merged in his jumma. I admit also the difficulties. expense, and the litigation attendant upon legal enhancement of rent, but a sensible zamindar would much rather face the difficulty, than leave things in such a state of utter uncertainty and thereby place himself entirely at the mercy of his tenants. As, however, the matter now stands, the zamindars of Pubna as a body are more sinned against than sinning—and so far as the charge brought against them of rack-renting their ryots is concerned, I think I will not be very far from the truth if I say that those zamindars, who have compounded with their ryots in that way, do not with all the cesses get by at least ¼ of what they would be legally entitled to. Now the ryot under the influence of designing men refuses to pay what he knows the zamindar cannot legally enforce, but what nevertheless he had hitherto acknowledged as part of his jumma, and paid with as much punctuality as he paid the other. If the Zamindar owing to his legal disability is obliged to forego the cesses and take from his ryot what he was in the habit of getting some 30 or 40 years ago, he would be punished not for any wrong that he had done to his ryot, but for having made a compromise with him on terms, which though morally right, were not legally so. I think, Gentlemen, his case is a very hard one, and deserves the special consideration of Government. Such differences between the zamindar and ryot as have arisen in Pubna and also in some other districts cannot be adjusted by the application of the ordinary laws of the country. Special Officers armed with special powers should be appointed to adjust such disputes in an equitable manner, and, to guard against a recurrence of the like, changes should be introduced in the rent law of the country. With the sunset law, (enforceable quarterly) staring him in the face, the zamindar in his turn has been deprived of all the facilities which he possessed under the prior rent-laws, of enforcing his demands upon his ryot either by the arrest of his person immediately on institution of a suit for rent, or by distress with the aid of the Police of his moveable property wherever the same might be traced. These powers might at first appear to be too stringent, but bearing in mind that at the time of the settlement and for a long period subsequently and in many instances even at the present day, the zamindars had to pay into the public exchequer from sixty to ninety Rs. out of every hundred he had to collect, nothing short of such powers was considered by the legislature adequate for the purpose. Even when armed with such summary powers it was not unoften that the zamindar was kept at bay by combination formed amongst his tenantry known in the country by the familiar phrase of *Dharma Ghut.* Under the present state of the rent law, which gives *carte blanche* to the ryot to pay his rent, whenever it suited his convenience, and withhold it as long as appeals to different courts and the dilatory process of the execution of decrees, would admit of his doing so, the wonder is, not that such rent difficulties should have taken place in Pubna but that they did not arise long before. I must say that this fact of itself speaks highly in favour of the conciliatory disposition of the zamindar evinced though it might be said under the dread of serious consequences befalling him if the ryots were given the opportunity to combine and withhold the payment of rent, and to this dread, it might be added, it was mainly owing that the zamindar agreed to receive from his ryot increased rent due to him on account of the increased value of agricultural produce, in the shape of abwabs or cesses, rather than enforce the same by the legal remedy open to him viz, institution of suits for the enhancement of rent. It is not my wish at present to indicate the nature of the changes which should be introduced in the rent laws of the country,but simply to point out the imperative necessity thereof, or the spirit which has already manifested itself amongst the ryots of Pubna and elsewhere to coerce the zamindar to their own terms however extravagant, will I am afraid spread like wildfire and envelope the whole country.

The early cessation of the rains in 1873 threatened Bengal with a disastrous event. In that great rice-country, no-famine or famine is a yearly question decided by the fall of a few inches of the autumn equinoctial rains or otherwise. The heavens withheld them in the above year, and men waited with anxious expectancy till the Kali Puja new moon. There was no fall. Sir George Campbell at once wired the fact to Lord Northbrook at Simla. His Excellency made not a minute too late in coming down to cope with the evil. Day by day progressive scarcity passed into starvation. The Government opened relief-measures with all the means and appliances at its command. Great stress was at first laid upon the old stores in the country, and loud and bitter cries were raised against the hard-hearted men supposed to hold them. The British Indian Association submitted a representation against the erroneous impression to the Bengal Government. Two communications were received in reply, in one of which the Association was invited at the instance of the Government of India to "state the grounds on which they had based their estimate as to the food prospects, and to make a comparison between 1865-66 and 1873-74." Digambar took up the task on behalf of the Committee, and so ably got up the paper that Sir George Campbell acknowledged its receipt with his "best thanks for the care and labor taken to sift and collate all the information," and further remarked that "he attached much value to the views held on the all-important question." It is one of the most valuable papers in the archives of the Association, which reflected great credit upon that body* Digambar was engaged in its laborious preparation for upwards of a week without an intermission to his toil. The adduction of the

* See Appendix E.

evidence of facts and figures in demonstration of his arguments, was a work of such severe strain upon his health that shortly afterwards he fell ill of a serious mental complaint. The memorial was submitted in the last week of December 1873, and he became affected early in January 1874. He remained unwell for many months, and kept away from every business till he attended the annual meeting of the Association in August 1874, when in his presidential address he made the following allusion to the famine of that year :—

GENTLEMEN,—In meeting you again after nearly a year, allow me to congratulate you on the changed condition of things in the country. The famine has passed away, and plenty now smiles over the land. It was about this time last year that grave apprehensions were entertained of the calamity then impending, consequent upon the scanty produce of the *amun* crop, the staple food of the country, and there must have been very few indeed, if any, amongst those who had devoted any thoughts upon the subject, who were sanguine enough to predict that the calamity would be tided over without a terrible loss of life. Judging from the past such apprehensions were far from being groundless. It was, however, left for the nobleman at present presiding over the destinies of this vast empire to prove for the first time that such visitations could be successfully coped with without any loss of life—and at the same time without deranging the free course of trade. I will not detain you gentlemen, by going over those measures which were adopted by His Excellency, and which resulted in this marvellous achievement. We all know what English instinct is on such occasions, and which was so laconically but graphically given expression to during the famine of 1866 by the same nobleman who happened to be the Secretary of State then as now. "Spend freely, and save human life," was the short message, which was then flashed forth to the Government of India by Lord Cranborne, but it was reserved for the head of the present Government to give a thorough practical effect to such a noble and humane policy. Gentlemen, I doubt not you will agree with me, when I say that it is impossible to express in a suitable manner the deep sense of gratitude which we all must feel for what His Excellency has done at so much self-sacrifice. Our thanks are also eminently due to His Honor the Lieutenant-Governor for so admirably and successfully carrying out the policy laid down by the Government of India. Gentlemen, I need hardly remind you that, however wise and sound that policy might have been, it would scarcely have borne the fruit it had, if it had not been so loyally and ably seconded by Sir Richard Temple at considerable self-sacrifice, consequent upon his personal supervision of the relief operations throughout the anxious period of the famine. We have heard it said that the administration of famine relief has not been without great waste of money, and that the large profits made by some of the contractors in the transport of grain have been adduced in proof thereof; but I ask you, gentlemen, whether it was possible to conduct operations on such an unprecedentedly large scale without any previous experience, against time, in such out-of-the way places, and over such a vast area, if the Government had gone to work in a niggardly spirit. High though the contract rates were, let it not be supposed that it was all profit, and no loss with the contractors. These men had undertaken immense risks, and I can tell you I know of one contractor and many of you, perhaps will have no difficulty in guessing whom I mean, who had confidently calculated upon a profit of Rs. 50,000 by his contract, but instead of making any profit, he is in a fair way of losing very nearly that amount, unless Government take a lenient view of his case, only because he was too late by a few days in making the necessary arrangements for carrying out the contract.

With the close of 1874 Digambar's public career may be said to have closed, unless his appointment to the Shrievalty, which took place a few months before this time, be regarded in the light of a continuation. His was the first instance in which the honor of Sheriffhood was conferred upon a Bengali gentleman The duties of this office terminated in December 1875, but not without giving him a rare opportunity for a crowning conclusion, and a proud privilege falling to his lot. His Royal Highness the Prince of Wales was about to visit India. The mythical Company-Jehan was without a bodied form or pressure on the Indian imagination—it lived in name and tradition. The advent of the Heir-Apparent called forth an outburst of loyalty throughout the Empire, such as had never been known in the annals of British India. To consider the necessary arrangements for welcoming and giving a suitable reception to His Royal Highness, the public of Calcutta held a meeting on the 31st July 1875. As Sheriff, Babu Digambar had the honor of opening its proceedings:—

With your permission I will read the requisition under which this meeting has been convened. "To the Sheriff of Calcutta. Sir, We the undersigned, have the honor to request that you will be good enough to convene on an early date a public meeting of the inhabitants of Calcutta for the purpose of considering what arrangements should be made to do honor to H. R. H. the Prince of Wales on the occasion of H. R. H.'s approaching visit to this City."

This has been signed by the Lieutenant-Governor and the representatives of the different sections of the community of Calcutta. I will not anticipate the gentlemen who will address this meeting, but I will beg permission simply to observe that I consider it one of the happiest events of my life that I happen to hold the office of Sheriff at such an auspicious time as this, and that I thereby enjoy the privilege of summoning this meeting to do honor to the Heir-Apparent of Her Gracious Sovereign, our future King. Ever since the establishment of the British Empire in the East, only once, about five years ago, a distinguished member of the Royal Family honoured us with his august presence; but this is the first time that the Heir-Apparent of the Crown has expressed a wish—nay declared it to be the dream of his life—to visit this countrry, and I have no doubt that this auspicious event will be hailed with rejoicings and fitting demonstration of loyalty amongst all classes of Her Majesty's subjects throughout the length and breadth of the country (cheers). Without detaining you with any further remarks I declare the meeting open, and I beg to move that the Hon'ble Sir Richard Temple be requested to take the chair.

Various were the processions, and illuminations, and rejoicings on the arrival of the Prince. But the most gorgeous of all spectacular displays was made in the Chapter for the presentation of the crosses and ribands of the Star of India. It was held on the morning of 4th January 1876. The grand Viceregal Darbar pavilion was pitched on the race-course maidan. There was combined the magnificence of Asia with the refinements of Europe to adorn the pageant with a splendour and beauty worthy of the ceremony. The Viceroy, along with the Prince, represented England's Suzerainty, amidst an assembly of the highest rank, intelligence, and authority of the realm. The most brilliant sight was made by the crowd of Rajas and Chiefs in their richest dresses and jewels. But the rows of female beauty, the brightness of their eyes outlustre-ing and shaming the glittering diamonds --made up a show that is never witnessed in any Asiatic Court. Many a worthy of the land was honored before this august gathering, among whom Digambar Mitra was decked and dubbed a C. S. I.

Soon after the Prince of Wales had left Calcutta, Lord Northbrook wired his resignation to England. His administration was distinguished by many acts of wisdom and beneficence, for which the community of Calcutta held a public meeting on the 8th April, 1876, to vote a fitting memorial to His Excellency. Many European and Native speakers came forward to bear their testimony. In moving the third Resolution, Babu Digambar thus expressed his sense of His Lordship's eminent public services ;—

Hon'ble Sir, Ladies, and Gentlemen,—I have been asked to move the third resolution, which I do with, great pleasure :—That the following address expressive of the sentiments of the community of Calcutta on his Lordship's administration of this country be presented to the Right Hon'ble Lord Northbrook :—

* * * * *

I need not read the address, as I find printed copies of it are already in your hands. It sets forth the chief characteristics of Lord Northbrook's administration. If, however, there is any one point more than another in his Lordship's Indian career, which has vividly impressed the minds of the people of this country, it is the single-mindedness of purpose, the purity of intentions, and the high conscientiousness which have marked that career. Others might have been more bold, more dashing, more brilliant; but, as an honest and conscientious ruler, pursuing his work quietly, unostentatiously, but uncompromisingly, sympathising with the people, and advancing their best interests, Lord Northbrook yields the palm to none. His Lordship assumed the reins of Government at a time when the public mind had been unhinged by a course of over-legislation, over-taxation, and over-activity in administration, so much so that petitions were sent forth from different parts of the country for a Royal Commission of Enquiry; but our retiring Viceroy, threw, as it were, oil over troubled waters by his wise and considerate measures. This of itself was no ordinary moral achievement. Others might have sought glory in making new conquests, or adding new territories; but he sought his in soothing the public mind, which was irritated and discontented, in lightening the burthens upon the people, who were groaning under taxation, in combining retrenchment with reform, and placing the Empire upon the solid foundations of peaceful progress, enfranchised commerce, and steady prosperity. His Lordship was not a stranger to this land ; he felt an hereditary interest in it, and he showed his sympathy with the people in a most substantial and generous form. By his kindly demeanour and even-handed justice, he bridged the gulf between the rulers and the ruled. and imparted his spirit into the whole body of the administrative machinery, In the calamity which befell the country in 1873-74, when millions of people were without food to eat and water to drink, he literally proved the father of the poor. In conquering this calmity, he achieved a measure of success unparalleled in the annals of such visitations in any age or country. I consider it a national misfortune that such an enlightened statesman and good ruler, and, above all, such a warm friend of humanity, is about to leave our country, and I believe you will agree with me, that we ought not to allow him to depart without expressing to him our respect and gratitude, our deep sense of the eminent public services which he has rendered, and our fervent hope that, though away from this land, he will, God willing, yet continue to benefit the millions whom he has once ruled so well and so wisely, by lending them the weight of his authority, experience, and influence in the Imperial Parliament of England.

The inefficiency of the Mofasil Courts in Bengal was an old complaint. The want of improved tribunals was one of the most vehement objections taken by the non-official Europeans in their anti-Black Act memorial in 1857. On the Anglo-Indian community becoming amenable to the jurisdiction of the District courts, their reform became an urgent duty of the Government. Considerable improvement took place in the lower courts by the accession of Native Judges of great knowledge and ability, compared with whom the District Appellate Judge many a time presented the spectacle of occupying a lower position in point of training and experience. But still much remained to be done. In 1876, the question of their re-organization cropped up in connection with the Civil Appeals Bill. Sir Richard Garth, the then Chief Justice of our High Court, drew up a minute suggesting the constitution of appellate tribunals combining the three elements—the civilian, barrister, and native. The proposition for such a composite bench had long ago been made by Sir John Peter Grant, but the finances did not permit its being carried into effect. To meet the public demand, Sir Richard Temple proposed to have a bench of the English Civilian Judge associated with a Native Judge. Touching this question then under public consideration, the following extract preserves Babu Digambar's opinion expressed at a General Meeting of the B. I. Association on the 15th September, 1876.

Mr. Chairman,—The Hon'ble the Chief Justice has been kind enough to favor the British Indian Association with a copy of his Lordship's minute on the subject of the constitution of Appellate Benches for the Mofasil. This subject has for many years engaged the attention of this Association, and it is a matter of no small satisfaction to them to know that the sentiments and opinions, which they have from time to time expressed for the reform of Mufasal Courts, have been endorsed by such a high and distinguished authority as the Hon'ble and learned Chief Justice. Sir Richard Garth has approached the question with a thoroughly unbiassed mind, and the earnestness with which he has enforced his views deserves the grateful acknowledgments of this Association.

Amid the general improvements made to place the administration of justice in the Mufasal on a satisfactory footing, the District Bench alone remains untouched. The procedure regulating the Civil Courts has been improved, the Bar has been considerably improved, so has been the subordinate Bench which, in point of legal education and general efficiency, is considered superior to the District Bench; even the character of the ministerial agency has to a certain extent been improved; but the

District Courts remain what they were; aye these are even considered to have deteriorated; younger men are now appointed to the District Judgship, and not only do they bring less experience, but, devoid of the old Collectorate training they have not, if I may so express myself, the bone and muscle of the Mufasil Judge.

It is therefore in the highest degree necessary that the District Bench should be strengthened. It would have been certainly desirable if a composite Bench, such as Sir John Peter Grant had proposed, this Association has always advocated and Sir Richard Garth also prefers, could have been carried out; but that scheme would be very expensive. We must therefore for the present be content with the instalment of reform promised in Sir Richard Temple's scheme of Appellate Benches consisting of two Judges, a civilian and a native. But the Association have given their opinion that the *sine qua non* of such a scheme should be in perfect equality between the two Judges; and I am exceedingly glad to observe that Sir Richard attaches just importance to this point. His Lordship observes:—"In the letter of the British Indian Association, to which I have already referred, great stress is laid, and very properly so, upon the independence of the native Judge, and his equality with the European being duly preserved. Without such independence and equality it is impossible that the combination of the two elements would work satisfactorily." In fact the new Bench would then prove a curse instead of a blessing. If the position and prospects of the native Judges would in any way depend upon the good will of his civilian brother, he would necessarily feel himself fettered and therefore unable to act with independence and self-respect. His sense of subordination would always tend to repress his higher sense of duty, and the result would not unfrequently be "ditto to Mr. Burke." But it would not be sufficient to merely constitute the District Bench in the manner proposed. There is doubtless, a large body of legally educated native gentlemen from among whom the native Judge may be selected. There are able and experienced Subordinate Judges and first grade Munsifs, who would do honor to the District Bench; then the Bar of the High Court could supply competent men to any number. The question, was, could the Civil Service, under the existing system furnish men with the required judicial ability and experience for the District Bench? Sir Richard Garth, quoting Mr. Justice Markby, doubts very much whether the Civilian Judges can be found with sufficient experience and legal knowledge to perform the duties efficiently, and to command the confidence of the public.

Now the fault was not with the men, but with the system under which they have been brought up. There is no legal training provided for them; they begin as Assistant and Joint Magistrates, and, under the new system of parallel promotion, they are at once raised to District Judgships. It is of the utmost importance that a proper judicial training should be given to the Civilian Judges, and the Association ought to address the Government on that subject.

In December 1876, the epidemic question cropped up again. From time to time there were abatements, but the country still suffered from its outbreak in its malignity. The Government could not sit idly while villages were being depopulated and thinned from year to year. His Honor the Lieutenant-Governor of Bengal (Sir Richard Temple) invited Babu Digambar to an interview for consultation. It resulted in the following Memorandum submitted by the Babu:—

MEMORANDUM BY RAJAH DIGUMBUR MITTER, C. S. I., SHOWING THE MANNER IN WHICH IMPEDIMENTS HAVE BEEN OFFERED TO THE DRAINAGE OF SOME OF THE VILLAGES OUT OF MANY.—CALCUTTA, THE 16TH DECEMBER 1876.

Sibpore—Situate opposite Fort William. The impediment to the drainage of the village has been offered by the filling up of a big drain which was called the Chowdhery's Gurh. This was done by the Howrah Municipality between April and June of 1873, and the fever broke out in September following.

Bally—The drainage of the village is interfered with by the construction of a metalled road about four years ago from the railway station running southwards, crossing the drainage channel of the village. This road was kutcha before, and the monsoon water made its way to its out-fall—the Bally Khall—by making several breaches in the road which. having been filled up without substituting culverts for them, and the pucka road being much higher and stronger, the drainage cannot make its way over and through it into the khall, as it did when the road was Kutcha.

Besides this, the surplus low lands on either side of the railway line having been recently sold by Government, their present owners have converted them into tanks and gardens, offering additional obstruction to the passage of the drainage through them into the Khall.

The drainage is also obstructed by a number of Kutcha roads which have been constructed recently.

Connagore—Situate within the Municipality of Serampore. The drainage of this place ultimately discharged itself into its natural out-fall —the Bally Khal. Obstructions have been offered to the drainage in the interior of the village by roads without culverts crossing the drainage channel, by the gradual silting up of the drains and their encroachment by the owners of the adjoining gardens. Lastly, the surplus railway lands through which the drainage ultimately made its way into its natural out-fall—the Bally Khall—having been sold by Government about three years ago, their present owners have converted them into tanks and gardens, thus cutting off the villages completely from its out-fall. When in June last I had the honor of sending a similar memorandum to His Honor. I observed in respect of this village: "It is apprehended that the epidemic will break out with greater virulence after the next rainy season than it has done before." I am sorry to say that my prediction has been fully verified. Those that can afford are removing from the village,

A line of villages extending from Itchapore, adjoining the Nawabgunge Powder Manufctory, to Chagdah.

The Eastern Bengal Railway has intercepted the drainage of these villages from finding its way into Beels Burroti and Mathooraw. These places, which were noted for their healthiness, after passing through the active stage of the epidemic fever which broke out within a year or two of the railway embankment alongside of them, have like Choonakhaly, Bhatpura, Cossimbazzar, Kalkapore, Bamunghatta, and Sydabad, lapsed into a chronic state of unhealthiness.

Based on this memorandum, Sir Richard made a Minute for the appointment of a new Commis sion. But leaving Calcutta shortly afterwards for the Governorship of Bombay, his successor Sir Ashley Eden took up the matter. Desiring to know whether Babu Digambar could act in the Committee, the following reply was sent to his demi-official note :—

Calcutta, 31st January, 1877.

From—RAJA DIGUMBUR MITTER, C. S. I.,

To—THE JUNIOR SECRETARY TO THE GOVERNMENT OF BENGAL.

SIR,

I have the honor to acknowledge the receipt of your letter of the 24th instant, with its enclosures, and in reply to state that I would have gladly served on the Committee alluded to in your letter, if the nature of the duties which they are called upon to perform did not necessitate them to visit the different localities mentioned in the memorandum furnished by myself, and to hold enquiries thereon, which, in my present state of health, I regret, I do not feel myself competent to undertake.

Allow me, however, to request the favour of your conveying to the Hon'ble Mr. Eden my thanks for the kind consideration he has shown me by asking me to be a Member of the Committee.

In the room of Raja Digambar, the Government chose to have the services of Babu Hem Chandra Kerr He was an experienced and energetic public officer, who was put in the Committee to act both as its member and Secretary. The work of the Committee was restricted to the inquiry into the obstructions to drainage in the places around Calcutta specified in Raja Digambar's Memorandum. They began their labors in March 1877, and submitted their Report in next July. Believing that after repeated local investigation and long discussion his theory had at last been established and finally accepted by Government, the Raja had made the following excellent suggestion for working practically upon that theory: —"I have already alluded to the provisions in the Embankment Act of 1873 for the preservation of drainage channels, and the Circular of the Board of Revenue on the subject. But they are, I humbly submit, not sufficient. There ought to be a regular organised agency for the execution of this work, so essential to the health of the people. What is required is not large expenditure of money, but a careful, constant, and minute attention to the drainage of the villages; and this attention cannot be secured unless there be an agency whose duty it shall be to report every obstruction to drainage, and to remove it wherever and whenever it may occur. This work, I think, ought to be performed by the Municipal, the Road Cess, and the Embankment establishments acting under the orders of some central authority, be it the Sanitary Commissioner, or the Superintending Engineer. The work after all belongs to the domain of what is called the Sanitary Engineering, and if the Government through its Public Works Department should make it a rule that the proper drainage of villages shall be maintained by the agencies I suggest, and should now and then make small contributions in aid of local funds for the execution of necessary improvements of efficient drainage, the object aimed at will, I am confident, be attained." But, entertaining a difference of opinion, Dr. Lethbridge, the Officiating Sanitary

Commissioner and President of the Committee, was opposed to action based solely upon the Raja's recommendations. He could not "altogether accept Raja Digambar Mitter's views of the dampness of the village subsoil itself being the sole and only cause of the fever, or that this has altogether been brought about by roads and railways." Citing many facts and opinions, he tried his utmost, if not to upset the Raja's theory, at any rate to weaken the force of the conviction it had produced in men's minds. Happily, the Government came in to acknowledge that if the Raja's theory had not yet been proved to the fullest satisfaction, it had by no means been disproved so as to deserve no consideration.

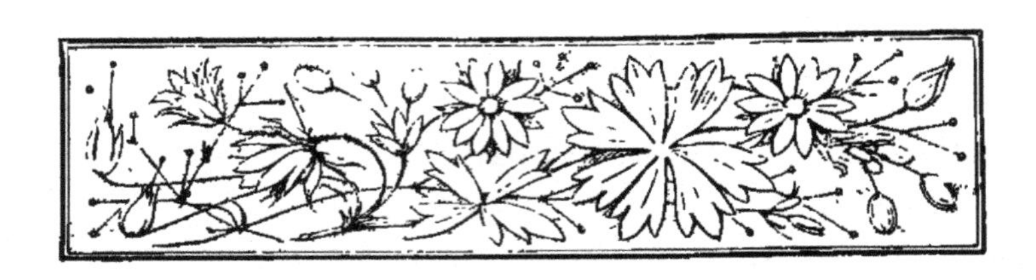

CHAPTER XIX.

THE PROVINCIAL PUBLIC WORKS CESS MEETING. THE INVESTITURE DARBAR. INTERREGNUM IN THE B. I. ASSOCIATION. THE MAHARAJA ROMA NATH TAGORE MEMORIAL MEETING. THE EXPENDITURE AND TAXATION MEETING.

BY the Decentralization of Finance in 1870, responsibilities were thrown upon the Local Governments for raising public revenues from within their provinces. Under "a juggle of names," new taxes were levied without "their nature being altered, or their burden made less sensible to the people." One by one the District Road Cess, the Embankment Cess, the Municipal Cess had been laid upon the shoulders of the Bengal Zamindars. The gradual development of the scheme at length promised the imposition of the Provincial Public Works Cess. It was the last straw upon the camel's back, and a loud cry of breach of the Permanent Settlement was raised by our Landholders.

Pursuant to notice a Special General meeting of the British Indian Association, attended by a large number of the general public, was held at the Hall of the Association on Thursday, the 17th April 1877, for the consideration of the Provincial Public Works Cess question. Raja Digambar Mitra C. S. I., was in the chair. He opened the meeting with the following speech :—

He regretted very much the necessity which had called them together. He could never believe that any measure would be initiated under the auspices of the present Lieutenant-Governor, a tried friend of the people of this country, which would call for a general protest. Unfortunately the financial considerations which have swayed the Government of India had, he feared, left the Lieutenant-Governor of Bengal no choice. As regards the two measures of taxation which have been introduced into the Bengal Council and which we have met this day to protest against, he could scarcely say anything which had not already been very well said before in the Bengal Council by his friend the Hon-ble Kristo Dass Pal. The Lieutenant-Governor's argument amounted to this, that the *Provincial Public Works Cess* would merely drive in the thick end of the wedge the thin end of which had been already introduced by the *Road Cess.* With regard to the Irrigation Bill the Hon'ble Mover of it justified the compulsory rate provided therein on the ground, first, of the immense benefit which the irrigation works were calculated to confer on the country by ridding it of periodical famines, and secondly, of the uniformly increased yield from irrigated lands. He would observe that in no year were the periodical rains entirely held off from any district in Bengal, hence it was that such a thing as an entire failure of the rice crop never occurred. One-fourth of the average produce of any particular district was the least that was obtained even in the worst year. But such a calamity seldom occurred, and never oftener than once in ten or twelve years in one district When, however, it did occur, the surplus produce of the neighbouring districts went towards meeting the deficiency, and the sufferings of the people from the deficient crop were never great and perhaps not known outside the limits of the district. It was only when such a calamity was widespread, that was to say when it extended over more than half the cultivatable area from which the staple food of the country was obtained that it assumed the proportions of a famine, and such a dire calamity was not known to have occurred in Bengal except once in 1769—70 and again in 1873—74 after more than one hundred years. We have no authentic records of the first, but our experience of the second has taught us that such a calamity might under proper management be tided over without any loss of life and with an outlay of some six-crores of rupees from the public exchequer. To ensure against such a widespread calamity it would not be enough to have irrirgation works in two, three or half a dozen districts; such works ought then to be extended over the whole of the provinces under the Government of Bengal. Now from the report of the speech of the Hon'ble Mover of the Bill we find that the total quantity of irrigable area covered by the existing works is 695,000 acres, distributed over three districts. He does not give the outlay, but the works already executed, he imagined, could not have cost less than two crores of rupees. Now, taking the cultivable area of each district at the moderate figure of 2,257,500 acres, it might be easily imagined what a vast outlay must be incurred for extending such works over two-thirds or even half of the cultivable area of the Bengal provinces to ensure them against famines, which after all occurred but once in every hundred years. It would be far more economical that the public should bear a loss of six crores or even double that amount every hundred years to meet famine charges than make a capital outlay of at least fifty crores, carrying a permanent charge of two crores per annum for interest, in order to avert that calamity by the construction of irrigation works. He could have also shown if time permitted that we could never hold a sufficient quantity of water in store for irrigating lands cultivated with rice, and this was to a certain extent made evident from the fact of the Mahanadi water held in store being sometimes found insufficient to irrigate the few thousand acres of land, leased for that purpose in the district of Cuttack, and the same result was seen more markedly in connection with the Midnapore works. As regards the Hon'ble Member's second ground of justification for the compulsory rate *viz.*, the uniformly increased yield of produce, he admitted that aided by seasonable showers of rain the yield of irrigated lands might be uniform, but doubted whether such lands would produce more than non-irrigated lands assisted by seasonable showers of rain—in fact, if the lands cultivated by means of canal water were deprived of the rain water at the time the paddy plants flowered, *viz.*, between October and November, the yield, notwithstanding the full supply of canal water, would be materially less, and the rayats naturally argued that in as much as the canal water, unless supplemented by seasonable showers of rain, failed to give the average produce, they did not see why they should be compelled to pay an irrigation rate in ordinary years, when the rainfall was abundant, particularly as experience showed that seasonble showers were missed perhaps once in eight or ten years. The canal water would certainly prove a great boon to the country if the rayat could by the use of it get two crops for one crop which he now gets from the *amun* paddy lands; but he did not see how such lands, which however constituted three-fourths of the cultivable lands in Lower Bengal, could be made to yield two crops. The Hon'ble member accounted for the repugnance shown by the ryot to the use of the canal water in spite of the manifest advantages derivable therefrom by the fact of the averseness shown by the people of this country to all kinds of improvement. He says "if they were used to sowing one sort of crops you could not get them to sow any other. Their caste prejudices were really very strong." He would respectfully submit that if the people of this country were really so strongly opposed to all kinds of improvement as the Hou'ble Member would make it appear, such articles of produce as tobacco, strawcoloured ottahate sugarcane, potato and many other articles that he could name, would not have taken such a deep root in this soil, nor would they have been so extensively cultivated as they had been since 70 to 80 years. He did not believe irrigation works would answer in Bengal, or would be ever remunerative to the State or the rayat, and before undertaking the further extension of such works the Government ought to appoint a properly qualified Commission to enquire into and report upon the subject. Without anticipating further what the speakers who would follow him might say, he would call upon Maharaja Norendro Krishna to move the first Resolution.

The Belvedere, originally Warren Hasting's villa, calls forth manv associations. It has been the scene of many interesting Darbars. One of them was held with every stately preparation on the 14th of August 1877. It was for the investiture of those who had received titles on the occasion of the Imperial Assemblage at Delhi. The muster of the *elite* was great and splendid. Several worthy men formally received the titles by which they were thenceforth to be addressed. Among those thus honorably distinguished, was Digambar Mitra. In handing to him the sunnud of his Rajaship, the Lieutenant-Governor (Sir Ashley Eden) prefaced it by the following short but not the less graceful peroration :—

Raja,—I have much pleasure in handing to you the title of Raja which has been conferred on you in recognition of your many and eminent public services. There has hardly been a single measure before the local Government of late years in which you have not been asked to assist with your counsel and advices, and as an old colleague, I can bear testimony to the invaluable assistance which you have always given, often at much personal inconvenience.

"In this land of jealousies," to quote Sir Ashley Eden, "where those selected for title and honor were so often made the subject of depreciatory remarks," * the creation of a Raja excites discontented grumblings amongst the disappointed candidates. The spirit of Kristodas Pal needs to

* His Honor's speech at the Maharaja Romanath Tagore Memorial Meeting.

be invoked to unfold the secrets of many Rajaships and Maharajaships. Raja Digambar did not owe his distinction to prestige of birth, to influence, to interest, to importunity, to euphuistic puff. It was purely *earned* by him—it resulted from an act of spontaneity on the part of Government in recognition of his valuable services. Digambar did not court it from a mere vulgar love of titles, but prized it as a testimonial of his achievements.

Maharaja Romanath Tagore died in June or July 1877. He had filled the chair of the Association for nearly ten years—the Presidentship then being a life-appointment. Than him there were wealthier, more talented, more influential, and more high-minded men, but they all acquiesced in his leadership out of deference to his age. On his death an interregnum followed in the Association. The succession to its Presidential chair became the subject of a notable squabble. With the restraint imposed on us in writing a contemporary biography, we cannot speak of it otherwise than as a contest waged between Talent or Nature's aristocrat, and Wealth or the world's aristocrat. The one claimed it as his heritage by right of seniority—the other held merit to be an arrogant intruder into the grounds of an exclusive aristocratic assembly. In this unseemly contentention for supremacy, it ought to have been remembered that "rank is (no more solely) the guinea's stamp." A new social creed hath been imported upsetting all old rules of distinction. Dignities and privileges are no more a hereditary monopoly of the rich. They are prizes open to all who can make themselves deserving. The man accredited by wealth now yields precedence to the man of public esteem. New men are being honoured, while ancient families languish in obscurity. A high-caste Brahman is nobody, and an enlightened Sudra is somebody in the present day. The two were tough antagonists, and hard was the tussle between them. At this time, the great master of finesse, like his immortal namesake, was up at Simla. He hastened down, and throwing oil over the troubled waters dexterously hushed up the scandalous party-strife that threatened the dismemberment of the Association The voice of the majority finally voted the apple of discord to seniority. In plain words, the warfare ceased on the elevation of Raja Digambar to the Presidentship.

The walls of the Vice-regal Council-room are hung with the portraits of every Governor-General from Warren Hastings. Similarly, the Hall of the British Indian Association is adorned with the portraits of all its Presidents. They wanted to perpetuate the memory of Maharaja Romanath Tagore, and a crowded and influential meeting of his friends and admirers was convened at the Town Hall, on the 20th August, 1877. Raja Digambar paid his generous tribute of eulogium to the memory of his respected friend and colleague in the following speech :—

Hon'ble Sir and gentlemen,—I feel a melancholy satisfaction in seconding this Resolution. For more than 30 years I was associated with my lamented friend both in private and public life. It was my privilege and pleasure to mix with him at all hours of every-day life, at the social board, in the council of friends, in the chamber of confidential consultations on the public questions, and in the arena of public discussions, and I never saw a frown on his look nor heard an angry word from his lips. He was a connecting link between the past generation and the present, and such was the winning grace of his manner, that all equally respected and loved him. He was thoroughly loyal to the State, and yet he was always independent and firm in the expression of his opinion respecting public measure and men. He knew well and fully appreciated the good points in the character of Englishmen. He always felt that they were not only our rulers but teachers, and that we could never hope to rise to the high platform of English citizenship without their co-operation and countenance. It was, therefore, the principle of his life to work hand in hand with the English, and how these appreciated him and his work was evidenced by the confidence and honors which the Government bestowed on him, by the eloquent testimony borne this evening to his worth and work by His Honor the Lieutenant-Governor and the Hon'ble and learned Chief Justice, by the presence of so many leading Europeans in the assembly, by the alacrity and good feeling with which representatives of European and American and other nationalities in this great city have joined the Committee to do honor to his memory. I leave it to other speakers, who will follow me, to dwell on his many public services and private virtues; suffice it for me to say that in him the country has lost a devoted patriot, the State a wise and trusted counseller, Society a most useful member, and most of us who have met this evening an affectionate and guileless friend.

A public meeting of the inhabitants of Calcutta and its vicinity was, in accordance with a requisition made to him, called by the Sheriff of Calcutta on Saturday, the 2nd March, 1878, at the Town Hall. There were present the leading men of all sections of the community. Over 1,500 gentlemen were present on the occasion. They met to make an humble representation against the impolicy of increased taxation which an over-burdened country could ill bear, and to urge the preference of a more economical administration in its stead. It was an important public theme of exposition and advocacy. Digambar made a great and comprehensive speech on the occasion, a speech at once the last and best of all his public efforts of the kind—it being remarkable for lucidity, elegance, conciseness, and simplicity of expression.

He said they had met to-day to consider a subject which affected all of them more or less. Somebody had defined the civilized man to be a tax-paying animal, and he himself was obliged to confess that if they wish to enjoy the blessings of civilized rule, they must pay taxes. Progress meant expenditure of money, and money could not be raised without taxation The Government under which they lived was a progressive, and necessarily, therefore, an expensive one They could not have protection from external attacks and internal commotion, good courts to administer law and justice, an efficient police to protect their person and property, a good system of education, good roads, bridges, and other means of inter-communication, and many other advantages for material and moral advancement, without paying for them; and all this entailed taxation. But while he admitted that taxation was the necessary accompaniment of civilized government, he must say that there ought to be a limit to taxation. It was the last straw, as the saying went, which broke the camel's back. If taxes were multiplied without regard to the circumstances and resources of the people, they could not but trench on the very means of their existence, and what could be a greater calamity than that millions of people in this country should be ground down into a nation of paupers by the over-grinding mill of taxation. A greater mistake did not prevail in times past than that India was "El Dorado," that it teemed with gold and gems, that one had only to shake the pagoda tree and he would reap a shower of gold. It was this reputation of India,—alas for it,—that tempted foreign invaders, fired with the lust for Indian gold, to pour their hordes into this country for carnage and plunder. But he believed this delusion had now been dispelled. The English nation that had governed India for about a century and a quarter had seen from practical experience that she was poor, very poor; that millions of her children though ever toiling from early morn to dewy eve, could hardly make two ends meet; that her untold riches were a myth; that her so-called millionaires could bear no comparison with the happy possessors of princely incomes in England and other parts of Europe; that in fact they were only just above competence. What could have been a better proof of the excessive poverty of the people of this country than the fact that a four per cent income tax upon two hundred millions with the minimum fixed so low as Rs. 200 or £20 per annum did not produce quite a million and three quarters of revenue. He admitted that under the benign rule of Great Britain, India had prospered; but what was the extent of that prosperity? A single years' drought and scarcity were sufficient to plunge millions of people into the most abject poverty—the most heart-rending misery. He had seen comparisons instituted between the rate of taxation per head in this country and that in the civilized countries of Europe; but such comparisons, however interesting from a philosophic point of view, were wholly fallacious. Now, how was India situated? There was a famine in Orissa in 1867, and about a milion of the population died for want of food. It was true that in that trying time there were not sufficient facilities for the transport of food, but it was none the less true that even if food could have been conveyed in time and in sufficient quantities, the poor sufferers had not the necessary means to buy it with. When the famine of 1874 occurred in Bengal and Behar the means of transport were not wanting, or, if wanting, they were promptly improvised, but about one-third of the population, directly or indirectly, depended upon public charity. It was the same last year in Madras and Bombay. And it should be remembered that the people would not have recourse to public charity unless driven to the last extremity. Lord Salisbury, in a public address on the Madras famine last year gave a faithful and harrowing picture of the condition and sufferings, of the people. His Lordship said :—"They have been stripped of absolutely everything I have heard tales of whole populations selling down to the roof beams over their heads in order to provide themselves with food, before they came to our relief camps for help; for to whatever motive you may ascribe it—and I hope it is, in the main, a creditable motive—it is only in the utmost necessity that they will come to Government for relief." Such being the case, he would ask whether a generous Government should multiply taxes upon a people so straitened in their means without first exhausting all legitimate means of economy? Our rulers were justly and laudably anxious to save the people from the horrors of periodic famines. The heart of the English nation had been stirred on the subject, and the splendid charity which it lately sent forth and for which all India was grateful to it, was the best proof of its earnestness. Now it had here been proposed to create a Famine Insurance Fund in order to meet like calamities in future. He would not now discuss how far the measures contemplated were likely to prevent famine, but he would ask their attention to what Lord Salisbury said on the subject. His Lordship remarked :—" Now, depend on it the only true remedy against occasional famine and scarcity is the frugality of the people themselves in times of plenty (hear, hear.) If they are too many for the land to support, tell then there must be emigration (hear, hear) You know in Ireland that was the case. There were too many people for the land to support. A great calamity came, great emigration followed, and there is no danger now of any such calamity being repeated. But if the people are not too many for the land, if the land can really support them, then it follows that they ought in years of plenty to make money enough to lay up against these times of famine and it is to the improvement of the civilization of the people themselves, to the improvement of their social condition, to rescuing them from the grasp of money-lenders, who now eat up their fortunes—it is to this rather than to any great and passionate expenditure on public works that I should look for a remedy and to prevent calamities of this kind from recurring (hear, hear.)" He need hardly say that he entirely concurred in these remarks. The conclusion which the Secretary of State had arrived at was worthy of the keen penetration, clear-sightedness and statesmanly view for which his lordship was celebrated. He need hardly tell them who were so well acquainted with the circumstances of the people, that emigration on a large scale was not possible in this country. The Indian had an attachment to his ancestral hearth and home which could not be easily uprooted. On the other hand, the people of this country had always been noted for thrifty and frugal habits; their wants were few and simple, and they could manage to live by eating even roots, plants and leaves. And yet a single year's disaster—he meant drought and famine—reduced them to starvation and brought them to death's door. Why was it that they were so helpless? It was because they could save so little. Lord Salisburv said that they ought in years of plenty to make money enough to lay up against these times of famine; but had they enough in years of plenty to live upon and spare? He was sorry to say they had not. And when such was the case, should taxes be multiplicd on them? Should not the required ways and means be provided by judicious retrenchments and economical administration? (hear, hear) He would not anticipate the speakers who would follow him by pointing out where retrenchments were practicable, and how far they would go to meet the necessities of the State; but one thing he could not refrain from mentioning. If they would examine the accounts of Government for the last eighteen years they would find that the more money it had got, the more it had spent, and the more it still wanted. It is incessantly raising the cry of the horse-leech's daughter, "Give. give." He was quite aware that the Government of India had a most difficult task to perform; it had to adapt the civilization of the West to the circumstances of the East; and in doing so it must employ an expensive foreign agency. Besides, it was not quite unfettered in its actions; it was dependant upon the rulings and behests of the Home Government, and not a small portion of the charges thrown upon India was due to the exigencies of the Imperial policy of England. In 1860-1861 the revenues of the country amounted to 39 millions; for 1877-78 they were estimated at 52 millions, showing an increase in round numbers of about 13 millions, or a little less than three quarters of a million per annum. And yet the Government had not been able to make the two ends meet. The finances of India were in a chronic state of deficit. If such had been the financial position of a private individual, the first thing he would have done, if he were wise, would be the reduction of his expenses. He did not say that the Government had not been mindful of the necessity for economy, or that it had done nothing in that direction; but after all, what was the practical result? It was in need as much as ever. It should be remembered, too, that in a period referred to, there had been no war, annexation of territory, no great emergency except the famines which from 1866-67 to 1877-78 had cost the State sixteen millions which carried interest amounting to 64 lakhs of rupeees per annum—an amount quite a fleabite compared with the enormous growth of income, that was to say 13 millions in 18 years. When the system of provincial finance was introduced in 1870 the people were led to believe that it would lead to economical administration and to the relief of the taxpayers. But how did they now stand? There had not been an increase of imperial taxation it was true, but there had been an augmentation of provincial taxation to the tune of about a million and three quarters per annum; and this year there had been an addition of a million and a half. The whole of this burden fell chiefly upon the land and partly on trade. But this did not represent the true measure of taxation. There was again heavy municipal taxation which was not shown in the imperial accounts, but which nevertheless pressed very hard upon the taxpayers. He hoped he had said enough to show whether the people could bear further taxation. Profoundly grateful as the natives of this country were for the manifold blessing which the British Government had conferred on them, he could not conceal that there was a universal feeling of dissatisfaction against this progressive increase of taxation, and this feeling was greatly aggravated by the circumstance that much relief could be afforded them by judicious economy (hear, hear.) The Government of India itself advocated ecnomoy, but, so far as the Home expenditure was concerned, it seemed to be powerless. He hoped therefore that this meeting would strengthen its hands. Their object was to approach Parliament in all humility and loyalty, to urge their claims to economical administration, and to an adjustment of the Home military charges on a fair and equitable basis, which, if conceded, he has no doubt would obviate the necessity of the additional taxation which the Government had lately imposed upon the country. It was needless for him to remind them that Parliament was the arbiter of their destiny, that as representing the British nation in the aggregate, it alone could give the redress and relief which they humbly prayed for. John Bill was both just and generous and, if he only knew how the people of this country were situated, how poor and helpless they were, he would not refuse to give them a hearing, or shirk his own legitimate burdens. The nation that could at a moment's notice pour forth such magnificent charity as it did last year would not, he was convinced, deny them justice. If they appealed to the British nation through its Parliament, he was sure they would receive justice (cheers.) With these remarks he begged to move the first resolution, "that, in the deliberate opinion of this meeting, the excessive poverty of the mass of the population is the chief cause of the widespread suffering which results from periodical drought and scarcity; and that it is imperatively necessary, therefore, that the growing demand upon the Indian Exchequer for the ordinary wants of the State and for insurance against famine should be provided by judicious retrenchments and economical administration, without permanently adding to the burdens of the people by further heavy taxation."

CHAPTER XX.

THE LAST ILLNESS AND DEATH. THE LIEUTENANT-GOVERNOR'S CONDOLENCE LETTER. OBITUARY NOTICES. COMMITTEE RESOLUTIONS. THE BRITISH INDIAN ASSOCIATION'S REFUSAL OF A MEMORIAL PORTRAIT. FRIENDLY REMINISCENCES.

RAJA Digambar's public life may be divided into two epochs: the period of his membership of the British Indian Association, and his years of office in the Bengal Legislative Council. Our narrative up to this time has consisted of the events belonging to those epochs. We now enter upon the remaining or last period of his life, and shall relate a few of those personal incidents which may not present the features of interest that his public appearances possess, but which, if passed by in silence, would be missed in an account meant to be biographical.

In 1878, Raja Digambar was old a few months over his sixty-first year. His strength of nerves as well as of mind, combined with his regular habits, bade fair to keep him at this age in better health than many feebler men who pull through to an octogenarian terminus. But he suffered from a break-down of his health under a strain of labor and excitement continuing without an interval of cessation for upwards of a quarter of a century, coupled with the aggravating circumstance of the death of his only son, which obliged him to keep off from all public labours for about a year. He was struck down by a nervous complaint in 1874, when both his body and mind were affected. In the words of Kristadas Pal, "he wasted away, and his mind began to wander. He lost control over his memory, he was sometimes so much oppressed with the fitfulness of this faculty that if he forgot the name of a person or place, he would send a messenger to some friend or other even at dead of night and from a distance of miles to know that name." To give an instance. The names of his old silk factories, ·Ramkhola and Rajaputty were not coming to his mind. He grew impatient to know them. It was past midnight, and he was at Cossipur, whence a man was sent some six miles off to Sibpur on the other side of the river to get the names from Babu Amrita Lall Bannerjea. Preferring homœopathic medicines, he placed himself under the treatment of his friend Babu Rajendra Dutt of Bowbazar, who was an amateur in the line To have a regular river-bath, along with the benefit of a change, he went and resided in Babu Heeralal Seal's garden-house at Cossipur, which was pleasantly situated on the bank of the Hughli. Every afternoon he enjoyed a trip up and down the river for some hours. Thus spending the hot months of April and May, he returned home on the setting in of the rains. He was not restored completely to his former health, but he got well enough to assume the office of Sheriff, and perform his duties on such important public occasions as the arrival of the Prince of Wales, the Northbrook Meeting, the Cess Meeting, the Indian Expenditure and Taxation Meeting by taking a prominent part in their proceedings.

He kept himself well enough under routine, and, silently suffering without any apparent symptom, pulled through up to the year 1878. But he could no longer bear up his enfeebled frame. In the beginning of 1879, he became ill all of a sudden. Two years before, he had purchased the estates of Holta and Sonakhali from the Morrells. "Whether," says Kristadas Pal, "it was the complications in the management of these new estates the rayats of which were notorious for recusant spirit, or from a natural decay of his constitution, his mind seemed to be oppressed and his body laden with disease." This originated in an attack of cold with cough, to which he was liable every cold season. Neglected, they brought on a low insidious fever. Lightly thought of at first to be no more than a simple excitement and scarcely cared, his illness in time rooted itself in the system as an obstinate consuming fever, under which his appetite gradually diminished, and his body thinned away. There was a perceptible relaxation of the energy by which he was distinguished. Later on, he began to spit blood. At this stage, Babu Rajendra Dutt, feeling alarmed, asked him to send for Drs. Charles and Payne. They found a sore within his throat, to which the application of medicine by means of a brush gave him excruciating pain. Still he trusted to his strong constitution, and ate his usual dinners, and drank his daily pint of champagne, which he always considered to be "a generous drink." They were not left off until within three weeks of his death, when he found that his disease in its final stage had resolved itself into an acute phthisis, and he was under the heavy hand of death. Towards his approaching dissolution, the usual diarrhœa made its appearance to give the finishing stroke. Four days before his death he made his will. His privileged friends and relatives now attended his bedchamber. To Babu Kristadas Pal his last words were "my time is come, take care of your health." "Being a spiritualist, he did not fear death. He looked upon death as the gate to a higher and better world, where those who had been here would meet again." The 19th of April, 1879, was his last day. He passed the night surrounded by the members of his family, retaining his sense up to three o'clock in the morning. Falling then into an unconscious state, he gave out groans in his last dying moments.

On the morning of Sunday, the 20th April, at 7-30 A. M., he breathed his last, and "his soul winged its way" to its future destination. He was upwards of sixty three years old when he died.

Next day, the following letter of condolence was written by Sir Ashley Eden, the then Lieutenant-Governor of Bengal, to Babu Mahendranath Bose, the Raja's cousin, and whom the Raja had appointed the Executor of his will :—

Belvedere 21st April 1879.

MY DEAR SIR,

I have just heard with very deep regret of the death of my old friend, your cousin, Raja Digambar Mitter. I was afraid from what I heard of his case that it was a very hopeless one. His death involves a great loss to his countrymen, whose best interests he uniformly advocated with independence and energy, and at the same time with an amount of moderation, reason, and tolerance which always ensured due consideration to his opinion.

Personally I lose in him a trusted and most efficient adviser, and I must ask you to accept yourself and to express to his family my deep sympathy for them in the loss which they have sustained.

I am, Yours faithfully,

ASHLEY EDEN

TO

BABU MOHENDRA NATH BOSE.

The *Hindu Patriot* on the same day came out with an obituary, the texts of which have been quoted at various places in this sketch.

Following is the notice of the *Englishman* of 21st April 1879.

'We regret to have to record the death, yesterday morning, of the Hon'ble Raja Digambar Mitter, C.S.I. at his house No. 1 Jhamapookar Lane, Thuntunia. The Raja had been suffering since last cold weather from a complicated disease (a sort of phthisis with severe congestion of the larynx). His loss will be universally mourned. The Raja died in the 64th year of his age. He has left a widow, a widowed daughter-in-law, and two young grandsons of 10 and 11 years old. Raja Digambar's only son, Grish Chunder Mitter, died some years ago."

The Editor of the *Week* in the *Saturday Evening Englishman* of 26th April 1869, made the following most appropriate remarks about the Raja.

"Native Society, and for the matter of that, all Europeans, who had the pleasure of his acquaintance, have sustained a severe loss this week in the death of Raja Digambar Mitter. He was about as unlike the general class of Bengalees as it is possible to imagine. Upright and stern in all business matters, never afraid to express his opinions before either Europeans or his own countrymen, and provided with plenty of good sense and arguments to maintian those opinions, at times the Bengalees hated whilst they respected him, and no native gentleman of Calcutta has ever been held in higher esteem by Europeans. For though he disdained to cringe or flatter, and had a very direct way of expressing his opinion, every European felt that he was dealing with one of nature's gentlemen, in whom was no guile. Of his public and private charities it is not for me to speak, but it is no inconsiderable call on one's pocket to maintain, as the late Raja did, eighty poor students of the University and schools in Calcutta. The British Indian Association will miss him more than any one else; for he was the backbone of all the business of the Association."

The following notice appeared in the *Indian Daily News* of 21st April 1879.

"It is with very great regret that we have to record the death of one of the most prominent and best known of the native citizens of Calcutta. The Honorable Raja Digambar Mitter, C. S. I., expired yesterday morning at the comparatively early age of sixty four years. His large estates, which were all the results of his own industry and attention to business, will be inherited by his two grandsons. The Raja's only son, the late Baboo Girish Chander Mitter, died a few years ago in consequence of a fall from his horse. For many years the name of Baboo Digambar Mitter has been prominently before the public of Calcutta, as that of a man who possessed in virtue of his own great abilities, an influence in the native community second to none. The election of the Raja to the post of the President of the British Indian Association in succession to the late Maharaja Roma Nath Tagore was but a recognition of the place he filled in native society. It is not too much to say that for sound sense, shrewdness, information, and sterling ability, Digambar Mitter was a man whose place cannot be easily filled. There has been scarcely any question affecting India, or Bengal, during the last quarter of a century, on which he has not left his mark, either as a legislator, or as a moving influence with the Association which he had done so much to raise to a position of acknowledged influence and usefulness. Entirely a self-made man, the Raja was in a special sense an ornament to native Society as well as one of its worthiest and best known representatives. His death at this time will be a loss not only to the British Indian Association, but to the Government and the country at large."

The notices of the *Indian Mirror* of 22nd April 1879, and of the *Bengalee* of 26th April 1879, have for their lengths been placed in the Appendix.

The following remarks were made in the *Amrita Bazar Patrika* of 24th April 1879:—

"The news of the death of our illustrious countryman Rajah Digambar Mittra must have spread by this time from one end of the country to the other. To us the sudden departure of the Rajah is a personal loss. To the country his loss can scarcely be supplied. Rajah Digambar Mittra was a philosopher, a patriot, and a philanthropist. There was no tinge of selfishness in his patriotism. Latterly he lived for the good of his country. Like all self-made men Rajah Digumber was intensely unpopular, but the number of his enemies had almost disappeared during the latter days of his life. It is needless to speak of the intellectual calibre of the departed, for it is generally known, but it is not known generally that he was as simple as a child and as tender-hearted as a woman. He was a spiritualist, and, therefore, unlike some of our educated countrymen, a believer in the future state of existence."

The following Resolution was passed at a Meeting of the Native Committee of the District Charitable Society held on Saturday, the 26th April, 1879 with regard to the death of the Honorable Raja Digambar Mitra. C. S. I. :—

"The Native Committee of the District Charitable Society beg to express their deep regret at the death of Raja Digambar Mitter C. S. I. who was connected with the Committee as one of its Honorary Secretaries from the year 1859, and the Committee feel greatly indebted to him for the valuable services rendered by him. He took a lively interest in the Society which is evidenced by his monthly grant of Rs. 25 for the relief of certain paupers. As a mark of the Committee's sincere sympathy with the Raja's family, the Committee resolve that a copy of this Resolution be sent to Babu Mohendro Nath Bose, Executor to the estate of Raja Digambar Mitter."

On Tuesday, the 22nd April 1879, the British Indian Association held a Special meeting to record its regret at the death of Raja Digambar. Maharaja Narendra Krishna Bahadur, Vice President in the chair, moved, and Babu Jaikissen Mukerjea, seconded, the following Resolution which was unanimously agreed to:—

"That the Committee of the British Indian Association desire to place on record the expression of their deep sorrow at the death of their esteemed President, Raja Digumbar Mitter C. S. I. The Raja was connected with this Association from its foundation; and during its existence, extending over a period of twenty seven years, he rendered valuable services to it successively as an Honorary Assistant Secretary, a Member of the Committee, a Vice President and President. Possessed of great intellectual abilities, rare knowledge of the country, strong common sense, and mature judgment, his opinions and advice always commanded attention of the Committee and of the Association generally. Among those who have contributed to the advancement of the Association in usefulness, and importance, Raja Digambar will be always regarded as one of the foremost, and his eminent services will be cherished with grateful remembrance by the members of the Association."

The Honorable Moharaja Jotendro Mohun Tagore moved, and Kumar Debender Mullick seconded.—"Resolved that a copy of the above Resolution be forwarded to Baboo Mohendro Nath Bose, cousin of Raja Degumber Mitter, for communication to the family of the deceased Raja."

But shortly after this warm tribute, the members of the Association stultified themselves by their cold refusal of the usual portrait with which it was their rule to honor the memory of all their departed and retiring Presidents, and of all their distinguished members. It is surprising that the man who had always been the foremost volunteer in bearing the burden and heat of all their onerous undertakings, who was their "backbone," and who had largely raised the Association in official and popular esteem, should at last be condemned to posthumous-ostracism. Thirteen years have passed away without his pictorial honor.* The

*In proof of the fact, we quote the following extract from the correspondence of the Amrita Bazar Patrika of February 26, 1892.

"I happened to go to the British Indian Association the other day on some business, and availed myself of that opportunity of catching a glimpse of every thing that presented itself to my vision. I was well pleased with what I saw, and must allow that the meeting room, the Committee room, the Secretary's office, and in short everything that contributes to the dignity of the Association, are not unworthy of the first Political Association of the country. But while I was looking at the portraits that adorn the walls of the Hall, and congratulating the Association on preserving in such a sacred manner the memories of so many distinguished men whose services to the cause of the Association and proposal for it formally came under consideration, but it was deliberately disallowed. The member who bore a grudge and bided his time to avenge himself, vetoed the proposal. He went into one of his violent opposition-fits, and the majority passively followed suit. How shall this warring with the dead be thought of by the Anglo-Indians in England—how shall the savants of Europe judging under enchantment at a distance regretfully find out their mistake. The Association ought to have calculated that they were going to make themselves vulnerable to outside criticism. "Better late than never"--and it is high time for them to make the amende honorable. In truth, with Raja Digambar died the last but one of the

---

their country were as good as anything, I was somewhat mortified in not finding in this group of dead celebrities the likeness of one, who from a very humble position rose to become one of the foremost and leading public men of his time, and who joined the British Indian Association from its very foundation, and from its Honorary Assistant Secretary rose to become its Honoured President—an office which he filled with honor to himself and to the Association—and in recognition of whose eminent public services the Government invested him with the title of Raja and decorated him with the insignia of the Companion of the Star of India. It is a mystery to me why the Association has not thought fit to vote an oilpainting to this great economist and politician of his time. I am not in the secret of the British Indian Association, and therefore cannot attribute any cause to this wonderful phenomenon, if I may be permitted to use such an expression. But, Sir, there is yet time to rectify this error, and in honor of the revered memory of Raja Digambar Mittra it should be done at once. To a man, whom they should have voted a statue to vote an oilpainting, is not much, and it would not tax the finances of the British Indian Association if they contribute towards such an expense. The likenesses of Sir Raja Radha Kant Dev, Rajas Protap Narian and Ishur Chunder, Babus Prosonno Kumar Tagore, Ram Gopal Ghose, Kristo Dass Pal, Joy Kissen Mookerjee and others which adorn the Hall of the Association will have their full complement when to them will be added the likeness of Raja Digambar. The absence of Digambar's portrait in the rooms of the British Indian Association produces the same sorrowful impression in one's mind, as that of the absence of the statue of Lord Ripon in this City of Palaces."

Titans of the British Indian Association—the others being Raja Radhakanta Deb, Babu Prasana Coomar Tagore, Maharaja Romanath Tagore, Babu Ramgopal Ghosh, Babu Harish Chandra Mukerjea, and Justice Sambhunath Pandit. And not more was the Titanic age in Greek mythology followed by that of the Liliputians, than it appears to have happened in the history of the B. I. Association. Nemesis, too, has seldom held the scales so evenly as that the attempt for a public memorial in favor of that bitter opponent should have ended in a complete fiasco.

Rather than write from imperfect knowledge, we have preferred to borrow the following memorandum, by Babu Rajnarian Bose of the Adi Brahmo Samaj, from Babu Ramgopal Sanyal's *General Biography* of *Bengal Celebrities*.

1 "He was a very affable, polite, and courteous man. When he went to visit his Zamindary at Orissa, he returned the visits of all the native gentlemen of Cuttack, even the poorest among them. He used to say the poorest deserved the greatest attention.

2. He was a very hospitable man, and kept an open table to which even the best men of Calcutta society did not hesitate to attend at times. He was kind and courteous to all.

3. He was a man of strong passions, and slander was very wide-mouthed against his cha-

racter. He used to express his greatest regret to me that he could not control his passions. He knew the wrong, but still pursued the wrong. I used to give him religious and moral advice to the best of my power.

Babu Mohendra Nath Bose, the Small Cause Court Judge of Narail, and the cousin of Rajah Degumber says, in connexion with this anecdote, that Raja Degumber was somewhat rough in exterior, but at heart he was a very kind-hearted man.

4. He used always to narrate to me (Babu Raj Narain) the great opposition he met with to his theory of the cause of the epidemic fever in Bengal from the other members of the Epidemic Fever Commission, especially the medicals among them; but a layman as he was, his views were at last adopted by Government. As a proof of the truth of his theory, he used to instance his native village of Konenugger, the climate of which improved on its drainage being properly attended to. With reference to the said opposition, he used to remark that the English were rather an intellectually dull nation. He also used to say that no nation is so selfish as the English.

5. He was a spiritualist. Spiritualism was his religion. Such was his firm belief in spiritualism, that he used to say that, in the future world, he will dine with his friends exactly as he did here. but, of course, on ethereal food. When one of

his grandsons was providentially saved from falling down from the top of his house, he said that his departed father Grish Chundra saved him.

6. He was a very strong-minded man. When his only son, Grish Chundra, died of a fall from his horse, the first thing that occurred to Degumber was to give notice to the police. He was very much grieved, but not to the extent that ordinary men are.

7. He was a very popular man and highly liked by his friends. When he was attacked by severe nervous debility, and retired to Babu Heralal Seal's villa at Burranaggur for a time, all his friends from the highest to the lowest flocked to see him. He was highly delighted at this proof of the attachment of his friends. He was very fond of music.

8. He practised deep breathing, a kind of *Yoga*. He taught me the same. The practice has salutary effect on the bodily system, but not to the extent he believed. He recommended me books on spiritualism."

The next has been supplied by Babu Hem Chunder Kerr, one of the friends of the Raja.

"The late Rajah's habits were simple and regular. He always had his meals at fixed hours. And before the clock struck 10, he retired into his bed, getting up the next morning at about

4-30 ; and a little after 5, he was seen walking every day on the maidan walks. Latterly, he used also to take a drive on the Strand of an evening, but he would invariably return home before candle-light. He was fond of music, and after dinner would listen to both vocal and instrumental music with a few of his friends.

His tastes were refined, and his habits of cleanliness were marked. He had his dresses made at the English tailor shops, and whatever was placed on his dinner table formed the very best. He would take nothing which he did not consider to be healthy food. It was not his habit to dine alone, and invariably he had a few friends at his table. He was a hater of foppery.

Rajah Digambar Mitter was a generous man in the true sense of the word, and was kindly and charitably disposed towards those who were real objects of charity. In short, he was generous but not indiscreetly so. We have been informed on reliable authority that there was hardly a day in which his charity to the poor of all creeds and castes did not come up to Rs. 5/, and sometimes to Rs. 10 or more. In cases of কন্যাদায়, মাতৃদায় and পিতৃদায়, Digambar was always glad to come to the rescue of the parties, not unfrequently contributing Rs. 50, and at times even more. His daily food to the poor and helpless students is well-known He was also in the habit of distributing Homœopathic medicines (he was himself a Homœopath) to the sick almost at all times of the day, and when necessary he would also pay for their diet. He was a leading member of the District Charitable Society, and as such was the means of affording relief to many respectable purdah Hindu widows. Several respectable females living at his native village Konnagor, were dependant upon him for their livelihood. He lived on terms of peace and amity with all his neighbours and friends, who frequently visited him at his house, and whose visits he regularly returned.

The Raja during his life-time made many friends, who as occasion arose called on him for advice, which, always sound, was never refused, and he in return took theirs when necessary. In this connection we may mention that the late lamented Dewan Rajib Lochan Roy, always consulted him on important matters connected with the Cossim Bazar Raj, and it is a well-known fact that he acted up to his advice. Maharaja (then Babu) Durga Churn Law and the late Raja were most intimate and trusted friends to each other. His brother, the late Babu Shama Churn Law was also another friend of his, and so was the late Babu Rama Prasad Roy, after whose untimely demise, he became the executor of his extensive estates. The late Raja Rajendra Lala Mitra C. I. E., L. L. D. was at one time one of his best friends, but latterly that relationship had undergone a serious change. The late Babu Kisori Chand Mitter, Babu Kunja Lala Banerji, Maharajah Norendra Krishna, the late Babu Chandra

Mohan Chatterji, his brother the late Babu Madan Mohan Chatterji, Maharaja Rama Nath Tagore, the late Nawab Amir Ali, Nawab Mir Mahommed Ali, Babu Rajender Dutt were also amongst his friends. The late Babu Dwarka Nath Tagore was his most esteemed friend. Several Moffassil Zamindars cultivated his acquaintance, and when for the first time he visited his estate in Katak, he made several friends, who when visiting the Presidency visited the Raja also.

CHAPTER XXI.

PERSONAL APPEARANCE AND CHARACTERISTICS. HIS ZAMINDARSHIP. HIS YOUNG BENGALISM. HIS POLITICAL OPINIONS. HIS PUBLIC CHARACTER AND PRIVATE BENEFICENCE. HIS SPIRITUALISM.

ONLY a few men are now living who remember Raja Digambar. He had a tallish bony make between the slender and the thickset, who looked more a spare than a bulky man. Neither fair nor swarthy, his complexion was an average of the two. The face, rather roundish, and suffused with a smiling glow, appeared more amiable than stern. The keen thoughtful eyes with the small chin beneath a firm nether lip, indicated the resolute inner man. He has left behind a portrait which is an exact likeness of him when he was about his fiftieth year.

"Possessed of an iron frame," Raja Digambar kept up his health by regular exercises. Riding is universal in Hindustan, but rare in Bengal. Fifty years ago, we remember seeing only Sibkissen Banerjea on horse-back. Digambar's favourite exercise was walking, and great were his pedestrian powers. Early every morning, either in the dry or wet months, he used to go over five or six miles of ground, with an umbrella in his hand. For many years his great walking-companion was Babu Romaprasad Roy. At this time he "knew not what ailment was—had not a loose stool or hot skin."* This health was enjoyed for more than thirty years, until it was upset by the shock of his son's death.

From the foregoing reminiscences, the reader may well form an idea of the principal lineaments of his character. Hardly a feature or two remain to which we need draw his attention. Possessing much human nature, Raja Digambar was a sociable man who knew many people. He cultivated chiefly good fellowship and association. By his business as a trader and speculator in early life, and by his public career in later years, he came in contact with many European gentlemen who regarded him with much esteem.

In the circle also of his own countrymen, Digambar met with much congeniality. He moved in the best society of Calcutta. The most friendly comrade with whom he often filled his glass was Romaprasad Roy, who, at the time of his death, gave proof of his great regard and confidence by leaving his large estate under Digambar's execu-

* The *Hindu Patriot's* obituary.

torship during the minority of his sons. He was also long united in warm friendship with Dr. Rajendralala. Not only were they fellow-Mitras and fellow-Associationists and fellow-walkers, but they became also fellow-stock speculators and fellow-Sunderbund grantees. Unfortunately, the Doctor had not the necessary wherewithal and experience for success in his last speculation. During his long illness for eighteen months in 1869-70, his grant became a losing concern and he surrendered its ijarah. The original grantee, Siddee Nazar Ali, next transferred the lease to Digambar. The property improving in his hands, Rajendralala asked to have back the ripe pear. Never was heard or known the like of such a request, to which a deaf ear was sure to be turned. Disappointed Rajendralala took the denial for "the most unkindest cut," and exaggerated it into a count of serious indictment. But "the very head and front of Digambar's offending hath that extent, no more." Rajendralala was no tyro to be easily humbugged. Could he find a hole, he would have moved heaven and earth for redress. We are at a loss to understand how he could have confounded worldly friendship with romantic friendship. Finding out his mistake, he attempted to turn the tables by the import of vilification.

Digambar was also "a personal friend and co-adjutor of both Prasana Coomar Tagore and Romanath Tagore; for two days in the week he had a fixed place at the splendid table of the former, and he was the right-hand man of the latter in all councils on public matters; he was the bosom-friend of Gopal Lal Tagore, whose son the munificent Kalikissen Tagore entertained towards him almost filial regard."* One other friend with whom he was on very intimate terms, was Babu (now Maharaja) Durga Charan Law, who speaks of him to have been a man of remarkable common sense. Latterly, Digambar lived in a style of considerable splendour. He kept an open table frequented mostly by his particular friends. The dinner was supplemented by a musical entertainment lasting for an hour or two. Casually, he may have had failings of temper, but he never repelled approach by a forbidding aspect, or dry speech, or icy manners.

One of the main points of view from which we should judge Raja Digambar, is his zamindarship. "Without any patrimony worth the name, he gradually acquired landed property yielding an annual income of about three-fourths of a lac. His estates lie in four districts, Twenty-four Parganas, Jessor, Backerganj, and Katak." There is an impression that he gathered this fortune round a nucleus of wrong. For aught we know, it is the want of a little social amenity in pecuniary dealings that were closed strictly according to the terms without any abatement. The rest is the thinking into which men are betrayed by their jealousies—is the insinuation of calumny that most new fortune-makers incur. Kristadas Pal, who knew Raja Digambar most familiarly

* The *Hindu Patriot's* obituary.

by constant and intimate association, says "he was a rare example of Young Bengal spouting Shakespeare and Bacon, and at the same time turning out a thoroughly practical and successful zamindar. The secret of his success as a zamindar lay in his thorough personal supervision of all matters connected with the management of his estates. He was a large Sunderbund grantee, and all the works executed in the grants were done under his personal superintendence. Until the last few years (that is before his nervous debility) he used to visit his estates frequently, and to attend to the development of their resources. He was tenacious of his own rights, but at the same time he was not hard upon his tenantry. He would take the uttermost farthing which the law gave him, but he would not kill the goose which lay the golden eggs."* He was not without tenderness towards those from whom no blood could be drawn. In Shapur, within Lot Dabipur, in 24-Parganas, certain poor Brahmans failing to show proper Bramatra sanads, became humble supplicants for favor. Digambar continued to them the enjoyment of their living rent-free He was not one of those sleepy absentee landlords who are dead to all interest in the improvement of their ryot's condition, and keep a look-out only to the realization of their rent. Digambar made himself popular with his tenants by his personal attention to, and active sympathy in, their well-being. He seems to have acted on the principle that the prosperity of the

* The *Hindu Patriot's* obituary.

ryots is the prosperity of the Zamindar. He did not confine his heed only to looking at things with his own eyes, but also took pains to master the knowledge of Zamindari rights and duties theoretically by the most inquisitive researches. His pamphlet on the Rent Case, his Minutes on the Road-Cess, his amendments of the Embankment Bill, his speech at the Anti-Cess meeting, are so many tangible and lasting proofs of his close study of the Zamindari question. The British Indian Association is largely indebted to him as the foremost volunteer, who went through the brunt on all important occasions and raised its prestige. Than him, there has not been a more zealous advocate of the Permanent Settlement, the adoption of which in other parts of India he consistently urged during his whole public career. But rent with numerous cess-holes, the Permanent Settlement is now a misnomer.

Next let us view him in the light of a Young Bengal, whose class sprang up into a new power in the State promising to act as the pioneer of reform and progress. The reader may recollect that Digambar read for a time under, and attended the Academic lectures of, Mr. Derozio. Unlike the teachers of the present day, that talented young East Indian moulded the minds of his pupils in new forms, fired new trains of thought in them, and opened a new prospect to their gaze. They were distinguished by the name of Young Bengal, who left their college inspired with liberal ideas and a feeling of country that were unknown to their previous generations. Coming to notice, the public eye was turned towards them to watch how far their promises were fulfilled by their performances. Of course, the nation did not extravagantly expect from them in the beginning of their career. They could not reasonably be called upon to turn thorough-going reformers putting every thing upside down. To have asked them at the outset to effect the introduction of widow-marriage or intermarriage, would have been to ask them to effect impossibilities. By a premature agitation of these questions in fiery words, a Young Bengal would have utterly misspent his energies, and disappeared under a fiasco like a burnt-out meteor, leaving not a trace behind. That which was possible for them they were required to perform. In the first stage of transition, nothing more was practicable for them than to take the initiative. It was for them to sow only, and not to reap. They were simply to clear and open a path-way through the tangled forest of ancient prejudices. Young Bengal made his *debut*, when the abolition of Sati-ism and Infanticide was a *fait accompli*. To him was left next to renounce idolatry, cast off superstitions, get over caste-scruples, abandon Kulin polygamy, encourage female education, and put down all sorts of barbarities. The Revd. K. M. Banerjea and Babu Keshub Chandra Sen went ahead to lengths to which they could scarcely be followed. Next to them rank Babu Ramgopal Ghosh and Pandit Iswara Chandra Vidyasagara. Let us see how far Digambar was true to his enlightenment. Barring the instance of his son's marriage according to the rules of Kulin-Parjaya, he appears to have got rid of all other caste-prejudices. "To him," says Kristadas Pal, "the old Hindu and Mahomedan, the Christian convert, the Brahmo, and the England-returned Indian were equally welcome." They were all invited to his entertainments and admitted to his table. Like the rest of his class he looked not with a jaundiced eye upon the Banias, but rather bore the following testimony in their favour:—"Several Zamindaris that I can name exchanged hands then for so many thousands, which are now worth as many lacs. This was not owing to any want of capital in the country, for the Baisaks and Mullicks of Calcutta, and the Karfarmas of Murshedabad and Dacca, had already grown very rich by their commercial connection with the East India Company; but because they religiously kept back from that field of speculation, leaving it to the more enterprising and unscrupulous."* Of his non-objection to a Bania invitation, we will give an anecdote from personal knowledge. In observance of a Hindu custom, on the occasion of his removal from his old Kalutola house to his new house at Bachu Chatterjee's Street, Babu Durga Charan Law gave a rich evening entertainment. Together with his relatives, he invited a large number of his friends of all castes. Both Digambar and Rajendralala were there. Digam-

* See his pamphlet *Observations on the Judgments of the High Court in the Rent Case.*

bar made no hesitation to go and sit to the repast. But Rajendralala, with his profuse professions of liberalism, was not what he was--he chose to keep away from the mess by remaining left alone in his Kayastha punctiliousness. Digambar felt no caste scruples to send his son to England, or take him back into the family on his return. "He greatly valued the pilgrimage of Indian youths to the temples of knowledge in Europe and America."

Young Bengal came out of his college weaned from all popular superstitions, and inspired with lofty conceptions of the Supreme Being. Digambar had no faith in the Hindu Pantheon or in the Brahmanical mummeries. He performed the daily Ahnik as no more than calling to God, or the annual Shradh as simply honouring the memory of the dead. They were performed, after taking his usual morning tea. He visited no tirtha. He was not an idolator like his next-door orthodox neighbour. But he appears to have failed in strict adherence to his principles. His revival of the ancestral Durga Puja was scandalously idolatrous. Ramgopal Ghosh belied his principle by committing the same gross inconsistency. But their conduct is not wholly without an apology. The party of Young Bengal was peculiarly circumstanced. Their class had merely budded, and was the natural product of their age, which they represented in its weakness and in its strength. They were inconsiderable in numbers,--without organization, money, credit, weight, or authority in the community. They had not ripened with notions of a definite theology. However eager for improvement, they were not likely to call for extensive reforms and risk serious inconveniences. Social considerations obliged them to yield to the pressure of their surroundings, to be lukewarm in their zeal, to be untrue to their cause. They had to be content with a limited progress—with a trimming career in which there was something to approve, and something to upbraid. Surrounded by difficulties, they had to determine whether they should put every thing to hazard, or incur the reproach of their conscience. With many inward struggles they decided to submit their feelings to the force of circumstances. It has been the fashion to consider them hypocritical in their professions. But it is impossible to believe that their idolatry proceeded from faith, or pious emotions, or conservatism. It may safely be pleaded in apology of their conduct, that both Ramgopal and Digambar celebrated their *pujas* as entertainments which gave them the opportunity for a display of their newly-acquired wealth in conformity to the tradition and taste of the country. Digambar discontinued his Durga Puja after the death of his son.

The only "subject on which his sympathies were conservative, was female emancipation and improvement. It was his cherished conviction that the Hindu women under the present system of moral culture possessed far greater virtues than they would possess under the modern system of improvement. If the object of female education, he would say, was to make the household happy, there was far greater happiness in the Hindu home under the old than under the new system. Nevertheless, he did not refuse his aid to female schools."*

"Divide with reason between self-love and society," says Bacon, "and be so true to thyself as thou be not false to others, especially to thy king and country." With this noble maxim for their shibboleth, young Digambar and his eminent contemporaries came out of their college with a feeling that each of them had to fulfil a little patriotic mission—that India expected every one of them to do his duty. Ramgopal Ghosh distinguished himself the most by his public spirit and services. Close at his heels followed Digambar. He was one of our public men who, as he advanced in life, worked like a devoted servant under an exacting master—his country, and justified himself by useful results. His fellow-Zamindars should accord him a vote of thanks for his able advocacy of their cause. By his waging a long and, in the end, a triumphant contest with the Government, with successive Commissions, with professional experts, in the Epidemic cause, he performed a noble achievement of historic character that is honourably and inseparably associated with his name. The State owes not a little to his industrious researches in matters of local legislation. Those who from a social or political point of view expect a patriot

* The *Hindu Patriot's* obituary.

of the first water from a Bengali representative, misapprehend his position and entertain unreasonable expectations. Raja Digambar was fitted by his characteristics to be one of our truest public men. He was a man of self-reliance who thought for himself. "Although not a lawyer by profession he was one by instinct, and the sight was not unfrequent in the Courts of the 24 Parganas that while he paid for a counsel, attorney, or pleader as his advocate in a suit, he would with the permission of the Court argue out his own case, and carry it to a successful issue."* Raja Digambar made the best of his opportunity in the Bengal Legislature, where no one is justified in accepting office unless there were some great probability of his being useful. He was by his nature better adapted to be an advocate of democratical than aristocratical interests. He duly respected authority, but never followed it blindly and servilely. In the Legislative Council he was manfully outspoken, and pressed his views without fainting in his resolution. He knew no compromises, no half-way dealings, no backslidings from slavish loyalty. Offers of distinction did not dazzle his intellect, or confound his judgment. He was not to be diverted from his zeal in the public interest, and seduced into lukewarmness or sham patriotism. A due sense of the responsibilities of his position, hearty devotion of his time and labor to his duties, great sagacity in forseeing events, energy and vigor in dealing with them, and an inflexible determination in the cause of

* The *Hindu Patriot's* obituary.

humanity, are the qualities which characterize his public career.

Raja Digambar "had fixed independent ideas of his own on almost every public question. Although a mouth-piece of the educated natives, he would not always fall in with the general run of educated native opinion on such questions. For instance, while the educated natives were to a man opposed to the annexation policy of Lord Dalhousie, he supported it, because he had no faith in the Native Princes and no sympathy for the cry of Native Government as a national institution. He was a thorough-going utilitarian, and made the greatest good of the greatest number his motto; and as he felt that the British Government followed that principle, he considered the substitution of that Government for a Native tantamount to the redemption of a whole population His sympathies were republican, but at the same time he did not care much for representative institutions in this country. In this respect he was often at variance with his educated countrymen. He was a staunch advocate of the freedom of the press, and held that the best vindication of the paramountcy of the British Power in the East was the concession of this privilege to the people of this country, and he was deeply grieved when Lord Lytton's Press Act was passed."* His love for free ventilation of thought disposed him to come to the aid of the *Amrita Bazar Patrika*. There was the

* The *Hindu Patriot's* obituary.

Hindoo Patriot occupying the field in autocratic supremacy. It professed to be a big gun, but which always fired with blank cartridges. Its milk and water editorials, without salt or sauce, had become extremely insipid to the Native community. The *Amrita Bazar Patrika* came to the rescue from the tyranny of the *Hindoo Patriot*, at about the same time that the Indian Association became "a brother near the throne to the Turk" of the British Indian Association. The *Patrika* was in its first struggles for a foothold. Its proprietor called on Babu Digambar. Let the rest of the story be told by the proprietor himself:—

"It was in the year 1872 that this newspaper, which had been hitherto published from the native village of its well-known editor, Babu Shishir Kumar Ghose, in the district of Jessore, had to be transferred to Calcutta. Pestilence, epidemic fever, and other causes compelled Babu Shishir Kumar and his brothers to adopt this course. He stood in need of patronage and encouragement in his new career; and the first man to whom he applied for moral help was Raja Digumbar. Babu Shisir Kumar knew the Raja to be a broad-minded and far-sighted statesman who would readily sympathize with his political aspirations and the aims of his journalistic career. He appealed to the Raja, and the appeal was not made in vain. The Raja lent his moral support to the paper as he thought that an outspoken and fearless journal like the *Amrita Bazar* was a *desideratum* at the time. Although Raja Digumbar was a staunch supporter of the British Indian Association, some of whose members looked with jealousy upon this new aspirant for journalistic distinction, he never hesitated to accord his support to the advancement of the best interests of the *Amrita Bazar Patrika*.

"Instances of such magnanimity are rare in these days. Here was one of the founders of the British Indian Association pushing up an editor whose paper was rising as a rival of the *Hindoo Patriot*, the organ of the Association which represented the interests of his own class. The foundations of the power which the *Patrika* has subsequently built up as an organ of Native opinion, were thus laid; and to Raja Digumbar Mitter is to be attributed not a little of the credit of placing in the possession of educated Indians, a journal which has done such staunch and invaluable services to this country."*

The *Amrita Bazar Patrika*, the *Indian Mirror*, the *Bengalee*, the *Reis and Rayat*, *the Nation*, have all extinguished the hope which the *Hindoo Patriot* might still have of recovering the position it once occupied. It has only the consolation that none of its rivals is, or would be able to supplant it. But its sceptre has not only been wrested from its hands, but it has been shivered into pieces.

* R. G. Sanyal's *General Biography af Bengal Celebrities*.

Besides his services of public value, Raja Digambar did much untalked-of-good privately. Daily he gave away a rupee or two to indigent paupers, generally writing out his orders on slips of paper torn from the *Exchange Gazette* in his hand. To "hard-up gentle-folks," his donations ranged from Rs. 10 to 50 according to the nature of their need. He released from arrest a few of such folks among whom was one of his old college friends, by paying off their debts amounting to some 5000 rupees. "His private charity to distressed relatives, friends, and dependants was large. Being in the fore-front of the community his purse was as a matter of course open to works of public usefulness, but the greatest and most useful charity which he founded was the maintenance of about 80 poor students whom he gave their daily bread, and enabled to prosecute their studies. He was one of the Honorary Secretaries to the Native Committee of the District Charitable Society, to which he contributed a fund called after his name, the proceeds of which were applied to the support of some twenty poor persons per month."* He helped the Albert School in its beginning with a few scholarships in order to attract pupils.

In his mature years, Digambar became "a spiritualist by faith, and he invoked the aid of spiritual philosophy for the preservation of his health. He practised deep-breathing for a stated period every day, and used to say that by the concentration of his mind upon the seat of any-

* The *Hindu Patriot's* obituary.

complaint he derived much relief."† Some may take this in a favourable light—others may laugh at it as the weakness of age. We are not inclined to say any thing on the subject beyond reciting two instances. In our boyish years we saw a remarkable *Mahapurusha* at Khidarpur. He sat in a cross-legged posture, with closed eyes, so absorbed that he seemed absolutely dead to all external influences. He looked a tallish handsome man, with not a single grey hair on his head or beard. He did not move, or speak, or eat. He had no perceptible inhalation or exhalation—smelling salt held to his nose without any effect of its pungency and immersion under water for hours without suffocation proved the one, and unwastage of body without food testified to the other fact. People saw him in this state for two or three months and worshipped him as a Jogi next to Siva, till his trance was broken by milk crammed down his throat, when he revived to die in a few days of dysentery. Let the reader account for his abnormal condition, in which he felt not the necessities, the cravings, the ills to which flesh is heir.

Than ourselves there was not to be found a greater pooh-pooher at spiritual existence. But one afternoon, while many of us were seated in Babu Heeralal Seal's room, one Hussein Khan made a heavy silver English watch, held fast within our own clutches, disappear by exorcism without our perceiving in the least the process of transformation from its materialistic condition. The watch

† The *Hindu Patriot's* obituary.

belonged to a Gossain, who regretted its loss with the most rueful countenance. He was at last told where to find it out, and driving home in a gharry, picked it from one of his puja-vessels, and joyfully returned with it back to the company. Subsequently, Hussein Khan showed many such feats—producing on one occasion cheques and notes from the Bank of Bengal before a nautch-party, and on another grapes from Cabul within an hour, and champagne from the Great Eastern Hotel while driving in a carriage. The last operation of his Hazrat in our memory, was the disappearance of a brass tumbler from our hands that returned again after some ten minutes into the hands of a friend (the late Babu Romanath Law) then sitting by us. He put us in such a puzzle, that ever since we have been disposed to think that "there are more things in heaven and earth than are dreamt of in our philosophy."

CHAPTER XXII.

CHARACTERISTICS AS A WRITER AND A SPEAKER. SUMMARY OF CHARACTER.

RAJA Digambar was more a man of the tongue than of the pen, and more a practical representative man than either. He was not a man of imagination or sentiment—one without a touch of romance and very little of the poetical element in his composition. Not a single line of poetry is quoted in his writings, or speeches. Literary fame was not his ambition, and he was therefore not a man of literature properly so called. In the walks of public life, he chose to confine his study to the mastery of public questions. Newspaper literature was therefore his favourite reading. He read most of the Calcutta papers, and the principal papers of the London Press. But after all he did not lack literary accomplishments. On every important public occasion he turned his literary stock to the best account. The two specimens by which he is to be judged as a writer, are his "*Observations on the Judgments of the High Court in the Great Rent Case*" and

"*The Epidemic Fever in Bengal.*" Both are small pamphlets not at all meant to be his intellectual and authorial monuments. They were ephemerals to serve the purposes of the occasions. Decidedly, the second is the better written of the two. Being engaged to break a lance with tough professional opponents, it is the outcome of conviction in earnest language not without elegance and finish. The statements of facts are lucid, and the illustrations appropriate. Digambar wrote neat simple English pruned of all redundancies, in which there is not a flower and in which there is not a weed. He argues plainly, but forcibly, with a touch of quiet humour. They ridicule and snub all Bengali English as *Babu English*. But like the Latinised English of Milton and Macaulay, the Gallic English of Hume, the Yankee English, the *Babu English* is no more than a new variety. The laugh is not on the side only of the rulers. But the Babus too, on their side, have a laugh at the profundity of European Sanscrit which concludes a down-right Sudra, from the surname of *Mitra*, to be "a Brahman and hereditary pandit" descended from the Vedic Viswamitra—and at the value of statistics compiled by an author, who confounds a Hindu *Dolkat*, or swinging frame, of stone for aboriginal Santal gods!

There were public debaters, like the Greek Sophists, in ancient India, but no political rhetoricians. To Young Bengal belongs the honor of introducing the rhetorical age Our noted Bengali public speakers of the past generation, were the

Revd. K. M. Banerjea, Ramgopal Ghosh, Romanath Tagore, Jaikissen Mukerjea, Kissory Chand Mitra, Rajendra Lala Mitra, Kristodas Pal, and Keshava Chandra Sen. The Revd. speaker was plain in his style, but philosophical and weighty. Ramgopal, born with the oratorical temperament, was indisputably pre-eminent among his contemporaries. Romanath Tagore was uniformly quiet, consistent, and careful not to utter unpleasant premises. Well-informed and self-possessed, Jaikissen gave utterance to truths boldly and sternly. Kissory Chand poured forth sentences in fine language, with great fluency and an excess of rhetoric. Rajendra Lala studied to be profound, gorgeous, and witty; but he never bore away the palm. With an equable temper and the stores of a retentive memory, Kristadas was a clever tactician who often succeeded with an imposing declamation to win over his audience. Inspired with generous motives and sustained by talent, Keshava Chandra Sen had trained him self to be an earnest, eloquent, and brilliant speaker, always heard with attention. "Digam bar," according to Kristadas Pal, "was neither a ready nor an eloquent speaker. But latterly it fell to his lot to speak at almost every public meeting held by the Native Community of Calcutta." Certainly, he was not qualified like Ramgopal, who, possessing a graceful personal appearance, united brilliant eloquence, set off by the silver tones of his voice, with an attractive delivery; who, concentrating his thoughts in a bold and vivid image, now appealed to the understanding and then to the imagination, producing thereby an irresistible impression that made him a general favourite, and earned him a wide popularity. Digambar lacked the gift of impromptu volubility—the power of immediate utterance. He required to meditate, to master his subject, to accumulate facts and put them in rhetorical shape and symmetry with appropriateness of epithets. He appealed to the intellect, and aimed to convince by reasoning.

Kristadas Pal opened the obituary of Raja Digambar thus:—"Another star of the first magnitude has passed away from the Indian horizon." In Kristadas' firmament, glow-worm twinklings, sparks, scintillations, flashes, meteors, are all luminaries adored with a hymn of admiration. In our firmament, the first-class stars are at such a distance that their light has yet to travel down to us. Gross exaggerated eulogy is rather trifling with, than doing justice to, the memory of the dead. The public writer who glozes and attunes his voice to flattering airs, sins as a public courtier by misleading to conceited opinion ending in a moral vertigo. The ungracious disenchanting censor, who honestly deplores his nation's shortcomings and tells unpleasant truths, is after all a well-meaning man intent upon producing a salutary effect upon their moral constitution and bringing about the wished-for results. No more is the consequence of applying the minimizer to our defects, and the magnifier to our little Alnascharian stock, than the inducement of the mischievous habit of over-estimating our achievements, and rating high our public men. Instead of generation after generation improving, Young Bengal of the Brag School is deteriorating in moral spirit and right-minded aspirations. He is now very much in the humour of old Æsop's "fly that sat upon the axle-tree of the chariot wheel, and said, what a dust do I raise!" * We have no objection to hero-worship, but first let us have a hero. Raja Digambar is not to be extolled because he was the architect of his fortune—many such architects there have been in their day. He is not to be extolled either for his speeches or his writings, which do not rise above mediocrity. He is not to be admired for his rising to the high and honourable office in the Bengal Legislative Council—many less merited persons have got in there. He is not to be admired because he earned a Rajaship—that honor has been reduced to the value of Brummagem. We may conceive a respect, but cannot assign him a niche in history, for those common-places. His claim to our remembrance rests upon higher grounds. How prevalent all round us is the want of strong-minded men—"which way we turn infinite weakness and despair" meet the eye. Of Raja Digambar we entertain a favourable opinion from an unused omitted point of view. We appreciate him most as a strenuous and sagacious man, who possessed

* Lord Lytton styled Young Bengal a *Lucifer Match*. We should so improve as to deserve a higher regard.

a heart approaching to an English stout-heart, and a force of will approaching to an English force of will. There are few Natives who would dare impeach a high Civilian, or raise objections in the Legislature to which he firmly adhered, or carry on persistent tilting against authorities and experts till "victory perched on his lance." He was one of the most consistent public men of the age, who did not change his colors, or veer about with every wind of doctrine, or worse still, sacrifice his principles and reputation to the sordid impulses of self-interest. Digambar is the hero of our epic on account of that manly character, which meets from Europeans with an enlightened appreciation. From this standpoint he appears to us to have left behind a mark—to furnish an example to his nation. India is greatly in need of men cast in a stern stuff, men who, resisting the temptations of emolument and honor from outside, can prefer to repose in the sunshine of an approving conscience within. "To be weak is miserable"—less so physically than morally. Now that we are in our regeneration, the strengths that we require to lift us into the status of a nation, are the strength of body, the strength of purse, the strength of intelligence, and the greatest of all the strength of moral virtue that draws us nearest to God.

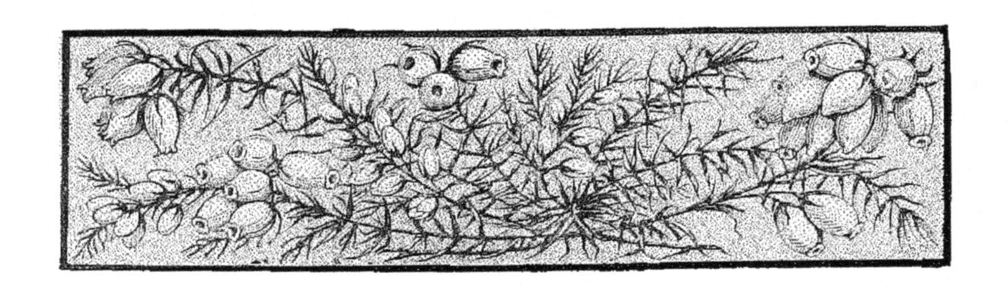

CHAPTER XXIII.

THE FAMILY AND HEIRS.

RAJA Digambar died leaving a widow, a widow daughter-in-law, and two infant grandsons. He had a son, Grish Chandra Mitra, who died in his lifetime. Grish Chandra had turned out a graduate of the Calcutta University, and taken to the profession of a Vakil or Pleader. Intending to qualify himself for the Bar, he proceeded to England in 1867, in the company of the late Babu Shama Charan Law, the brother of Maharaja Durga Charan Law. But after staying about a year they returned together. One morning in 1870, Grish Chandra rode out towards Sealdah on a powerful new waler. The animal shied at something, and becoming unmanageable, Grish Chandra tried to get down from its back. But unfortunately one of his legs got fixed in the stirrup, and the fiery horse running at full speed carried him along dangling on its side, his head violently striking against the road all the way. The horse was not stopped till it had gone thus over a mile of ground. Grish Chandra was brought home nearly dead-unconscious. The father received him with a shock that is to be conceived and cannot be described. He offered thousands of rupees to any one who could cure Grish Chandra, but who died a short while after his arrival. With great presence of mind the Raja sent information to the Police of his son's accidental death. The father bore the affliction heroically. But the mother became crazed from that day, and still survives a most wretched lunatic.

Grish Chandra left a daughter and two very infant sons. During the minority of the latter, Babu Mahendranath Bose, an ex-Sub-Judge, and the cousin of the late Raja, carefully discharged the duties of his executorship. Faithful to his trust, the estate, husbanded with economy under his administration, has prospered by the accession of new properties. The two young Babus, Manmatha Nath Mitra and Narendra Nath Mitra, have attained their age, and, taking over the possession of their inheritance into their hands, have considerably improved its income. They are very amiable and sensible young men, who promise to do well. They seem to cherish a sacred feeling for the memory of their grandfather, whose institution of charity to poor students they continue to maintain on the same liberal scale with the most punctual attention. Further, they have put up a charitable dispensary, called Grish Chandra Mitra's Charitable Aushadhalaya, in honor and perpetuation of the memory of their unfortunate father. Under the superintendence of a paid Kaviraj, native medicine, according to the Ayurveda, is every morning distributed to more than a hundred patients. Quarterly, a meeting of the most noted Kavirajes of the town is held to watch and direct its proceedings. Out of their generous nature, the two brothers also take a pleasure in supporting useful public institutions and projects by liberal donations and subscriptions. They have helped mainly to establish the Jhamapukur Library. The welfare of the Konnagar School is promoted by them with four scholarships of four rupees each. This conduct is in keeping with the traditions of their grandfather. Promising as they are, the two Babus should keep a steady eye upon his example, and endeavour like him to mark their lives by distinguished services to their country. Babu Manmathanath Mitra is already a member of the British Indian Association, and an Honorary Magistrate of the Sealdah Bench. Let him persevere to make good his claim to the public distinction that awaits all useful and honourable career

APPENDIX—A.

FROM E. C. BAYLEY ESQR., SECRETARY TO THE GOVERNMENT OF INDIA, HOME DEPARTMENT, TO THE HONORABLE A. EDEN, SECRETARY TO THE GOVERNMENT OF BENGAL,—(NO. 19 A, DATED GOVERNOR-GENERAL'S CAMP, AGRA, THE 14TH NOVEMBER 1866.)

—oo—

SIR,

I am directed to acknowledge the receipt of your letter No. 1848 T, dated 31st August, submitting, with reference to the correspondence marginally noted, the opinions of the Officers of Government and of the native gentlemen whom the Lieutenant-Governor has consulted on the subject of the Hindoo practice of taking sick people to the river-side to die.

From Bengal, No. 337T., dated 12th July last.
To Bengal, No. 903 dated 10th August last.

2. The Lieutenant-Governor, in conformity with the view taken by the great majority of those consulted, admits that, in the present state of Hindoo public opinion, it would be inexpedient to prohibit the practice of taking sick people to the river to die; but His Honor thinks that the Government should take some measures openly to discourage the practice, and he proposes, in this view, that the following regulations be

enforced by law, *viz*, that notice of the intention to carry any sick person to the river-side to die shall be given in writing to the nearest Police Officer, at least some hours before removal, and that, failing such notice, all persons concerned in taking any sick person to the river-side to die shall be liable to imprisonment of either kind for two years, or fine, or both; that the notice shall be signed by the nearest relation or friend in attendance on the sick person; that it shall give the name, age, and sex of the sick person; the time at which he or she is to be removed; the ghât or other place to which he or she is to be taken; that it shall declare the nature of the disease, and that there is no reasonable hope of recovery, and that the sick person, if capable of giving consent, has consented to his or her removal. If there is a kobiraj or other medical practitioner in attendance on the sick person, the notice to be accompanied by the certificate signed by the medical attendant to the same effect as the declaration contained in the notice.

3. The Governor-General in Council is of opinion, after reading the interesting papers which accompanied your letter, that it cannot be reasonably believed that there is any intention on the part of friends and relations to hasten the death of those who are taken down to the river-side to die. Whether, however, the removal to the river-side does not in some cases have a mischievous effect on the sick and dying person is doubtless more open to question. The whole subject seems to the Governor-General in Council to be discussed with much candour and impartiality in the following extract from the letter of one of the native gentlemen consulted by the Lieutenant-Governor:—"The subject may be considered under the heads—*first*, that of *Gangajatra*, or the practice of taking sick people to the river-side to die; and *second*, that of *Antarjali*, or the ceremony of immersing the nether limbs of dying persons in water at the moment of death. The first is but a prelude to the second, but taken by itself, there is nothing in it revolting or pernicious. As a general rule, it is resorted to only in the case of people advanced in years, who have been given up by their physicians, and whose dissolution is hourly expected. Men and women under forty years of age are seldom taken, and children never. If allowance be made for those, as also for sudden deaths, want of means, and other causes which interfere with the practice, bearing in mind at the same time that 50 per cent. of children

die before the seventh year of their age, and that three-eighths of the remaining 50 per cent. die before they grow up to the fortieth year, it will be found that but a very small number of sick people are taken to the river before their death. Nor are the majority of those who are so taken subjected to any avoidable hardship or suffering. The time selected for the purpose is generally the dawn or the night, and every precaution is taken that the means of the dying and their nearest relatives can afford to avoid exposure to the weather on the way and during their stay near the river. Medical treatment is never intermitted. This I state from extensive personal experience, and I have no hesitation in saying that the assertion of the Editor of the *Dacca Prokash* about unconcerned exposure to the fierce rays of the sun, and to the violence of storms and rains, is as unfounded as the rest of his remarks are high-colored and exaggerated. Such exposure may take place by accident, but never by design or culpable neglect. What the physical effect of a transition from the close atmosphere of a sick chamber to the river-side may be on a dying person who has been given up by his medical attendant it is needless to enquire; for admitting the medical man to be inefficient in many cases, they are the best the patients can command, and their chance of life must, therefore depend upon their treatment, whether at home or by the river."

"It is not to be denied that the mental effect of announcing to a sick man that he is about to die, and of taking him to the place which is most intimately associated in his mind with immediate death must be generally very depressing, but as they are not resorted to until the attending physicians pronounce the patient to be past all hope of recovery, their evil consequences cannot be great, nor can they overbalance the great good they otherwise effect by soothing the mind of the faithful at a time when, with eternity before him, he must need the succour of a higher power than that of man. The anxiety which dying natives often evince to be taken to the river at their last moment, the supplications they put forth to impel their relatives not to lose time in affording them the last solace of religion clearly shew that the practice is not so repulsive to those who are most concerned in it as it may at first sight appear to a foreigner. Certain it is that the announcement of the near approach of death to the dying cannot be avoided, for it is at that time that religion steps in, and whether it be in the form of religious consolation, the last mass, or the ceremony of crossing the styx *(voitarani)* invariably does long before, what the procession to the Ganges," but supplements in case of the Hindoos. It might offend our feelings of delicacy, but there is nothing in it that would amount to criminal neglect or render any party morally culpable. The Hindus believe that it is unfortunate to die within a room, and, therefore, in places where the river Bhaugiratee is not easily accessible, the dying are taken out of the house and placed in an open spot surrounded by toolsi shrubs with the body touching the bare ground. This, as regards exposure, is worse than the procession to the Ganges; for in the one case the patient is kept in a room, and in the other under the canopy of the sky, and for the sake of consistency, the one ought to be as soon suppressed as the other. The concern of the dying, however, at such a time is with his Maker, and Government cannot, without doing great violence to the religious belief of the people, interfere and legislate as to how and where a man should die."

"As regards *antarjali* it is no doubt a very offensive ceremony. As a religious observance it is not enjoined by the Hindoo shastras as absolutely indispensible, nor is any penalty attached to its neglect. From its very nature it cannot be observed except along the banks of the Bhaugiruthee, otherwise called the Ganges,—for it is there alone that the ceremony is enjoined, and consequently it is confined to but a few districts of Bengal; but it nevertheless exercises a potent influence on the minds of the community, and as a means of spiritual consolation to the dying it is most intimately connected with the religious fabric of Hinduism * * * * The ceremony, barborous as it is, has been in practice from time immemorial, and to suppress it a case ought to be made out sufficiently strong to justify legislative interference. This, I believe, has not yet been done, the mere fact of a custom being barbarous is not enough, it must be proved likewise to be criminal before legislation can be brought to bear upon it. I am aware that the European mind has been inflamed by exaggerated stories of enormities committed during *antarjali*. It is generally believed that the mouth, nostrils, and the ears of the dying are stuffed with clay and death is hastened by immersion of the head into water. These are, however, not facts. The nether limbs are all that are immersed, the body being supported on the lap of a relative, and nothing is put in the mouth but drops of water.

Further, the immersion is never thought of until the death-rattle had set in, and the dying is in his last gasp. It is a mistake to suppose that those who have to get rid of troublesome and obnoxious relations would wait till that moment, and then commit a gratuitous murder. There are ample opportunities during sickness, and at other times to effect their purpose, without the least apprehension of detection. The anxiety to get rid of a relation must be mild indeed which would patiently wait till that relation has the death-rattle set in his throat. It is possible that criminal neglect should take place in the cases of old prostitutes in populous towns who sometimes bequeath their property to their priests or gooroos, on condition of their taking them to the river at the time of their death, and performing the funeral rites, for in such cases, the persons employed in attending the sick at the river-side are the merest mercenaries, whose interest and that of their employer would be to get rid of their patients as soon as possible. But they are quite exceptional, and however much official interference may be desirable in such cases, it can not be brought to bear against the general practice of *Antarjali*, unprotected persons left under similar circumstances in their homes would be equally liable to the same neglect."

"It has been said, that persons who are taken down to the river-side to die, but who recover and return, are looked upon with disgust and excluded from caste. This, however, is not the case. I can, as a Hindu living in that part of the country where the practice in question is in every day observance, most positively declare that no person suffers any social inconvenience on that account. Such return entails no stigma, and no disgrace, much less any loss of caste ; indeed, I never heard of such a thing until I read of it in your letter. Perhaps the impression of loss of caste has originated from the visit paid to the Goddess Kali, and from certain other ceremonials observed on such occasions before returning home. They are, however, thanks-offering, and precautionary measures, and not expiations."

"Such being the case, you will perceive that what had been supposed to be a 'powerful inducement to the commission of murder,' does not exist at all. I do not deny that the practice is a very repulsive one, and I would hail the suppression of it as a blessing to the country. But I do not think that the time has come when it could be put down by

Government interference without giving serious offence to the religious feeling of the great bulk of the Hindu community of Bengal. Such interference, while it would prove intolerant and highly vexatious, would do little in favor of humanity and civilization. The evil is one of those which should be removed by education and enlightenment, and not by the hand of law. It has already begun to die out, and if left to itself will soon disappear, while legislation on the subject is sure to give it an adventitious importance, and evoke the most serious discontent."

4. Taking this to be essentially a correct account of the custom and of the mode, in which it is carried out, the Governor-General in Council would be very glad to see it discontinued ; but he is not prepared to say that it is desirable to have recourse to special legislations for its repression. and particularly by recourse to what, in India, would be the highly preventive measure of a compulsory notice to the Police.

APPENDIX—B.

I.

ON LOCAL CESSES.

It is not questioned, I suppose, that all lands, whether mal or lakhraj, are liable to the cess.

As regards mal lands, the cess should be levied upon the gross assets of every estate, that is, upon the amount realized from the tillers or immediate occupiers of the land.

To obtain the necessary data, the Collector should be empowered to call on those by whom the revenue of the different estates on his towjee is payable to produce within a specified time, and under certain penalties in case of default, the rent-roll of the estate. Should the entire estate, or a part thereof, happen to be let out in putnee or ezara, the Collector, at the requisition of the zemindar, is to call on the putneedar or ezardar to file the requisite paper.

In the same manner, at the requisition of the successive superior landlord, each intermediate tenant is to be called upon to produce his own rent-roll, until a statement containing the rent payable by all the immediate cultivators or occupiers of the land of an estate is secured.

There could be no possible room for doubt that the return so made was, for the time being, a correct one, since by understating the rent the zemindar or his intermediate tenant, as the case may be, will be the eventual sufferer, as the rent-roll filed by him will be referred to in suits for the recovery of the arrears of rent. In case of deterioration or enhancement in the assets from time to time, the party charged with the filing of the rent-roll is to report the increase or decrease to the Collector, and the rent-roll at the Collectorate will be accordingly amended.

The gross assets of the district or sub-division (if for the better administration of the tax it should be found convenient to sub-divide the district into circles) being thus ascertained, the rate of assessment is to be regulated, from time to time, according to the requirement of the district or sub-division. Perhaps it will be convenient not to alter the rate of assessment until at the expiry of every five years.

The cess or assessment upon the gross rental is to be paid quarterly by the proprietor, he recouping himself of the same from his tenants, intermediate or otherwise. For default or delay in payment, the rules under which the dawk tax is now realized should be made applicable. The zemindar is to realize the cess along with the rent payable by the tenant, and under the same rules and conditions as he now observes in the recovery of the arrears of rent.

At first sight it might appear that the zemindar and the intermediate tenant would escape the incidence of the tax, and that it would fall entirely on the tillers of the soil; but it should be borne in mind that the latter, except in rare cases, are tenants-at-will, or with rights of occupancy only; any tax therefore upon their rents will have the effect of diminishing in that proportion their capacity to pay the zemindar, since in determining the rent the tax levied will constitute an item of outgoings.

It is only in the case of tenures, with fixity of rent, that the zemindar really escapes the incidence of the tax; but considering the burden imposed upon him of paying punctually, under a severe penalty, the whole amount of the cess levied upon the estate, whether the same is laid waste by drought or devastated by inundation, the concession will hardly be appreciated as a boon, except perhaps in the case of such districts (three or four in number) where, in many instances, the whole or a major part of the estate is let out in putnee. As regards such tenures, it should also be recollected that the zemindar is simply an annuitant, and does not in the least benefit by any improvement effected on those tenures by the application of the cess.

With regard to lakhraj, the zemindar is to submit to the Collector the names of all the lakhrajdars in his estate, and they are to be called upon by the Collector to file rent-rolls in the manner prescribed for mal lands. They are also to be called upon by an *Am Istahar* to file rent-rolls within a certain time. As a check against omission to comply with the order, it should be provided that no lakhrajdar would be entitled to institute suits for the recovery of rents from his tenant unless the name and rent of such tenant appeared in the rent-roll previously filed by him. The zemindar is to be empowered to collect the cess which may be imposed upon the lakhraj lands.

By the above scheme, the lands covered by the houses will be taxed with the cess. I would not therefore levy an additional tax in respect of them, nor would tax them separately. That would necessitate the retention of an expensive agency. The tax levied, even under close supervision, will be unequal in its incidence, vexations, and utterly unremunerative.

DEGUMBER MITTER.

August 13th, 1870

APPENDIX—B.

II.

MINUTE.

I DESIRE to record a few observations on certain points on which I do not agree with my colleagues.

First, with regard to the Draft Bill.

Section 7.—This section interdicts the right of the zemindar to sue for rent if he fails to file a return after the expiry of three months from the service of notice The consequences of this outlawry, it might be, easily imagined, would be very serious. Being shut out from the court the zemindar has no remedy when his rents are withheld ; and if he should fail to meet the Government revenue, his estate would be sold out. And this outlawry, and the disastrous after-consequences, may fall upon a person who may have had no knowledge of the issue or service of notice. When it is seen how cautious have the Committee been in enforcing the daily fine for default in filing papers mentioned in section 6—for section 9 provides that every order for the levy of a fine passed by a Collector under the proposed Act shall be appealable to the Commissioner of Revenue within one month of the service of the first process for the levy of such fine, and that no estate shall be sold for the levy of such fine pending an appeal without the special order of the Commissioner—I cannot but say that they are strangely inconsistent in prescribing for the defaulter the infliction, *sans* ceremony, of the heaviest civil punishment that could be passed on a subject. It needs be remembered that this is one of the several penalties prescribed for ommission or refusal to make returns; firstly, the defaulting person is liable to a daily fine of Rs. 50· secondly, to pay all the expenses which the Collector may incur in ascertaining the rental of his estate by employing his own agency; and thirdly to forfeit the right of suing for the recovery of his rent. The first two, penalties are more than sufficiently rigorous, and will prove quite efficacious. I would therefore recommend the omission of the clause under comment.

2. *Section* 18.—I am one of the minority, who object to the recovery of the cess as an arrear of revenue. Our objections have been set forth in the report, and I do not therefore wish to repeat them. I may, however, add that the responsibility thrown upon the zemindar for the collection of the cess is very great, so much so that the assessment of their profits at one-fourth of the rate, in consideration of their risks and trouble on this account, does not reconcile to it some of the most intelligent, practical, and public-spirited zemindars, whom I have had an opportunity of consulting. They argue that the zemindar would be required to pay the amount of assessment practically in advance, which he would be competent to recover as an addition to rent; that when there was scarcely an estate which had not considerable outstandings carried on as a book-debt from year to year, he would necessarily suffer loss on that score; that as in times of drought or flood he could not realize his own dues, he would much less be able to recover the cess;

that he would also suffer loss in case of desertions; that while the Government would possess the summary remedy of selling his estate in default of the cess, he must, in case of similar default on the part of his tenants, recover the amount he has advanced on their behalf, by going through all the processes of Act VIII. (B. C.) of 1869, which would necessarily involve a delay of months, expense, and harassment, particularly under the present system of trial by the civil court, though in cases of municipal taxes municipal bodies possessed much more summary power for the recovery of the same. Looking to these difficulties and risks they would rather pay a uniform rate in common with the ryots than undertake the duty of collection, although it would carry exemption from three-fourths of the rate. They also question the right or the justice of the Government holding the zemindar's estate responsible for the liabilities of his tenantry, and of burdening him with the duty of collection by a compulsory law. The question of collection they hold is one of contract, and should be left to the option of the two contracting parties—that is, the Government and the zemindar. Let the Government, they say, lay down a scale of commissions for collection, and if the zemindar find it to his interest to contract for collections, he will do so of his own accord. Should the zemindar refuse the contract, it might be offered to other persons. Although I do not subscribe to all that they urge, I must admit that the difficulty of realizing any dues from the ryot is great; and because it would be a source of convenience and economy to employ the zemindar's ready-made agency for the collection of the cess, it would not be fair to make his estate liable to sale for default. Under no law that I am aware of is real property held liable to sale for the realization of municipal dues, much less the property of a person, who is made for convenience' sake the tax-gatherer, for the liabilities of others. Even in the Draft Bill prepared by the Committee the house is not declared liable to sale in case of the non-payment of the house tax. I do not therefore see why an invidious distinction should be made in the same law between the realization of the cess on land and the same on house in case of default. I do not believe that any difficulty is experienced in the realization of the dawk cess; on the contrary, I think the penalty prescribed for default made in the payment of that cess is a source of gain to the dawk fund, and rarely, if ever, is resort had to further measures than the issue of a warrant against the defaulter. As the zemindars with whom the Government will deal are generally propertied men, they possess as a rule personalty many times more than enough to cover the dues recoverable under this Bill. I would accordingly propose that the road cess be made recoverable from the zemindar in the manner of the dawk cess, and that only goods and chattels of the defaulter be liable to seizure and sale for the satisfaction of all demands under the proposed law, whether on account of the cess or of fines and penalties levied under any of its provisions.

3. With a view to enable the zemindars to pay in the cess with facility, I would make it payable in two half-yearly instalments.

4. I now come to the question of general taxation.

I do not think that the Committee in devising the proposed scheme of road cess on land and house have carried out the instructions of the Secretary of State in their integrity. I am not privileged to discuss the principle of the cess, but I may be permitted to point out that the Secretary of State justifies the imposition of the cess on permanently settled estates on the ground that they will be assessed, as in the case of the income tax, in common with all classes of property accessible to the rate. But the Committee have practically singled out land for assessment, and, in order to give a sort of fictitious general character to the tax, have nominally included house. There can be no comparison between the proportion of assessment on house and the same on land prescribed in the Bill. Besides, the house tax will materially fall on the landholding class, for the great centres of trade, the towns and cities, being exempted, the trading classes, who are greatly interested in facilities of internal communications, will, as a matter of course, go untaxed under the proposed scheme Although the Secretary of State has not indicated the mode of taxation, it is clear from the circumstance of his basing the justification of the proposed cess on the precedent of the income tax that His Grace intended it to be as general in its incidence as the other. And the Committee have followed the same course, as far as the assessment of land goes. The proposed cess is in effect an income tax of a little more than two per cent. upon profits derived from land, and if the landed class is to be thus taxed, why not the trading and the fund-holding classes, who own property of a nature accessible to the rate? When the Secretary of State uses the word "property," he cannot mean real property alone, and in this view I am supported by the decision of the Governor-General in Council. How the property of the trading or the fund-holding classes may be reached for purposes of assessment is a different question.

As the income tax is the form which has been selected by the Committee for the purpose of taxing the profits from land, the same form, in my opinion may fitly be adopted for the assessment of persons holding other species of property. It may be urged that the income tax is a source of imperial revenue, and the local Government would be trenching upon imperial resources by resorting to it, but this objection has not been held by the Committee to apply to the assessment of profits from land for the road cess, and if not in the case of one class of profits why in that of other classes of profits? The object of the Secretary of State was not certainly to palter with the landed classes by practically taxing their property exclusively, and letting off other species of property. Considerations of justice and expediency alike require that the road cess should be imposed upon all classes of property equally, and as the Committee have adopted the principle of the income tax for the assessment of profits from land, I would extend the same principle to the assessment of profits from other sources or species of profits, and would assign the duties of assessment and collection to the District Committee to be constituted under the proposed Bill.

5. I am fully alive to the evils of the income tax. Indeed nothing is more distasteful to the people of this country than direct taxation. But as I see no prospect of the abolition of the income tax, although the percentage may be considerably reduced next year for the relief of the tax-payers, and as the principle of that tax has been adopted by the Committee for the assessment of profits from land under their scheme, I would take this opportunity to recommend a plan which, by combining the income tax with the salt tax, could be made to yield a maximum of revenue with a minimum of oppression and without subverting the principle laid down by the Secretary of State, that, as in the case of the income tax, all classes of the community should be made to contribute to the road cess. My plan is this. I would raise the salt tax for local purposes by 8 annas per maund, so as to leave no member of the

community beyond the reach of the cess; for instance no other tax, direct or indirect, touches the artizan class, who have profited most under British rule, as they neither come under the income tax, nor will they come under the proposed road cess, but they cannot escape the salt duty, for salt they must consume; while the amount to be contributed by each individual would not be such as to cause any hardship. The produce of this tax would not however suffice for our requirements, and as it would be impolitic to raise the salt tax by a higher figure for the present, I would supplement the increased salt duty by levying an income tax for local purposes one per cent. upon profits from all classes of property subject to the present limit of exemption, on the same principle on which the late Mr. Wilson applied one per cent. income tax of 1860,--the assessment and the administration of the funds being left to District Committees to be appointed for the purpose. The burden on the ryot of the enhanced duty on salt would not be more than that of the proposed road cess, while it would be free from all the evils of direct taxation, which press with greater severity upon the man the more limited are his means and the less his capacity to cope with the administrative agents. The two taxes combined would, I believe yield about 50 lakhs: salt tax 40 lakhs in round numbers, taking the average annual produce of the salt tax in Bengal at Rs. 2,51,53,080, on a calculation of the receipts for five years, that is, from 1864-65 to 1868-69 (*vide* finance and revenue accounts Part III.,) and the income tax at 1 per cent. 10 lakhs if not more for Bengal, exclusive of Calcutta. As a concurrent measure to this system of local taxation, I would abolish the numerous municipal taxes now levied in the mofussil, which, in spite of the checks the legislature have provided, have proved fertile sources of injustice, hardship, and oppression, and have necessarily tended to render the Government more unpopular than any single act of it during the last hundred years. This combined income and salt tax—the rate of assessment being graduated from time to time according to their requirements—would take the place of these petty and irritating imposts, and constitute the one general local tax for Bengal. The majority of the Committee estimate the produce of the road cess on land at 20 lakhs of rupees, (I do not take into account the house tax, because the way in which it is sought to be imposed will scarcely render it remunerative after deduction of charges of assessment and collection), while the two-fold taxes I propose would yield 50 lakhs, or 30 lakhs in excess. I have not before me statistics to shew the yield of the different municipal taxes and the chowkidari tax under Act XX of 1856, and the probable result of the village chowkidari tax under Act VIII (B C.) of 1870, but whatever the aggregate, the balance of 30 lakhs indicated above would go a great way to meet it if it did not entirely cover it. If the sum of 50 lakhs should not however suffice, the resources I recommend would be so elastic, that they might be easily augmented by a slight increase or extension.

6. I am aware of the strong objections entertained in certain quarters to the salt tax on the ground that it is a tax on a necessary of life and presses with special severity upon the poor. We have to deal with fact and not with theory, and from my knowledge of the sentiments and feelings of my countrymen on the subject of taxation, I make bold to say that they prefer the salt tax ten times to any direct tax, whether levied in the name of a municipal or imperial impost. Indeed, high as the salt duty is, its pressure is scarcely felt, and the bulk of the population, who do not read official *Gazettes* or *Newspapers*, scarcely know that they pay a tax on the salt, which they eat as a condiment of food. I don't believe that the philanthropists, who object to the salt tax, contend for the total exemption of the poor from all taxes; they cannot be unaware of the variety of local taxes levied on the poor, which I have enumerated above, and if they knew the hardship and oppression caused in the assessment and collection of these taxes, they would be the first to recommend this indirect tax, which while it is highly productive, because none can escape it, and because the charge of collection is almost nominal, sits very lightly upon every individual tax-payer, is not open to any of the evils of a direct tax, and has one merit above all others—it protects the poor man from the always unwelcome visits of the tax-gatherer. Of course there is a limit to the salt tax as to every other tax, but I feel satisfied that the proposed addition of 8 annas per maund would not appreciably increase the burden on the poor, which I may observe would be diminished, as facilities for transport would be improved. I can confidently state that were my countrymen polled on the question as to whether they would prefer the proposed road cess and its present oppressive municipal taxes, or an enhanced salt duty of 8 annas,

they would unanimously vote for the latter. I need hardly point out that I have recommended a local income tax as a supplement to a local salt tax with a view to make the rich bear their fair share of the burden both in the shape of increased salt tax and income tax, and thereby reduce to a great extent the pressure on the poor.

7. I feel so strongly on the subject of the present system of municipal taxation, and am so sensitively alive to the widespread discontent which it has produced, that even if my plan of the combined income and salt tax were not adopted, I would still recommend the abolition of the existing municipal taxes and their replacement by a general local cess both on land and other kinds of property, for all local purposes, instead of their multiplication as the ruling ideas of the moment might prompt.

CALCUTTA,
31st October 1870.

DEGAMBER MITTER.

APPENDIX—C.

As one of the majority who recommend the scheme for levying the proposed road cess, I desire to offer a few remarks on the able minute which our colleague Mr. Bell has recorded on the subject.

Mr. Bell objects to the scheme of the majority on the grounds of its being both unsound in principle, and tedious, complicated, and impracticable in its details. He apprehends that it will be exceedingly difficult to work it out, and that it will cause a great amount of irritation and evoke widespread discontent. He therefore proposes to substitute in its place a scheme of his own, which, while practically free from all the defects inseparable from the other, is in his opinion sound in principle, and will work harmoniously on a self-acting principle.

For the sake of convenience, I will notice his scheme first. He starts with the premise (paragraph 8) that "when land was made over to the zemindar, there were no under-tenures." If an estate, he in substance says, is now sub-divided and split up into a hundred tenures, the zemindar has done so for his own convenience. Such being the state of facts,

2

Mr. Bell concludes that in levying a cess on land it is with zemindars alone that Government should deal; and he emphatically denies that Government is under the circumstance bound to recognize the existence of these under-tenures for the purpose of levying a tax on land, or is called upon "to distribute the tax fairly between the zemindar and the under-tenants."

From the foregoing one would understand Mr. Bell to mean, that so far as a tax on land is concerned, he would have the whole burden of it imposed upon the zemindar, he being presumed in the eye of Government to be the sole and absolute proprietor of the land. This view of Mr Bell's meaning is further countenanced by the fact of his instancing, in support of his position, the principle of the Dawk Tax Act: in reference to which he says—"Did the Government attempt in any way to distribute that tax rateably between the zemindars, putneedars, and other middle-men?" But strangely enough, in the very same paragraph he again says—"All that the Government is bound to do, is to impose a fair assessment upon the zemindar, and to give to the zemindar an easy means of recovering from the under-tenants a fair proportion of the rate."

With every deference to the experience of my colleague, I must observe that a great confusion of ideas like the above is observable in such parts of his minute, where an attempt is made to lay down a basis whereupon to construct his scheme. In section 4 of paragraph 9 he reiterates, in spite of the admission to the contrary in paragraph 8, the ground on which he would nevertheless have the tax imposed wholly upon the zemindar, and why he would object to the Collector having anything to do with the assessment of the under-tenures. "Because," he says, "under-tenures having been created by zemindars for their own convenience, the Government in imposing a tax upon the land is in no way bound to take into consideration under-tenures, which they had no share in creating, and which are *ipso facto* void in case the zemindar defaults in the payment of his revenue." Now Mr. Bell knows perfectly well that it is not a fact that all the under-tenures have been created by the zemindars, and that "when the land was made over to the zemindar there were no under-tenures (paragraph 8). Should there be any doubt about the matter, he has only to refer to regulation 8 of 1793, and he will find that the estates when they were settled with the zemindars were heavily encumbered with under-tenures, over which the zemindar would exercise no control, and which subject to the payment to him of a fixed rent, were the sole and absolute property of their owners. A series of laws have also, from time to time, been passed, confirming the rights of the owners in those under-tenures, and even protecting them from being null and void in case of a sale of the parent estate for arrears of revenue. It is now, therefore, too late in the day to say that Government has nothing to do with them.

Such being the state of facts, the imposition of the tax wholly upon the zemindar would not be warranted even on the only ground on which Mr. Bell would justify it.

But I contend that even if the under-tenures, in which we find the zemindarees are split up, were all created by the zemindars, and not, as I have shewn, handed to them from before the settlement, still that of itself would not be a sufficient ground for levying the cess exclusively upon the zemindar. It does not matter under what title they exist; there can be no question that all the undertenants do enjoy, as a matter of fact, a beneficial interest in the land, and many of them derive larger profits from these holdings than the proprietor of the parent estate himself; and I do not see what possible ground of exemption from taxation could be pleaded on their behalf which did not equally apply to the zemindar or anybody else in the enjoyment of property yielding a profit. Were Mr. Bell's dictum to hold good, all putnees, &c., should be exempted from the incidence of the income tax, though they are not.

But it is useless to dilate further upon this point, since Mr. Bell, though arguing upon principle for the exemption of the under-tenants from the tax in question, would nevertheless subject them to taxation upon a plan of assessment which appears to him "to be essentially fair and remarkably simple." (Paragraph 13.)

The plan is developed in paragraphs 11, 12, 13, 14, 15, and 16, and is in substance as follows. He would not issue any notice, but simply by a proclamation call upon the zemindars "to produce, within three months, before the Collector the collection papers of their estates. If these papers be not produced within the appointed time, the Collector should be authorized to estimate the zemindar's annual rental at three times the sudder jumma of the estate." "There are many estates," Mr. Bell proceeds on to say, "which were almost waste in 1793, and which now produce a rental of fifteen to twenty times the sudder jumma. In such cases I would allow the Collector, with the previous sanction of the Commissioner, to take as the standard of valuation a higher estimate than three times the sudder jumma; but in all such cases a special notice should be served on the zemindar, giving him the option of paying the higher assessment or producing within a specified time his papers."

In distributing the tax "among the various classes of middlemen, the distribution must be made upon a self-acting principle;" and towards that end Mr. Bell says: "We shall not therefore be far wrong if we strike a general average and allow the zemindars to assume for the purpose of assessment that their under-tenants' profits are 20 per cent. or one-fifth of the rent they pay," and he would allow the zemindar therefore to recover from his immediate under-tenants the prescribed cess on one-fifth of their rent. As regards what the zemindar's under-tenants are to recover in their turn from the under-tenants below them, he says: "If we assume that 20 per cent. of the rent is a fair estimate of the putneedar's profits, we should not be justified in taking more than 10 or 15 per cent. as the estimate of durputneedar's profits. I propose to take the latter figure, and to allow the putneedar to assess his under-tenants on an assumed profit of 15 per cent of their rent, and any under-tenants below the durputneedar I would assess upon an assumed profit of 10 per cent. There would thus be three general scales for assessing under-tenures:

1st.—Primary tenants, or tenants holding under the zemindar, would be assessed by the zemindar on 20 per cent. of their rent.

2nd.—Secondary tenants, or tenants holding under primary tenants, would be assessed by their landlords on 15 per cent. of their rent.

3rd.—Tertiary and all other tenants on 10 per cent of their rent."

Now I deny that, as a rule, the zemindar's rental is three times the sudder jumma payable for their estates. I would even make myself bold enough to say that, with the exception of two or three favored districts, it would be an over-estimate if we take more than 60 per cent. of the estates on any collectorate towjee, as bearing a rental of double the revenue payable upon them respectively. The correctness of my statement could be easily tested by a reference to the records of the Court of Wards. A statement could be easily prepared from the materials available at the Board's office, shewing the rental and the sudder jumma of the estates that have come under the management of the Court of Wards for 60 to 70 years, and it would, I doubt not, exhibit a goodly array of estates in all the permanently-settled districts of Bengal, from which to derive an accurate idea of the relative proportion between the actual rental and the sudder jumma. In many instances, and notably in that of the Rajah of Burdwan, the profits scarcely come up to one-fifth of the revenue; and if such estates are assessed at an estimated rental of three times their sudder jumma, it would almost amount to a confiscation, and probably bring them all to the hammer within the first decade. On the other hand, there are several estates the profits of which exceed the Government revenue by more than three-fold, and these would be let off with light cess, to the injury of the public and the heart-burning of the people, for the sake of convenience only, the provision suggested by Mr. Bell to meet such cases being utterly insufficient, as the Collector can have no means of knowing them.

This being the case, I question the justice and fairness of assuming, for the purposes of assessment to the local rates, the rental of an estate at three times its sudder jumma; and this is what Mr. Bell recommends on default being made by a zemindar to produce his rent-roll on the issue of a general proclamation calling upon him to do so.

If the several processes recommended in the Bill for the service of special notices following, it must be remembered, the issue of a general proclamation, are, in Mr. Bell's opinion, insufficient to justify the penal consequences attached to the non-compliance with the requisition contained in the notice, surely he would not for a moment countenance, even in a single instance, the infliction of a penalty, however light, for non-compliance with an order conveyed through so inadequate a channel as a simple general proclamation; and yet, according to his scheme, a zemindar in case of default made in responding to such an inaudible call will be assessed on an assumed rent-roll of three times the sudder jumma payable for the estate, though in reality the rental may not be half as much.

That I am not dealing in extreme or imaginary cases, I give in the margin the names of half a dozen large estates within the collectorate of 24-Pergunnahs alone, and such as occur to me whilst writing these remarks, the rental of which, to the best of my belief, is considerably below their respective sudder jumma.

Pachacooly.
Burreedbatty.
Mothoorapore.
Alipore.
Chalooria.
Capenugger.

It is plain therefore that, for the purpose of obtaining and fixing the assessable assets of a district, the scheme under comment is not at any rate less calculated to give rise to irritation and heart-burning than the one it aims to supplant.

In distributing the tax upon a self-acting principle, Mr. Bell would assume the profits of the under-tenures held immediately of the zemindar at 20 per cent. of the rent payable for them, and so in a graduated scale of 15 and 10 per cent. for under-tenures of the secondary and tertiary class, but he would not go further. Mr. Bell's reasons for the assumption are the most flimsy possible. He entirely ignores the existence of innumerable under-tenures as old, if not older than the parent estate, and held on as good a title as the other. This being admitted, any assumption made in reference to the present probable assets of the zemindaries must apply equally to those under-tenures. It is not unknown that when the permanent settlement was made for the zemindaries, there was hardly any margin left, for profits. Various favorable circumstances have since contributed to enhance their assets, but the same causes have also been at work in improving the resources of the under-tenures. Why then, I ask, should the profits of zemindaries be estimated uniformly at double their sudder jumma, and of the under-tenures only at 20, 15, and 10 per cent. of the rent payable for them. Even putnees, durputnees, &c., which Mr. Bell would appear to think the under-tenures were principally composed of, though in reality they do not form one per cent. of the latter, have a much larger margin of profit than he would estimate it at, except in cases (as in indigo districts) in which such settlement is sought and concluded for objects other than the profits derivable from letting out the lands to the ryots at the prevailing rates; such being the state of facts, and not as they have been most arbitrarily assumed by Mr. Bell, it would not, I trust be contended for a moment that such wholesale injustice should be done for the sake of a "self-acting principle."

To turn now to the alleged defects of the scheme adopted by a majority of the Committee. In paragraph 17 of his minute, Mr. Bell discusses the propriety of levying three-fourths of the rate from the ryots, and in reference there to, says: "Is it that the ryots are in such affluent circumstances that we can justly ask them to pay for three-fourths of the roads in Bengal?" The argument is no doubt telling at first sight, but it does not stand the test of a thorough scrutiny. The question at issue is, who derives the greatest benefit from the land, who is likely to feel the advantages of good roads most in the disposal of produce, and is therefore bound to contribute to their construction and maintenance? To decide it rightly, it is necessary to enquire into the legal status of the zemindar and the ryot. Had Mr. Bell looked at the question from this, the only fair point of view, I am sure he would not have thought the distribution so manifestly unfair, nor would he have expressed his surprise at the injustice done to the ryot in the way he has done. The best test is the Rent Act of 1859, and its effect on the landed tenures of the country. That law, I hesitate not to say has reduced the zemindar to the condition of an annuitant, and I make little doubt but that Mr. Bell would be of the same opinion if he would only go over its several provisions with the light which a host of conflicting decisions of the High Court has thrown upon them. It is sheer folly in a zemindar now to attempt to enhance the rents of his ryots. There are no doubt certain sections paraded in the Act purporting to assist the zemindar in enhancing under certain conditions the rents of his ryots. But everybody interested in land knows well enough that they are worthless for all practical purposes. What with interminable law-suits, combinations of ryots under *Dhurmoghut* to resist payment of rent, false criminal charges and breaches of the peace leading not unoften to murder on the one hand, and the utter uncertainty of the law, with its out-crop of a whole host of conflicting and sometimes diametrically opposite decisions on the other, the cost, the labor, and the worry, are infinitely greater than the chances of enhancement. There can be no question therefore that, as matters now, stand, the ryots are more directly interested in the construction and repairs of the roads than the annuitant zemindars.

Another reason which swayed the majority in the distribution of the tax, and which has been entirely overlooked by Mr. Bell, is the most troublesome and vexatious task which has been thrown on the zemindar and the under-tenants, *viz:* of furnishing the materials for levying the tax, and the burden which has been imposed upon the former alone of collecting and paying tax at fixed periods, whether he is able to collect it or not, and to be responsible for losses for default committed by third parties, over whom he has no control. In fact. the zemindars consider this burden to be so onerous, that some of them of high standing and intelligence have expressed their readiness to pay the tax at uniform rate in common with the ryots, rather than be burdened with the collection and payment under the heavy penalty of the sun-set law.

Mr. Bell next proceeds (paragraph 18) to discuss the impropriety of taxing the ryots at all, and in support quotes a passage from the despatch of the Secretary of State, which, so far as I can see, has no bearing at all upon the question raised. In that passage His Grace simply lays down a ruling, that no rate should be levied from the agricultural classes over and above the land revenue, which is not imposed as equally as possible upon all holders of property accessible to the impost; or, in other words, any extra taxation upon land can be justified only by reason of its being imposed equally upon all other kinds of property. To avoid the difficulty, Mr. Bell denies that any property is taxable over which the owner does not possess a transferable right. According to this no entailed property in England is amenable to the income tax, nor any landed property in this country either, the owners of which are governed by the Mitackshara laws.

Arguing on his assumption, Mr. Bell comes to the conclusion that, inasmuch as many ryots (not all) in Bengal do not possess a transferable right in the land they occupy, therefore no ryot according to the plain instructions of the Secretary of State can be taxed with rate. I have not quoted his own words, but this in substance is the position which Mr. Bell takes in disposing of the question as to the liability of the ryots to the road cess. He entirely ignores the existence of the innumerable ryottee tenures, which by contract or by the operation of section 4 of Act X, of 1859, have acquired a fixity of rent and have necessarily become transferable; and as for non-transferable tenures he would not regard them as property, and therefore not amenable to the rates, whatever may be the profits derivable from them for the time being.

The corollaries deducible from Mr. Bell's distribution of the rate between the zemindar and under-tenants are—

1st.—That the more an estate is split up into sub-tenures, the greater is the proportion in which the landlord recoups himself of the amount of tax which is imposed upon his estate.

2nd.—That in the case of estates which have a few or no under-tenures attached to them, as is the case with all the Khoordah mehals, which in number form the bulk of estates on a Collector's towjee, the owners thereof bear the burden of the tax principally or exclusively.

Now, more than 70 to 80 per cent. of estates in Bengal consist of Khoordah mehals, or mehals the area of which being small are let out to cultivating ryots, and not to under-tenants. The owners thereof must under Mr. Bell's scheme, bear the burden of the tax exclusively; and as in the cases in which the privilege of recoupment is conceded, the zemindar should have still to bear on an average 90 per cent. of the tax. I do not think that they would at all grudge to relieve their under-tenants, and bear the whole burden themselves.

The cultivating ryot, and the under-tenants as well, being exempted from taxation, the work of assessment will be simpler still, as the Collector has only to multiply the sudder jumma by 2, and assess the rate for the time being upon the product, which, according to Mr. Bell, represents the profits of the estate. So far as simplicity and economy are concerned, no mode of assessment can be better. In fact, one of the members of the Committee did propose such a scheme, and it was not entertained only because the other members thought that simplicity would be dearly paid for, when it could be purchased only at the cost of justice.

I fully admit that the scheme of taxation adopted by the majority is beset with difficulties in working it out practically, but I do not believe the difficulties are such as ordinary tact and diligence cannot overcome. Nor do I believe that the irritation, heart-burning, and discontent, which the enforcement of that scheme is likely to cause, are at all comparable to what would be given rise to, under any scheme of taxation which did not contemplate for its ruling principle the distribution of the burden of the tax equally upon all. As for the delay which will be entailed in completing the assessment under the scheme of the majority, dwelt upon at such length by Mr Bell, I am quite willing to admit it : nor would I grudge, were it even two-fold as much, if thereby I could ensure the attainment of a basis of taxation, which would produce the maximum of revenue with the minimum of injustice. But I cannot, on the ground of difficulty of serving notices, subscribe to the fairness, justice, or propriety of letting off those who are not easily accessible, and doubling or trebling the tax on those we can readily reach. This would be to cut the knot by a fiat of arbitrary power and not to unravel it.

In paragraph 6 of his minute, Mr. Bell says—"It must be remembered that highly penal consequences are attached to those notices. If they are not complied with, the under-tenant is placed under a legal disability to sue for his rent, and he is further subjected to a daily fine of Rs. 50. It is therefore but a bare act of justice to the under-tenant that the notice should be served upon him. It would be a mere mockery to say that a notice served at the zemindar's cutcherry, or at any other place, was a sufficient service upon the under-tenant." None will deny the force of this argument, and I am glad to see it so tellingly set forth ; but I beg to ask, is the remedy suggested at all effectual ? If three months' notice served on the person, or on his agents, or suspended at his ordinary place of business, or at the zemindar's cutcherry, be a "mockery," what would be the proper epithet for one published in the *Calcutta Gazette* or some such other medium, calling upon the whole body of zemindars of Bengal to file their rent-roll within three months, and punishing those who neglect to attend to it, by assessing them upon a profit calculated at double the suddar jumma, when the actual profit in many cases was not one-sixth as much.

I heartily subscribe to almost every word which Mr. Bell has recorded in paragraph 7 regarding the effect of the cess on the people at large, but the evil should be attributed to the policy, which insists upon the cess, and not to the scheme, which has been devised to carry it out. A general cess has been ordered to make it just to all parties;

but because a general cess is sure to cause irritation, let us therefore tax only a few, and confine the annoyance, irritation, and injustice, among a small number of tax-payers, is a principle of action which I regret I cannot admire. If the Committee, or any member of it, is convinced that a cess of the kind proposed would be a source of disaffection or discontent, it is clearly their duty to report the same for the information of Government, and not to devise a scheme which will make the incidence of the tax press unequally and unfairly on the people.

I am as anxious as Mr. Bell is to relieve the poor from the pressure of taxation, but I do not see how it can be successfully achieved unless the necessities for a local tax were to be provided by indirect taxation alone. For it is under the incidence of that system of taxation alone that a man can suit himself to the burden of the tax he was capable of bearing. No scheme of direct taxation would, in my opinion, be equitable which did not contemplate to tax one and all according to one uniform rule and standard, and if any exemption was to be allowed, it must be solely in consideration of such exemption lightening, instead of adding to the general burden of the tax. It is upon this ground that the exemption from taxation of incomes under a certain amount is justified, because the cost of assessment and the collection thereof, often exceeds the aggregate produce. But as no such consideration can weigh with the assessment of profits from land uuder the scheme proposed by the majority, no exemption has been allowed, and it is expected that under such a principle of assessment the produce of the cess will be comparatively large, even at small rate of assessment. The only mode, however, which occurs to me by which to relieve the poor from much of the pressure and oppression of the contemplated local cess is what I have recorded in a separate minute.

CALCUTTA :
8th November 1870. DIGUMBER MITTER.

P. S.—Since writing the above, I have received a copy of a revised edition of Mr. Bell's minute. There is no change made in it in the main principles of his scheme, I shall therefore confine my remarks to such additional arguments as have been put forth in further support of them.

Mr. Bell has withdrawn his original remarks regarding the under-tenures being the creations solely of the zemindars.

In paragraph 7 he illustrates the difficulty of serving notices by quoting the case of Jessore, where it is said there are 4.112 estates, which, at ten under-tenures each, would bring in over forty thousand returns, and completely swamp the Collector's establishment with an utterly unmanageable torrent of work. Had he selected Chittagong instead of Jessore, he would have found 43.000 estates and 4,30,000 returns to deal with. Sylhet would have afforded better illustration of his position, for there are 77.226 estates, which, at the rate of ten under-tenures each according to his calculation, would have given 7.72.260 returns. But the case is not so bad as these figures would indicate. Most of the estates which swell the Collector's towjee are the most insignificant farms possible and have no under-tenures at all. Taking the case of Jessore, I find from the annual report of the Board of Revenue that in 1852-53 there were altogether 4.551 estates in the district, and of these eighty-three paid under 8 annas a year, 148 from 8 annas to 1 rupee, 1.739 from 1 to 10 rupees, 1,540 from 10 to 50 rupees, and 712 from 50 to 250 rupees,* leaving only 329 to represent estates which are likely to have under-tenures of value.

*Under 8 annas	... 83
Above 8 " under 1 Re,	148
" 1 Re. " 10 Rs.	1,739
" 10 Rs. " 50 "	1,540
" 50 " " 250 "	712
Total	4,222

Other districts shew the same overwhelming preponderance of Khoordah over really large zemindaries. In fact over eighty per cent. of the so-called zemindars are no better than the poorest farms: and the eloquent appeal of Mr. Bell in behalf of the poor ryot applies to them with greater force than to the tillers of the soil; for owing to caste rules and other causes, they get less from their little holdings than those drive the plough themselves. It is possible that estates paying over Rs. 100 a year may have an under-tenure or two; but in the absence of returns it is impossible to determine how many should be included in our estimate on that ground. I shall not deny that even after excluding the Khoordah estates, there will be an enormously large number of returns to deal with; but will Mr. Bell's remedy recommended under an assumed profit of two-fold the revenue for zemindaries and fifty per cent. on their rent for under-tenures cure the evil? The estimates are the merest assumptions, and practically every zemindar and under-tenant will contest the assessment as excessive, and bring in as many returns and accounts as they would under the scheme of the majority.

The danger from the over-statements of rent by zemindar upon which Mr. Bell dilates in his 9th paragraph is not manifest. The ryot may be ignorant of law and was morbidly suspicious, but the zemindar is not. He knows perfectly well that his own return to the Collector cannot be used as evidence against his ryot, and he will therefore never over-state his demand and render himself liable to a larger cess than he can help.

The greatest objection I have to the scheme developed in Mr. Bell's 11th paragraph is, that it is based on the merest assumption, and that manifestly wrong. I have already suggested the propriety of preparing a return of the result of the Court of Ward's administration of the estates of disqualified landholders for the last 60 or 70 years, which I expect will at once demonstrate that the average profit of a zemindar instead of being twice the revenue is considerably under it. From the report of the Board of Revenue which I have above quoted, I find that in 1852-53 199 estates belonging to disqualified proprietors paying a revenue of Rs. 7,29,291 had a mofussil recoverable hushbood jumma of only 11,00,296-7-4, giving scarce 63 per cent. of profit. That in other years the case was very much the same I have every reason to believe, and believing it I cannot accept the estimate put forth by Mr. Bell, and upon which he bases his self-acting scheme.

As regards under-tenants, Mr. Bell's assumption is equally wide of the mark. In his first minute he remarked that the usual practice with the zemindars was to allow a profit of 15 to 20 per cent. when letting out estates in putnee, and therefrom inferred that a cess calculated on 20 per cent. of their rent for primary, 15 per cent. for secondary, and 10 per cent. for tertiary class of under-tenures, would be fair and just. He now proposes 50 per cent. all round. The increase is from $\frac{1}{5}$th, $\frac{1}{9}$th, $\frac{1}{10}$th to $\frac{1}{2}$, a goodly spring no doubt, but what have we before us to shew that the last is correct, or approximately so, and will answer for the purposes of a self-acting scheme.

It is not to be denied that the scheme of the majority accepts the measure of the ryots' profits at cent. per cent. of the jumma on an assumption founded on the experience of the members. But I was not prepared to see it objected to on that ground by Mr. Bell, whose whole scheme is based on a series of the merest assumptions, in which $\frac{1}{10}$th and $\frac{1}{2}$ are made convertible terms. Mr. Bell must be well aware that there is no possible means of ascertaining the profits of the ryots by written record of any kind, and it must therefore be taken at a guess whatever the scheme proposed; whereas in the case of zemindars and under-tenants reliable papers are accessible, and it would be a mistake to reject them or to call for them, simply because we cannot have them in the case of ryots. The proposition formulated would amount to something like this. Reliable evidence cannot be had in all cases, therefore evidence should be altogether dispensed with. Nothing has been advanced to shew that the estimate of the majority is wrong. If it can be proved to be so, I shall be glad to modify it.

Knowing how general is the belief among a certain class of publicists, that the zemindars are a class of hard-hearted extortioners, I am glad to note that Mr. Bell has "invariably found that a zemindar's ryots pay a lower rate of rent than the ryots of an under-tenant;" but I fail to perceive how he wishes to make that an argument for taxing the zemindars more severely than under-tenants. Surely it would be an awkward measure of reward for their leniency towards a class for whom he has pleaded so ably. The fact is in Bengal "land seeking for ryots is far more common than ryots seeking for land," and few zemindars or putneedars can raise the rent at will. There is a limit beyond which none can go, and no legislative enactment will help the zemindars to raise one pice more than what his land can bear. Whenever the proposed cess on the ryots will exceed the rack rent, the zemindars and their under-tenants will have the alternative of either foregoing the cess from the ryot or seeing their lands lying fallow. I think therefore that the argument founded, on some ryots being rack-rented, is totally beside the questions of issue.

DIGUMBER MITTER.

APPENDIX—D.

C RCULAR No. 5

FROM SURGEON-MAJOR W H. GREGG,
Offg-Sanitary Commiss oner for Benga

TO THE HA RMAN OF THE MUNICIPAL TY.

Da ed Calcutta, he 18th January 889.

S R,

Wh le read ng hrough the annua reports of my predecessors, one of he poin s that struck me most forcibly was the ery large r of deaths h ur ally fom fever malaria), and the consequent es that in y instances follow fever, viz. ia, diabetes, dropsy, enlargement of the spleen, &c. Taking the las five years, it will be sen from the statement given below that the death-rate from fever ey ar was nearly th-fourths of the entire death-rate of the province, or re n twice as much as the death-rate of all the r diseases put together :—

N ME OF DISEA E.	NUMBER OF DEATHS D RATIO PER 0 OF THE POPULATION OF BENGAL WHICH ACCORDING TO THE CENSUS OF 1881, IS 66,163,884.									
	1883.		1884.		88		86.		1887.	
	ber of deaths.	Ratio.	Number of deaths.	Ratio.	Number of deaths.	Ratio.	er of deaths.	o.	Number of deaths.	Ratio.
Cholera	90,439	1·36	134,421	2·03	173,767	2·62	118,368	1·78	172,578	2·60
Small-pox	[illegible]	·14	18,533	·28	9,863	·14	4,049	·06	3,846	·05
Fever	[illegible]	13·81	966,233	14·60	1,042,142	15·75	1,057,296	15·97	1,087,768	16·44
Bowel-complaints ...	55,270	·83	58,376	·88	63,808	·96	55,693	·84	56,893	·85
Injuries	23,670	·35	24,674	·37	28,956	·43	29,081	·43	26,630	·40
O her causes	152,817	2·30	176,373	2·66	186,209	2·81	190,818	2·88	204,813	3·09
Total ...	1,245,676	18·82	1,378,610	20·83	1,504,745	22·74	1,455,305	21·99	1,552,528	23·46

These facts are very startling and when it is remembered that every death from fever probably represents 20 or more attacks, it will be seen what a very large proportion of the population must have suffered. The question at once arises, what is this fever or malaria which exercises such a terrible influence on the health and prosperity of the people; what causes it; and how is it to be prevented?

2. Malaria is thus defined in Webster's Dictionary:—"Bad air; air tainted by deleterious emanations from animal or vegetable matter; especially noxious emanations from marshy districts, capable of causing fever or other disease; miasma." Dr. Maclean, a celebrated medical authority, says malaria is "an earth-born poison, generated in soils, the energies of which are not expended in the growth and sustenance of healthy vegetation." "By almost universal consent," he continues, "this poison is the cause of all types of intermittent and remittent fevers, commonly called malarial, and of the degeneration of the blood and tissues resulting from long residence in places where this poison is generated."[1] A great deal of discussion has from time to time taken place as to the intimate nature of malarial poison, and much light has been thrown on the subject by the researches of Professors Tommasi Crudeli in Rome, Klebs in Prague, Laveran in Algeria and Italy, Osler in the United States of America, Vandyke Carter in Bombay, and other scientific authorities who have made the physical cause of the poison to which malarial fever is due the subject of careful investigation. Tommasi Crudeli and Klebs have found a germ in cases of malarial or intermittent fever, which they assert is to be met with in the soil and air of malarial districts, and can be demonstrated in the blood of affected patients.[2] Dr. Vandyke Carter of Bombay says that malarial infection can be acquired through both air and water.[3]

3. Whatever may be the active principle of causation of malarial fever, sufficient is known of the conditions under which such fevers occur to warrant the conclusion that the agent is, as stated in Parkes' *Practical Hygiene*, "associated with some kind of decomposition or fermen-

[1] Quain's *Dictionary of Medicine* page 913.
[2] Ziegler's *Pathology*, page 2ç7.
[3] Paper on "some Aspects and Relations of the blood-organisms in Ague."

tation going on in the soil, especially when conditions come together of organic matter in the soil, of moisture, heat and limited access of air." There can be no doubt whatever that a humid soil is proverbially unhealthy, and marshy and water-logged lands have been recognized, the world over, as a cause of paroxysmal fevers. Professor Max von Pettenkofer's opinion is that humidity of soil is a necessary factor in the etiology of fever epidemics. Dr. David Smith, who was for some time Sanitary Commissioner for Bengal, says "there is constant and close connection between humidity of soil and high rates of sickness." The same authority asserts that "the fever of the Bengal districts is beyond all doubt an endemic malarial disease due to local causes, chiefly want of drainage, partial or complete stagnation of water-courses and saturation of the soil with moisture."[4] The late Hon'ble Rajah Digamber Mitter, C.S.I., a well-known and greatly respected zemindar, writing of the causation of malarial fever in Bengal, says "the type of fever met with in the epidemic districts is solely due to a something in the soil, and the condition most favourable to the development of that something is excessive or abnormal humidity of the sub-soil. The cause which operates most powerfully to produce that condition is impeded drainage: it is the inordinate humidity of the sub-soil of towns and villages, and not of the *paddy-fields* and *jullas*, which contributes to the outbreak of the fever with epidemic intensity." [5] Dr. K. Mcleod, the late Health Officer of Calcutta, says that "nothing in the etiology of malarial fever is more certain than that excess of rain or inundation is followed by excessive prevalence and fatal type of fever."[6] The Council of Hygiene of the City of New York reported, after a most carefully-conducted series of hygrometrical observations, "that any marked degree of excess of humidity in any locality was without exception found to be associated with an excessive constant sickness rate, and with all kinds of contagion and infection." Mr. Simon, Medical Officer to the Privy Council, considers that "an undrained or damp state of soil in populous localities is dangerous to public health."[7] In olden times Hippocrates stated

[4] Sanitary Report of Bengal for 1868.
[5] Digamber Mitter on the Origin of Epidemic Fever in Bengal.
[6] Report of the Health Officer of Calcutta for 1879.
[7] Sterndale on Municipal Work in Bengal.

that "the spleens of those who drink the water of marshes become enlarged and hard," and Rhazes not only asserted the same thing, but also affirmed that fevers were generated from the same cause.[8] In more modern times Lancisi has expressed the opinion that the air of marshes is the sole cause of intermittent fevers. Dr. Maclean, however, says "that marshes are not, as a rule, dangerous when abundantly covered with water: it is when the water level is lowered, and the saturated soil is exposed to the drying influence of a high temperature and the direct rays of the sun, that this poison is evolved in abundance"[9] The production of malaria on a great scale in this way was seen in the district of Burdwan not many years ago. The soil is alluvial, but dry; and until within the last few years Burdwan was more salubrious than the central or eastern districts of the Lower Gangetic Delta. The drainage of the district became obstructed by the silting up of its natural and artificial outlets, the result being a water-logged condition of the soil, the development of malaria, and an alarming increase in the death-rate.

4. I think I have quoted enough from high sanitary authorities to show that malarial fever is associated with the effluvia from marshes and lowlying and badly drained situations, which must be improved before any improvement in the health of the people can be hoped for. In the words of the late Hon'ble Raja Digambar Mitter, who has already been quoted, "there is a perfect unanimity now amongst all those who have devoted their time and attention to the subject as to impeded drainage being one of the chief causes, if not the sole exciting cause, of epidemic fever." Dr. K. D. Ghose has also pointed out in the course of a lecture delivered by him in 1885 at the Bethune Society on the sanitary outlook of Bengal that "the cause of fever in Bengal is the want of proper drainage of the soil." "Drain the land," wrote Dr. J. M. Coates, who was Sanitary Commissioner for Bengal in 1874, "so that the rain runs quickly off, or keep the sub-soil water so far from the surface soil that the supersoil does not remain damp, decomposing and evaporating, and healthy people are the result"[10] Sir Ranald Martin in his admirable work on the influence of tropical climates writes as follows with

[8] Parke's *Practical Hygiene*,
[9] Quain's *Dictionary of Medicine*.
[10] Report of the Sanitary Commissioner for Bengal, 18 74.

regard to the question of draining lands in the vicinity of marshes :—"It is not sufficient to convert the ground into a state of soft, low, meadow land; for the most dangerous exhalations are those which are retained and occasionally emitted from under a crust of earth during the drying process, whereby they would appear to acquire unusual concentration and prove the origin of the worst fevers. It is necessary that the grounds be thoroughly drained, leaving none of the characters of marsh." In all countries experience points to drainage as the chief preventive of fever epidemics, and shows that the population of towns has grown in health and in comfort, with the progress of drainage and reclamation. Hippocrates states that the City of Abydos had been several times depopulated by fever, but the adjoining marshes having been drained by his advice it became healthy.[11] Dr. William Fergusson tells us that in the colony of Demerara, within six degrees of the Equator, the efforts of man directed towards drainage and agriculture have "rendered the deepest and most extensive morass probably in the world a healthy, fertile and beautiful settlement." We have a good many memorable illustrations of the same fact in England. Important reclamation and drainage works have been executed in Lincoln, Norfolk, Suffolk, Kent, Essex, Somerset, Cambridgeshire, Huntington, Nottingham and Yorkshire. These lowlying and so-called "drowned lands" and poisonous swamps have been embanked, drained, and cultivated with the most happy results. The great level of the Lincolnshire fens, some 2,000 square miles in extent, which was once dreary and pestilential, is (since it has been drained and reclaimed) no longer the lurking place of disease, but as salubrious as any other part of England.[12] It is not, however, necessary to search in the history of olden times, or even to look out of India, for good results from thorough and systematic drainage. The City of Calcutta itself is a remarkable instance of the diminution in mortality from fever and improved health since the city has been thoroughly drained. While the number of deaths from fever in the suburbs of Calcutta and the surrounding districts where there is no drainage, or the drainage is defective, shows no diminution,

[11] Parkin on the Causation and Prevention of Disease

[12] Dr. D. B. Smith's Report on the Drainage and Conservancy of Calcutta.

but rather a tendency to increase, the mortality from this cause in Calcutta grows less year by year with the extension of the drainage system. "Since the year 1879," writes Dr. J. O'Brien in his annual Health Report of the Town of Calcutta for 1884, "there has been a very remarkable and sustained reduction in the fever mortality of the city. During the years 1874 to 1879 the average annual number of deaths was 5,030: in the four succeeding years, 1880 to 1883, the average fell to 3,655, or nearly 1,400 less, and in the past year (1884) the total was 3,618. The diminution in mortality from diseases of this class would appear to keep pace with the extension of the system of underground sewers, and with the improved surface drainage and reduced soil moisture which follows the introduction of sewers into undrained localities." Numerous other instances could be quoted to show that wherever sub-soil drainage is effectually accomplished good results, in a sanitary point of view, are conspicuous. But it is not necessary to multiply the examples already given.

5. It is of course not to be expected that mofussil municipalities with their limited resources and many urgent needs can accomplish as much in the direction of drainage as the Calcutta Corporation and other wealthy municipatities have done in as short a time, but with steady perseverance there is no reason why, in the course of a few years, the surface and sub-soil water which now saturates the areas of mofussil towns and villages may not be drawn off, and damp habitations thus rendered dry and an amount of salubrity obtained which these localities have never known. If surface and sub-soil drainage accomplished nothing else, it would be worth all the money expended on it as marking an era in the history of Indian sanitation. But there can be no doubt whatever that improved health and better physique would follow its introduction. Where now are to be seen wretched beings of sallow and ghastly countenance, looking twice their real age, with attenuated frames, shrunken limbs, muscles thin and powerless, tongues of silvery whiteness (certain index of deadly marsh fever), pulses feeble and irregular, spleens and livers enormously enlarged, and pitiable languid gait, would be found men well-knit, with their muscles developed, and their vital organs sound—altogether powerful, vigorous, healthy and happy.

In many towns great difficulties, other than monetary, will no doubt be met with before the desired result can be attained, but these should not be allowed to overbalance the advantages to be derived from a thorough and systematic drainage system. Great difficulties were at first experienced in England, but they gradually disappeared as improvement advanced. Not many years ago drainage improvements were as little known in many parts of England as they are at present in India, and much controversy and opposition preceded their introduction; yet populous and now flourishing districts have been drained in the face of great difficulties. There is no reason why similar results should not be obtained in India; and in inviting the earnest attention of Municipal Commissioners to the matter I would urge them to do all in their power, and devote as much of the municipal income as they possibly can towards improving the drainage of their municipalities,—the only means by which the present enormous death-rate and suffering from fever can be diminished, if not altogether prevented.

I have the honour to be,

SIR,

Your most obedient servant,

W. H. GREGG, SURGEON-MAJOR,

Offg. Sanitary Commissioner for Bengal.

APPENDIX—E.

FROM

THE HON'BLE RAJA JOTENDRO MOHUN TAGORE, BAHADUR,

Honorary Secretary to the British Indian Association.

To

R. KNIGHT ESQUIRE.

Assistant Secretary to the Government of Bengal.

SIR,

I have the honor to acknowledge the receipt of your letters nos. 3638 and 3871, dated the 2nd and 9th current, respectively, and to submit, in reply, the following statement of the grounds on which the

Committee of the Association have based their estimates as to the food prospects of the people in the present drought.

The two facts which the Committee sought to bring to the notice of Government most prominently and pointedly in their last letter were: *Firstly*, their views as to the stock of old rice in the country; and, *Secondly*, the probable outturn of the new crop.

The Committee relied upon the following facts in forming their opinion upon the first point. They know it for certain that the great bulk of the people take to the new rice as soon as it is harvested and available for use, as it becomes available in the case of some descriptions ever since the middle of November. That rice recommends itself by its superior flavour and taste, and even a considerable number of the upper ten thousands take it after the ceremony of *Novarna*, or harvest home, which is celebrated in December; and, indeed, there are very few people that in sound health continue the use of the old rice beyond the months of Bysack (April). People in a delicate state of health, particularly those who suffer from disorder of the digestive functions, do not take new rice, but it is not positively unwholesome, and even those that can afford to use old rice at a considerable difference in price prefer the new. The difference in the price of the old and the new rice is, at the commencement of the harvest year, from 6 to 8 annas, rising to a rupee and more by the month of April and May in favor of the former; this places the old rice quite beyond the reach of the masses of the population, even if they had a preference for it. This rise in the price can only arise from the stock being extremely limited, not above the requirements of the small number of persons who find it necessary for their health to take old rice and make it worth the while of the merchant to hold it on for them for a long time. The Committee also know for a fact that, after the arrival of the new rice into the market, not a chattack of the old rice is bought for export by sea, except in the case of the moonghee rice, which, on account of difficulties of transport from the part of the district of Dinagepore in which it is grown, does not commence to arrive into Calcutta till the rains had set in, that is between July and August. Arguing upon these data the only conclusion the Committee could arrive at was that the stock of old rice in the country was not such as in any way materially to supply the deficit in the yield of the current year's crops.

The Committee are well aware that there is a belief current among district officers and others that the yield of an average annual crop is considerably excess of the requirements of the country for home consumption and export. If so, and the excess be estimated at about three month's supply, the question would arise where does the old rice go to. The only answer that can be returned to it is, that it is held in the country. If so, the accumulations for four successive average years, such as the people had for the last four years at the estimated annual surpuls, would amount to 12 month's supply for the whole population. Now, it cannot be denied as a fact, that, except in the eastern districts, that estate will be considered prosperous where fifty percent of the cultivators can after harvest hold grain for a whole year's consumption, that is to say, sufficient for food, as well as for the purpose of purchasing by the sale thereof, or by barter therewith, other necessaries of life for the ryot and his family, and for payment of rent. The remaining cultivators can only hold from four to eight months, and, at the lowest calculations, about 10 percent of them have to part with all they reap to meet their creditors; and then subsist from year's end to year's end by advances from the mahajons and their personal labor. If then, as a rule, the ryots are not in the habit of holding rice for more than a year, and that even not in the case of all, the accumulated savings of four years, as assumed above, must somehow find their way into the hands of mahajons, who in the mofussil, are engaged in the sale and purchase of rice, or in lending out the same on the *baree* system, that is, on the condition of getting back the quantity they lend out with an addition of 50 percent by way of interest. Now, however large may be the number of such mahajons, scattered all over the country, that number cannot exceed one in a 4,000 of the population, representing, say, 1,000 families at four souls to a house. In this calculation, the Committee do not include the petty dealers or shop keepers, who retail by purchasing from mahajons and from four to eight maunds at a time or even less. The number of these mahajons cannot, therefore, at an average, exceed 500 in each district representing two millions of the populations. Now, to suppose that rice, equal to one year's consumptions for two millions, is at all times held by these 500 men would mean, taking the consumption at four maunds 20 seers per annum per head, that is, at half a seer per diem and rice at cost price to them at Re 1-4 a maund—that they, the 500 mahajons, keep between themselves upwards of 11 millions of rupees always idle. Applying this test to the whole population of the country, and taking the total of the rice-eating population at 57 millions , a year's store for them would imply the locking up in the hands of 14,000 mahajons of Rs 31,3500,000 from year to year. The surplus of every succeeding year would *pro tanto* depriciate the value of the old stock, and make the merchant not only lose the interest but also a portion of his capital ; and there is no such extensive export trade as can remedy the evil. Under these circumstances the Committee are of opinion that it would be grossly absurd to imagine that such a state of things can exist in a country notorions for its poverty, a more incontestible proof of which could not be had than the income-tax returns.

That such is not the case the Committee have every reason to believe. They know for a fact that mahajons who deal in *baree*, like other merchants, calculate their stock of supply according to their calculation of demand upon it, and they consider it a great loss, if, after lending out for the season, any large stock is left, because that stock represented capital left unemployed for the year. As for mahajons who make purchases for the purpose of selling at a profit, it would be absurd to suppose that they would ever keep a stock merely for the purpose of holding it on from year to year. In a country where the normal value of money is from 25 to 50 per cent, as the *baree* system still in full force in almost all district proves, it is hard to believe that so much capital should be kept idle, unless it be to sell the reserved rice at its weight in gold, an opportunity which, however, according to past history, might not occur once in 100 years.

The Committee would here take leave to observe that, if rice or rather paddy, (for *osna* rice cannot be held more than a year without being materially damaged) equal to a whole year's consumption, ever happened to be held in the country (as it must periodically be, even on so modest a supposition as a surplus of three months over demand', and that by 14,000 Mohajans, or on an average of 400 men in every district, the stock of paddy in the country would so to say so obtrude itself upon every man's observation, (the article being bulky and requiring large space for storage) that there could not possibly be room for such an uncertainty on the subject as has unfortunately prevailed from time to time resulting as in the case of Orissa Famine in a serious loss of human life.

That under the natural conditions of commerce, in passing through the hands of the different classes of traders, there must be a quantity of rice, like other commodities under similar circumstances, in circulation in the country, the Committee are ready to allow, but its measure cannot be equal to a three month's supply for the whole country or anything near it. To test this inference by the experience acquired during the Orissa Famine, if the supposition of a surplus of three months over home consumption, and export by sea, were at all correct, there must have been a stock sufficient at least from two to three year's consumption, when the deficient crop of 1865 was harvested, since there was no marked failure of crop in Bengal for a very long period previous to that year; and yet, in consequence of the scarcity caused by the failure of crop in a few districts, the price of ballam rice in Calcutta rose from Rs 3-1 in October 1865 to Rs. 5-8 in September 1866, and it reached the highest point, *viz*, Rs. 5-12 in November following. Could such a famine-price have been possible on the eve of a magnificent harvest, such as the crop then about to be reaped promised and turned out to be, if there had been any large stock left in the country? And how could the old stock have been exhausted to meet the deficient harvest of a few districts only, which, on the supposition of an annually recurring surplus of three months over consumption, must have stood in 1864 at two to three years' consumption for the whole population? It might be said that scarcity in 1866 was ushered in by a failure of crops in 1864 and 1865 successively. So far as Lower Bengal is concerned, it is true that in 1864 the southern part of the country was visited by a terrible cyclone, but as it happened about the beginning of October when the rice-plants had not even flowered it had little or no disastrous effects upon them, except in a very small part of the 24 Pergunnahs and the Midnapore district, where injury was done by the innudation of salt water. It did no harm elsewhere, except what a shaking of the plants without ears would cause wherever the cyclone had extended. So that the cyclone of 1864 could have made no sensible impression upon the stocks of previous years, as the prices which ruled until October

1865 would otherwise plainly show. It was only in November following, when the prospect of the ensuing crop was pretty correctly ascertained, that the price of grain rose above the normal rate. In no year, the Committee believe, is there an equal or seasonable distribution of rain in every district of Bengal, nor even in any part of the same district, and the consequence is that there are bumper crops in some districts, or in some parts of a particular district, and more or less a deficient crop in others, and by a complicated system of interchange the normal price is pretty uniformly kept up. When, however, once in a long series of years, the crop of the whole country happens to be much in excess of the average one, it is instantly indicated by a great fall in the usual price, and the surplus is soon disposed of either by larger export by sea or land, or by increased home consumption, both in Bengal and the North-West, where with some it is a luxury for which they can only afford when the price is lower than usual, or when there is a deficient rubbee harvest. In this way the surplus, whatever it be, is soon disposed of, and is never, to the best of the Committee's knowledge, held from year to year. It may be added also that a pretty correct knowledge of the requirements of the country, as also other economic causes, adjust the breadth of rice cultivation in the country, and a considerable surplus is not usually possible. As a rule, the Committee have no hesitation in asserting that it does not exist, and there is nothing exceptional in the history of the present year to justify a different assumption.

With reference to the second subject of enquiry, namely the probable outturn of the standing crop, the Committee beg leave to observe that the *aman* crop is cultivated upon three descriptions of land: 1st, the very low lands or heels which are sown broad-cast; 2nd, lands, not so low, that is, lands in which monsoon water does not collect with the first heavy showers of rain, and are therefore reserved for cultivation by transplantation of seedling previously reared in seed-beds; 3rd, lands still higher, but which are also cultivated precisely in the same way as the second. Now, a sixteen-anna crop means that, by a seasonable fall of rain from May to November, all the three descriptions of lands have proved equally fruitful. But this consumption is seldom realized. The crop from the first description of lands is uncertain. The crop in such lands is ensured, only when there are slight showers of rain from the middle of Bysack (April) to the end of Jeyt (May), so as to admit of the lands being ploughed up and sown, but no such heavy showers in Assar (June) as to swamp the young plants. If there be heavy showers in Bysack and Jeyt, then the monsoon water collects in those hollows and they cannot be sown for the year; or, if after the plants had come up, there be heavy rains in Jeyt and Assar, so as to drown the plants, then the crop is destroyed, and the lands cannot be re-sown. The rains in Bysack and Jeyt this year were all that could be wished for the cultivation of this description of land. For the proper growth of paddy on the two other descriptions of land there must be seasonable rains from Assar (June) to Kartick (October). The transplantation is commenced from the middle of Assar, and carried on even so late as the middle of Bhadar (August) as in the Sunderbunds. From other lands, unless the transplantation is finished by the end of Sraban (July), the yield must be less than the average. It is seldom that the rains held off during the time transplantation is carried on and finished. But in some years the rains set in late, as was the case this year. Transplantations in many part of the country could not be commenced before nearly the middle of Sraban (end of July). But, in the meantime, the soil had become so much enriched by the action of alternate sun and rain owing to scanty rain-fall that the transplanted plants attained in 15 days the growth of a month. From the latter end of Bhadar (beginning of September) the rains held off; still the plants did well till nearly the end of Assin (beginning of October). In Kartick (middle of October) the plants on the third description of land began to suffer, and gradually withered away in most places by the middle, and entirely by the end of that month. It is only in the first two descriptions of lands that the plants freely flowered and put forth ears. But to enable the plants to flower freely, and for the proper development of grains in the ears, it is not enough that there should be moisture in the land, for the fall of a shower or two of rain is needed from the latter end of Assin to the close of Kartick to help this development. So, by the cessation of rain from September, the crop even on the first and second descriptions of lands must have suffered, and the more so on the second than on the first. Accordingly, a large breadth of cultivation on lands of the second description, which began to be denuded of moisture from the end of Kartic, only partially flowered and put forth ears which did not promise to contain properly developed grains. It was the crop on the first description of lands only, and such as are irrigated by fresh-water, tidal streams, as in Backergunge, that promised to do well, and has done well, but not so well as it would have done, if at the time of flowering it had been helped by a good shower of rain. With these data it would be easy to make a fair estimate of the probable outturn of the crop this year, if the respective area of the different kinds of land under cultivation could be accurately ascertained. This is, however, not practicable. No record exists in the country to show the respective areas devoted to particular crops, and even the extent of cultivable lands existing in the province of Bengal can only be indicated by a guess.

In the absence of records the Committee have to depend upon individual experience. Relying on it they venture to state that the total area of the first description of lands is very small, hardly one-tenth of the whole area of amun lands of the country, and of that small area some portion is very often left fallow on account of the uncertainty of securing a crop therefrom, and as regards such portions as have been cultivated, the plants on the margin of those hollows cannot but have materially suffered in such a year of drought as the present. So that it is the crop obtained from the second description of land which will determine the question of the probable food supply for the ensuing year.

Knowing as the Committee do from actual experience that the average outturn from lands of second class in such a year of drought cannot exceed 8 annas, they thought that it would not be safe to estimate the new crop of the whole province at a higher figure than 6 annas of the average crop. This they did after taking into account the better produce of the lands of the first description, and the crop of the districts that promised a full average crop, and making a due allowance at the same time for the utter loss of crop on the third description of lands. The last class embraces a very large breadth of aman cultivation in every district, and almost entirely that of the Behar districts of Lower Bengal, such as Dinagepore and Rungpore.

The Committee are deeply sensible of the difficulty, nay, the impossibility under the present circumstances of making an accurate idea of either the stock or the probable outturn, but in forming an estimate of them the Committee thought that it was much safer to go upon the grounds mentioned above than to hazard mere guesses. Without any large stock at the close of the year, and with a 6 annas amun crop, the staple food of the country, to commence the year with, the Committee thought that the absolute deficiency in the food supply of the country for some months was almost inevitable, which could not be met, except by importation from abroad. It is true that the Behar districts are not entirely dependent upon rice, and that the rubbee crop of Bengal and Behar, and of all India, as also the two other rice crops, *viz boro*, which will be harvested in April, and *aus*, which will be harvested in September, should be taken into account in calculating the food supply for 1874. But it must be borne in mind that the rubbee crop of Bengal consists principally, if not wholly, of pulses and oil seeds, and very little, indeed, of wheat; and as regards that of Behar, where wheat is produced, —even if it should turn out to be favorable—still it would only go to supplement, as it does every year, the staple food crop (rice) of the country, but cannot make up for the deficient outturn in it by more than one-half, leaving the other half to be made up either by reduced consumption or importation from foreign countries. The same remark applies to the two other rice crops of the year, the breadth of cultivation of one of which *viz., aus*, has been materially reduced of late by the lands formerly devoted to it being appropriated to cultivation of jute and oil seeds.

The Committee will now put the case in another form. Let it be granted that the aman rice crop, which is harvested from November to the beginning of February, the rubee crop which is harvested in April, and the two rice crops which are harvested in April and September, go towards supplying the country with food for the whole year without leaving any heavy stock at the end of the year. Let it be also granted that the rubee and the two rice crops which are in prospect would yield an average outturn; and the prospects of the people will stand thus: Of the four sources of supply, the aman crop will yield less than half the usual average crop, and it is well-known that this crop constitutes, $\frac{12}{16}$th of the food supply of the country. The rubbee crop is sown in October and might be delayed at the most till the middle of November; but no sowing after that period, even under the most favorable circumstances, can be expected to yield an average outturn. At the date of the

Committee's letter to Government, the 21st November last, it was but a small breadth of rubbee lands in the Behar districts that, for want of moisture in the soil, could have been sown, and what little had been sown had not come up, and what had come up was infested with insects. Under such circumstances the Committee thought that it would not be wise to calculate upon more than an 8 annas of the average rubbee crop. The ensuing *boro* rice crop is also not likely to turn out an average one. This crop is entirely dependent upon irrigation, and hence it is planted in the neighbourhood of beels and other reservoirs of water. But as most of these must have dried up this year, the cultivation of this crop must of necessity be limited to a very small area As for the *aus* crop, it might be depended upon to meet the deficiency in the amun crop to an appreciable degree, if the cultivation of it were extended to all the lands suitable to the growth of that crop, which means the cultivation of all the lands with aus paddy, which are now appropriated to jute and oil seeds in addition to its ordinary breadth of cultivation. Taking the lands which may be disengaged from jute and oil seeds at one million of acres, these lands if cropped with *aus*, may under favorable circumstances, yield 15 days' additional supply of food for the whole population. This is, however, not at all likely to take place, and the Committee have therefore, no reason to alter the estimate which they submitted to Government in their letter of the 21st. ultimo.

The Committee are willing to admit that some little benefit may be derived by drawing a supply from the rubbee crop of the rest of India; but they are not without apprehension that like that of Bengal the rubbee crop in these parts, cannot, even under favorable circumstances, be much in excess of the requirements of the people. Be that as it may, when the Committee addressed to you their letter of the 21 st. ultimo, they were under an impression, from accounts then available to them, that the crop in several parts of the other provinces of India was not likely to turn out an average one. But as the prospects there have since improved, supplies mav be now looked for from them.

These are the grounds upon which the Committee came to the con. clusion, which led them to approach Government with their views on the subject. They may be mistaken, and nothing would give them greater pleasure than to find themselves really so; but unable as they were to take a sanguine view of the position of things, and knowing as they did the difficulties, not to say the expense, of procuring supplies from abroad sufficient to feed 60 millions for two months even, (leaving out Orissa and Assam), they humbly thought that no time should be lost in placing the results of their enquiries, views and opinions at the disposal of Government, in the belief that, if they had erred, it was an error on the safe side, which was better than fancied security, the mischief of which it might be too late to repair.

If the Committees estimates, of the stock of old rice, and of the probable outturns of the present crop, as shown above, are at all reliable, the total stock will be only sufficient to feed the whole population for six months; and taking the ensuing rubbee, boro and aus crops as sufficient for two months more, there is every apprehension of a deficiency occurring in the food supply for four months. This deficiency might be easily met without unduly sending up prices and thereby causing starvation to many, if the whole available supply could be equally distributed. For people in that case would have only to live upon two-thirds of their usual rations, which might be safely done without any detriment to health or loss of physical powers. But, as a matter of fact, this needful economy is never practised, until, in the natural course of things, high prices render it utterly unavoidable. It is then only that, according as the prices rule, it is only a comparatively small number of persons that supply themselves with full rations, a great number representing the bulk of the population, must according to their respective purchasing powers, live upon two-thirds, half or one-third of their ordinary allowances, and many are reduced to a condition, when they have no means left to purchase any food for days, and starve until relieved by death. The duration of such a period, and the proportion of the population that must pass through the different stages of destitution, must mainly depend upon the degree of economy exercised from the beginning of the deficient harvest, and their respective purchasing powers. But, as in the usual order of things, rigid economy and equal distributions of food sufficient for eight months to do service for a whole year is not possible, prices must gradually rise to that pitch, which will render food unattainable to many, and to a very large proportion of the population attainable only in quantities insufficient for the due preservation of the vital energies. By providing works on a gigantic scale, and at wages rising with the rise in the price of food, the Government might effect a more equal distribution of the food left than can otherwise be the case; but since the food stock is not sufficient for the proper sustenance of all, the pressure upon it will increase with the rise in price to the suffering and starvation of thousands over thousands, and that calamity can be averted only by pouring in grain into the country sufficient at any rate for a three month's supply. The Committee say for three months, because the outturns of the rubbee and aus crops are yet uncertain, and imagining that one or two months deficiency might be made up by the economy, which would be necessarily exercised in consumption.

The Government is in a better position than the Committee to Judge whether the supplies in the other provinces of India would not be sufficient to meet the deficiency in Bengal. The Indian continent is so vast, and its populations so numerous, that, if a small contribution were made from each of the different provinces, it would go a great way to relieve this province; if, however, the food supplies in this continent be not sufficient, the Government, the Committee respectfully submits, have no other alternative than to import food grains from abroad, if it considers, as the Committee have had abundant testimony to believe it does consider, its sacred duty not to allow a slngle one of its subjects to die of starvation.

Since writing the above, the Committee have been honoured with a further communication on the subject, dated the 9th. instant, forwarding copy of a letter from the Government of India, and requesting the Committee's reply to the questions contained therein. The Committee have also to thank the Bengal Government for a copy of Mr. Geddes' Compilation to assist them in making a comparison between the crops of 1865-66, and those of 1873-74. The Committee humbly think that they have, to a great extent, anticipated in the above the information and opinion called for by the Government of India.

The Committee have given above their own impressions as to the prospects of the crops and food supplies in the country at the date of their letter *viz.*, the 21st. November last, drawn from their own knowledge and observation. They will now, in compliance with the invitation of the Government of India, endeavour to institute, a comparison between the crops of 1865 and 1873 with the aid of the official reports published by Government. They must, however, remark that the official reports are far from clear or full, and do not therefore, afford sufficient data for an exact comparison. Even the reports connected with the Famine of 1866 do not give the exact outturn of crops in all districts, while the reports on the crops of this year are more indistinct. The Bengal Government seems to be alive to this defect. In the Special Narratives of Drought, dated the 21st. November last, it is stated that "the district reports are very unequal in clearness and fullness ; some of them, notably that from Bhaugulpore, are very distinct, while from districts where the sub-divisional system has not yet been fully introduced, the information is imperfect. The estimates offered by the district officers are confessedly rough and imperfect, and do not pretend to arithmetical accuracy. It must be borne in mind, moreover, that farmers when they speak of a full average crop really mean a bumper crop, such as is very seldom harvested, and therefore a three-quarter crop (or twelve-anna crop, as it is called), is in reality a good average yield. In one point most of the replies are more or less incomplete, namely, regarding the comparison between crops, the prices, and the general outlook of the present year with 1865." Thus, the materials for a fair comparison are wanting. The Committee have arrived at the following conclusions upon the official *data* now before the public.

The Commissioners appointed to enquire into the Famine in Bengal and Orissa in 1866 described the result of the crops of the autumn of 1865 in the following general terms: —"In the eastern districts (beyond the *delta* of the Ganges in that direction) material injury was not sustained. In the central districts of Bengal, that is, the districts of the delta and those to the North of the Ganges, although there was, on the whole, a very serious shortness of crop and consequent enhancement of price, and a good deal of alarm was experienced in several quarters, scarcity amounting to famine did not result, except in a comparatively minor degree and in a comparatively limited tract in what may be described as the most Western section of the delta not far from Calcutta. This was chiefly in the Nuddea district. It lies in the midst of a rich and accessible country. Time and liberal measures of a relief were adopted, and happily all considerable mortality was avoided." "The low-lying alluvial portions of the districts to the West of the Hooghly escaped with comparative impunity. It was only in the still more western districts of Orissa and higher parts of the western districts of Bengal, where the alluvium gives place to a laterite soil that the full extremity of famine was reached." The Committee have compiled the annexed table from the extracts from official papers on the Famine of 1866, and the returns published in the *Calcutta Gazette* on the prospects of the crops of 1873.

The Committee deem it necessary to observe that in preparing the table they have been compelled to assume the proportion of probable yield of some districts from the absence of precise information in the official returns. They have, however, endeavoured to make as approximate an estimate as they could form from the character of the official reports.

To elucidate the subject further the Committee propose to review the position of the different districts in 1865 and 1873.

MIDNAPORE.

1865.—"The main rice crop of 1865 is estimated to have been about - half crop; taking the whole district in the Jungle mehals, it is said to have been about six-sixteenths; in the Eastern parts somewhat better."

Mr. Geddes' Compilation p. 35

1873—"Reports received from all police stations show (after allowing for exaggeration) that the out-turn will be from about one-fourth in the worst to three-fourths in the best of an average crop. Taking the district as a whole, the crop will probably be a little over one-half of an average crop."—*Calcutta Gazette, October 22, 1873.*

Since then no improvement is reported from this district.

This is an exporting district, and failure of crops there mean scarcity not only for itself but also for neighbouring districts which depend upon surplus. With half a crop in 1865, Midnapore, according to the Famine Commissioners, stood " next in point of intensity of suffering, as well as next in Geographical position," to Orissa and Maunbhoom.—Vide report of Orissa Famine Commission, p. 105.

Geographical Sections—Physical [illegible]s.	Districts.	1865-66. Proportions of yield of — Each District.	1865-66. Proportions of yield of — Average of the Geographical Section.	Source of information—Geddes' Compilation.	1873-74. Proportion of yield of — Each District.	1873-74. Proportion of yield of — Average of the Geographical Section.	Source of information—Calcutta Gazette of 1873.
				Page.			
The [illegible]wer Delta and Littoral Districts.	M dnapur	1/2 or ·5	Total 3·875, average ·775 or 77 % (M dnapur to Chittagong)	35	1/2 or ·5	Total 3·25, average ·65 or 65 per cent. (M dnapur to Chittagong)	22nd [illegible]
	J ssor	3/4 or ·75		40	1/2 or ·5		17th [illegible]
	Backergunge	7/8 or ·875		72	3/4 or ·75		[illegible]th [illegible]
	Noakhally	7/8 or ·875		72	3/4 or ·75		26th Nov
	Chittagong	7/8 or ·875		72	3/4 or ·75		3rd Dec.
	Catak	1/3 or ·33	Total 4·874, average ·6092 or 60 per cent.	18	7/8 or ·875	Total 5·75, average ·7187 or 71 per cent	26th Nov
	Balasor	1/3 or ·33		18	3/4 or ·75		17th Dec.
	Puri	1/3 or ·33		18	7/8 or ·875		10th Dec.
							17th [illegible]
Wes Bengal [illegible] he Up-ands.	Bardwan	3/5 or ·6	60 percent.	3	1/2 or ·5	50 per cent.	
	[illegible]						
	[illegible]rah						
Cent[illegible]l De ta Districts.	24 Pergannas	1/2 or ·5	Tota 1·958, average ·391, 4/10 or 39 per [illegible].	39	1/4 or 25	Total 2·162, average ·432 or 43 per [illegible]en	26th Nov.
	Nadia	2/5 or ·4		40	[illegible] or 437		17th Dec.
	Murshidabad	1/4 or ·25		43	[illegible] or 375		3rd [illegible]
	Faridpur	7/8 or ·875		172	3/5 or 6		3rd [illegible]
	Pub ia	1/3 or ·333		43	1/2 or 5		26th [illegible]
	Ra [illegible]ye	[illegible] or ·875	Total 2·958	42	7/16 or ·43	Total [illegible]	3rd Dec.

JESSORE.

1865.—The Collector of Jessore reports as follows on the crops in the sub-divisions of his district :—

Jessore. —Only a six-anna rice crop expected. Cold weather crops cannot be sown for want of rain.

Magurah.—A twelve-anna crop. As in Jessore, the winter crops cannot be sown.

Narail.—More than an average crop, the lands of this sub-division being low. Cold weather crops promise fairly.

Jenidah.—The worst sub-division of all—not so much as a six-anna crop. The prices are already more than double those of an average year.

Khoolna and Bagirhat.—Believed to be very good, the ground like that of Narail, lying low.—*Mr. Geddes' Compilations*, p. 40.

1873—The outturn of the rice crop may be expected, on the whole to be an eight-anna one.—*Calcutta Gazette, December* 17, 1873.

The position of this district is .thus worse in 1873. Compared with 1865.

BACKERGUNGE.

1865—This district is included in the Dacca division. Its outturn in 1865 was an average one ; but Commissioner reports that the crop was an "about an average one throughout the division."—*Mr. Geddes' Compilation*, p. 102.

1873.—On the whole, it seems almost certain that there will be a twelve anna crop all over the district."—*Calcutta Gazette*, December 10, 1873.

Thus Backergunge is comparatively worse off this year.

NOAKHALLY.

1865.—This district is included in the Chittagong division. According to the Chittagong Commissioner's report dated 2nd June 1866, "the rainfall last year was about the usual average in amount, but it was unequally distributed, being in excess in the early part and deficient at the end of the season. This caused some failure of the crops here and there."—*Mr. Geddes' Compilation*, p. 172.

From this statement the Committee concluded that the crop of 1865 was an average one in this district.

1873.—"In 106 of the 382 villages in Sudharam ten-annas of the (Rojhsail and Chaplais) late paddy are said to have been destroyed, and similar loss is reported from 21 villages in Hatia. Loss of 4 annas of the crops is reported from Sundeep, Luckipore and Ameergunge, and some loss (nowhere said to exceed 2 annas) from the remaining Thannabs of Ramgunge, Begumgunge, and Bennumie."—*Calcutta Gazette, November 26, 1873.*

"In Sudaram, Begumgunge and Raimgunge, the prospects are much what they were last week. The average loss at Sundeep and Ameergunge is still reported at 4 annas."—*Calcutta Gazette, December 3, 1873.*

The Committee did not take into account of the crops of the Orissa Districts in their letter of the 21st. November last, and so they omit here a comparison of these districts. It will he seen that the chief exporting districts named above are worse off this year than they were in 1865.

BURDWAN.

1865.—Over the whole district it probably did not average less than two-thirds of a full outturn.—*Mr. Geddes' Compilation, p. 31.*

1873.—No definite information is given in the official returns of this district, but it is stated in Appendix B. to the Bengal Government's Special Narrative for the week ending on the 21st. November 1873, that the "total yield of the food crops of 1873 will be under one-half of the full average crop."

This district was considered a distressed district in 1866 with two. third of an average crop in 1865.

HOOGHLY AND HOWRAH.

These two districts import rice. The Famine Commissioners remark with regard to the Hooghly district that "so much of the soil is devoted to the fruits and more valuable products, (sugar-cane, jute, potatoes, plantains, and fine rice), that coarse rice is always imported from other districts and those supplies having been curtailed by the failure in the adjoining districts the price of the food of the people was greatly enhanced. Howrah also much in the same position.

Thus the scarcity in other districts will necessarily tell upon the districts of Hooghly and Howrah, which were considered distressed districts in 1866.

24-PERGUNNAHS.

1865:—The result of the enquiries which the Magistrate and Collector made throughout his district was that a failure of half the crop was expected.—*Mr. Geddes' Compilation, p. 39.*

1873.—"In Diamond Harbour Sub-division about a 7 anna crop is expected, and some distress is apprehended in the Southern parts of thannas Sultanpore and Mathoorapore, where more than a 2 anna crop cannot be hoped for. From Barripore the Deputy Collector reports that the paddy cut contains very little grain, and that the outturn will be very poor. Cold weather crops have been sown here and in Baraset, wherever water was available. In the latter Sub-division the rice crop on the high lands is comparatively destroyed, but some good crops will be taken from the heels and low-lands. In Satkhirah and Baseerhaut prospects are reported to be getting worse and worse as the drought continues."—*Calcutta Gazette, November 26, 1873.*

No improvement has since been reported. It is clear from the above statement that this district is also worse off this year. In 1866 it was considered a distressed district.

NUDDEA.

1865:—The outturn would not be quite half of that produced in ordinary years.—Mr. Geddes' Compilation, *p.* 40.

1873:—The accounts are very indistinct. In the *Calcutta Gazette* of the 17th December 1873, it is stated that the late crop in the Kooshtea Sub-Division is expected to yield a 6 anna outturn.

This district was considered a distressed district in 1866.

MOORSHEDABAD.

1865:—"In Moorshedabad the late rice is chiefly grown on the right bank of the Bhagiruthy. The crop will, I much fear, not be more than one-fourth of an ordinary one. In the neighbourhood of tanks and wells irrigation has saved a part, but I can state from personal observation that a large portion of the area sown will produce nothing."—*Mr. Geddes' Compilation, p. 43.*

1873.—"The outturn of the late rice crop in the Jongipore Sub-Division is still expected to be 7 annas; in the Ramporehat Sub-Division not more than 5 annas crop is expected."—*Calcutta Gazette.*

FUREEDPORE.

1865:—About an average.—*Mr. Geddes' Compilation, p. 172.*

1873.—Harvest of this year will be three-fifths of an ordinary year.—*Calcutta Gazette, December 3, 1873.*

This district is thus worse off.

PUBNA.

1865.—One-third —*Mr. Geddes' Compilation, p. 43.*

1873.—It will be about an 8 anna crop—*Calcutta Gazette, November 26, 1873.*

RAJSHYE.

1865:—Eight-annas.—*Mr. Geddes' Compilation, p. 42.*

1873.—"The early portion of the amun or late rice crop is being reaped. What little has been saved in the lowest lands in the Burhind has yielded from one to two annas. In Nattore the yield will be from 6 to 8 annas. In Pootea and the East of Beauleah, about 6 annas. In parts of Barraigoon paddy is good, and from eight to twelve annas will, it is hoped, be harvested. In Charghat and Beelmaria, from six to eight annas."—*Calcutta Gazette.*

MALDAH.

1865.—"In Maldah little late rice is grown, but the cold weather crops are suffering much from want of rain. The early rice crop was a good one, but owing to the large exportation which has lately been going on from the chief marts of the district, the retail price has been much enhanced."—*Mr. Geddes' Compilation* p. 43.

1873.—Four-anna crop of amun rice.—*Calcutta Gazette, December 3, 1873.*

DINAGEPORE.

1865.—One-third.—*Mr. Geddes' Compilation*, p. 42.

1873.—The reports from this district are very indistinct and very gloomy. It would be scarcely safe to assume more than a three-anna crop all round in this district as in Rungpore.

BOGRA.

1865.—In Bogra, as in Rungpore, half an ordinary rice crop may be looked for.—*Mr. Geddes' Compilation*, p. 42.

1873.—From this district the reports are also indistinct but it may be safe to assume the probable yield at one-fourth the usual average.

RUNGPORE.

1865.—Half crop as observed above.—*Mr. Geddes' Compilation*, p. 42.

1873.—"The state of the rice crop is extremely bad, not much more than a three anna crop can be expected. In one or two parts of the district it is hoped that a six-anna crop may be obtained, but in other parts it is expected that it will be as low as one anna."—*Calcutta Gazette, November* 26, 1873.

DACCA.

1865.—Average crop.—*Mr. Geddes' Compilation* p. 172.

1873.—No precise information is given in the official returns. The Committee estimate half crop for this district.

MYMENSING.

1865.—Average crop—*Mr. Geddes' Compilation*, p. 172.

1873.—No precise information is given in the official returns. Crop estimated at one-half.

CACHAR.

1865.—Average crop.—*Mr. Geddes' Compilation*, p. 172.

1873.—An outturn of 10 annas on the average crop or more is expected.—*Calcutta Gazette, November* 26, 1873.

TIPPERAH.

1865.—Three-fourths—*Mr. Geddes' Compilation*, p. 42.

1873.—The reports from this district are indistinct. Crop estimated at three-fourthes.

BANCOORAH.

1865.—This district suffered more from exportation than deficient crops.

"In ordinary years the district exports some little rice from the east primarily into Ghatal, a large mart in the Hooghly district. After the cutting of the cold weather crop of 1865 much more than usual was carried away to supply the deficiency in Midnapore and Manbhoom. Those who, as in ordinary years, had kept stocks for their own consumption through the coming year, were tempted by the high prices to sell, for which they suffered severely a few months later."—*Mr. Geddes' Compilation*, p. 32.

1873.—"In part an eight-anna crop is hoped for. But in others not more than three or four anna is expected."—*Calcutta Gazette, December* 10, 1873.

This was a distressed district in 1866.

MAUNBHOOM AND SINGBHOOM.

1865.—In Maunbhoom the distress in 1865 was intense, next only to the Orissa District. Outturn one-third.

"The outturn of cold weather crops all over the district is estimated by the Deputy Commissioner to have been between one-third and half of a full crop; but it varied much in different parts of the district. Over a considerable tract the yield could not have exceeded one-fourth."

In Singhboom it is stated that, "at the best of times, the majority of the people, cultivators and others, live from hand to mouth, and grain is rarely stored."—*Mr. Geddes' Campilation*, p. 29.

1873.—Maunbhoom nine-anna crop. Singbhoom half crop.—*Calcutta Gazette, December 10, 1873.*

BEHAR DISTRICTS.

1865.—"In the years 1864-65, the general average rainfall throughout the districts under notice was both deficient in quantity as compared with that of previous years and unseasonable. The rain commenced so late in June that the sowings were generally backward, and this was followed by such an abundant fall in July that the young rice plant in the low lands was swamped. The rains in both years ceased for the most part early in September, and there was none at all in October in either year. This resulted in the crops in the higher lands, from which the water had been completely drained, and which from the main area of the rice cultivation in these districts, dying up, so that the outturn of both years was more or less deficient, varying generally from two-thirds to one-third, and in some exceptional cases, such as the north of Tirhoot and Champarun, not exceeding one-fourth of the ordinary produce."—*Mr. Geddes' Compilation, p.* 15.

1873.—Trans-Ganges tract * is highly cultivated, and very thickly peopled. In belt of lands which lies just under the Himalayas and ordinarily produces a vast surplus of rice, the late rice crop has almost entirely failed. Over the rest of this tract the yield of the late rice may be from a tenth to one-twentieth of an ordinary year's out-turn"

*Including the districts of Tirhoot, Sarun, Champarun, parts of Bhaugulpore and Monghyr, Purneah.

"South Behar contains much less indigo land; and it contains, moreover, a very great rich area which is annually inundated by the Ganges, and on which excellent crops of food are produced in ordinary years. The early (September) crops of South Behar were for the most part bad, ranging from one-quarter to one-half of a full average year. On the inundated lands, the September crop, as it is very often the case, was utterly destroyed. † The late rice over the whole of this tract will not yield one-quater the out-turn of a full average year. The rubbee crops sown on the inundated lands, will, if we get December rains, give a fair crop; but the area actually sown with spring crops is below the average of ordinary years. In the Gya district there is a certain amount of artificial irrigation, and in the Sahabad district some 80,000 acres of rice and wheat lands will have been watered from the canal. If copious rain does not come before Christmas (by that it almost always *does* come in Behar) the total yield of the food-crops of South Behar can hardly exceed from one-quarter to one-third of the out-turn of a full average year."—*Appendix B to Bengal Government Special Narrative of the Drought, dated the the 21st. November 1873.*

†Including the districts of Patna, Gya, Sahabad, parts of Bhaugulpore, Monghyr.

It will be seen from the above whether the Committee were justified in assuming at the date of their letter, *viz*; the 21st. November last, that the average amun crop for the whole of the Bengal territorries, excluding Orissa and Assam, would be six annas, and that, believing as they did that there were not left much old stores in the country generally, there would be a deficiency of food for sometime for sixty millions of the population in round number, comprising those territories, after the harvest of the year was exhausted.

The Committee observe that great stress has been laid upon the manner in which they expressed their sense of the heavy responsibility imposed upon Government in supplying any deficiency, which might occur in the food-supply of the immense population inhabiting this vast country. when they said that "the task of feeding 60 millions of people may well appal the stoutest heart." It is superfluous for them to say that they could not have meant thereby that the whole population of the country would even for a day be without food. Such a contingency was absolutely impossible Instead of dividing the whole province under the Government of Bengal into areas of scarcity and sufficiency, which they could not well do, as neither of them was uninterrupted in its range or uniform in degree, the Committee formed their own estimate of the probable average outturn of the crop in the whole province and calculated therefrom the possible deficiency arising amongst the whole population, taking for granted that the existing supply was equally distributed amongst all, the deficiency of some parts being met by the sufficiency of the other, which, to a great extent, must be the case. But, supposing that the famine area was accurately defined, and the calculation of deficiency was confined thereto, the actual result would be exactly the same, inasmuch as any reduction in the number of sufferers would be made up by a corresponding rise in the duration of their suffering. So that, if, upon the former supposition there should be no food for 60 millions for one month, there would be no food for two months if the famine area were confined to a population of 30 millions. The price of the food any how must be kept within a reasonable figure, and that figure the Committee consider to be at the most 50 per cent. above the normal price in the different parts of the country. With such a price for 3 or 4 months aided in the shape of works liberally provided by Government, the people might tide over the crisis. Any price beyond that figure, and even with such a price for longer period, must reduce thousands to the point of starvation.

While on this point the Committee would invite the attention of Government to the following extract from the report of the Famine Commission of 1866, showing what proportion of deficiency of crop will produce a famine in India :—

What is the minimum extent of deficiency in crop, and what the minimum depletion of reserve stocks that will entail famine in India?

"A most important lesson is, we think, distinctly to be learned from the study of Colonel Smith's report. We are not quite sure whether, in estimating the losses, he takes fully into account the great distinction of the inferior grains of the rainy season, which depend solely on rain, or chiefly refers to the subsequent crop, of which he saw the failure before him—the wheat and other main staples, a great portion of which is always kept alive by artificial irrigations; but his estimates seem to show that in his opinion the failure, taking broadly the whole of the distressed districts, did not exceed that which was from the first admitted in the most sanguine estimates to have occurred in Orissa in 1865, viz. half the produce. He specifically states the loss in several of the bad districts at about four-tenths; in some it was more, in some it is estimated to have been less. The famine country of 1861, is generally speaking, a grain-producing country; with the exception of a good deal of cotton in some portions of it (and the cotton cultivation had not then been abnormally extended), food grains may be said to be the main staple throughout, and in good years there must no doubt be a large surplus produce. Particular estimates apart, it is that the failure of the produce of the whole tract was not complete—that there was in parts (good and bad being intermixed) a very considerable yield. Yet it is abundantly evident that if there had been no importations and no relief works, the famine would have been frightful and very fatal. It may be assumed, then, as the result of Colonel Smith's enquiry, that in the ordinary modern condition of things in India, something much short of the entire and absolute failure of the whole crops of a year in any province will suffice to produce that state of extreme famine when food is scarcely to be had for money, if the market be not relieved by importation from provinces more abundantly supplied. Still more will this be the case when either by previous short crops, or by exportations, or both, the stocks have been already reduced belove average; and as respects a famine caused by absence of grain as distinguished from one caused by absence of money, the effect of previous short crops and of exportation is much the same. Modern enterprize and means of communication, in relieving countries insufficiently supplied, drain those in which grain is more abundant to an extent which probably did not occur in the old days of Native hoarding. In fact in India, where famines have generally been present to the memories and traditions of the people, the want of means of communication was much countracted by the dispostion to hoard largely the grain for which little could be got in years of abundance. An unhappy combination of circumstances which renders exportation in time of abundance large, but brings no importation in time of want, produces such terrible calamity as has just occurred in Orissa."

As to "whether the status of 1873 in the provinces under the Government of Bengal be materially worse than that of 1865-66," the Committee venture to submit that they have adduced sufficient evidence and facts to leave any doubt on that point. The disastrous effects of the failure of rain in 1865 were considerably more circumscribed than could be said of the same in the present year, and remembering that the population now affected is immensely greater than that in 1865, it would, the Committee are humbly of opinion, be scarcely reasonable to take a more sanguine view of things in this year.

But supposing that the status of 1873-74 would not be worse than that of 1865-66, the mortality which followed in the last mentioned year was appalling. In Orissa the lowest estimate was the loss of one-fourth the population by starvation. In Maunbhoom and Singbhoom the death amounted to eighteen-percent. and twelve and half-percent., respectively. Of the other distressed districts no mortuary returns are given, but in the Behar Districts the mortality was very heavy :—

DISTRICTS.	Number of death from starvation or disease engendered by want.
Champarun	56,000
Gya	3,387
Monghyr	1,247
Sarun	8,175
Sahabad	4.424
Tirhoot	60,321
Total...	1,35,554.

Mr. Gedde's Compilation p. 54.

If such was the disastrous effect of the drought of 1865, with a crop of from one-third to two-thirds in the Behar Districts, the gravity of the present crisis may be easily imagined when the probable outturn of those districts in 1873-74 is estimated by Government from one-fourth to one-third.

In submitting these remarks the Committee gratefully acknowledge the judgment, energy, and liberality, which have marked the proceedings of Government to meet the threatened crisis, and they desire to record their humble belief and hope that every thing will be done which can be done, to mitigate suffering, by a Government, rich in resources, and always ready to do its duty by the millions entrusted to its care by a merciful providence.

British Indian Association Rooms
No. 18 BRITISH INDIAN ST.
The 24th December 1873.

I have the honor to be,
Sir,
Your most obedient and humble servant,
(Sd). JOTEENDRO MOHUN TAGORE,
Hony. Secy. British Indian Association.

APPENDIX—F.

I.

(*The Indian Mirror.—22nd April* 1879.)

A great and good man has passed away from among us. In every political, social, or religious reform that has ever taken place in any country where civil rights, manners, or creed have suffered deterioration, the men who have initiated, headed, and led the movement have invariably been distinguished, beyond their generation, by energy, by force of character, and intensity of will, to influence and carry away the unstable public opinion of the age with the strong current of their own advanced views before they have settled down into definite principles. Luther, Calvin and Knox, Voltaire and Rosseau, Robspeirre and Danton, wrought out their appointed tasks with no gentle hands; but so thoroughly and completely that the men who followed them could only round, and polish, and adapt the sound general principles which their masters had laid down to the capacity of the generation who had embraced the new doctrines. But the interval between the masters and the disciples in point of intellectual strength, was as decided as the superiority of the disciples to the masters in point of intellectual culture and general refinement. It is to the men who lead, as it were, the "forlorn hope" in a revolutionary movement, and not to the men who follow a safe beaten track, that the chief credit of a successful reform is due; for it falls to their painful lot to beat down, or break through, the prejudices of their age, and to raise popular feelings in arms against the novel principles which they profess to inculcate. Although of the three chief Presidencies of which the British Empire is composed, Bengal was the last Province that came into direct contact with the influences of Western Civilization, so was it the first Province that became deeply impregnated with those influences which worked like leaven in elevating the intellect of its people, and imparting a new and more vigorous vitality to its decaying and enfeebled institutions. Ram Mohun Roy, Dwarkanath Tagore, Sir Raja Radhakant Deb, Ram Komul Sen, etc., were confederated into a band, whose gigantic intellects and energies, like the highest mountain-tops, catching the first rays of the rising sun, grasped and realized at once the incalculable advantages which would ensue to their country and their countrymen from the introduction of Western literature, sciences and arts into India. Each in his own circle and according to the measure of his intellectual gifts, co-operated in acclimatizing the restless and progressive civilizations of the West to the torpid condition of the moral and social systems of the East. To them is due the entire glory of the victory which is attested in the marvellous advancement of the people of Bengal in moral and intellectual progress. That great race has passed away, and a few of the men who helped in their good work are still lingering on but filling conspicuous positions among the new generation that is springing up, with new aspirations and new views of life. Not the least conspicuous member of that great fellowship was the late Raja Digamber Mitter C. S. I., whose remarkably instructive life, chequered by every vicissitude of fortune, entitles him to a most honoured place in our memory.

Deriving his descent from the same stock as Dr. Rajendra Lala Mitra, the first Native scholar and antiquarian of his age and country, Raja Digambar Mitter came from the branch of the family which had long settled down at Connaghur, in the District of Hooghly. Though the family of the Connaghur Mitters is a well-known one in Bengal,

Raja Digambar succeeded to the inheritance—not of a patrimonial estate,—but of a paternal debt. His father, a man of most honest principles, was in the service of a zemindar, on receipt of a small pay. With a very fair amount of education he had received at the Hindoo College and had profited by more considerably than most men of his time, Digambar began life as a school master at Berhampore in Bengal —a fact which of itself bore testimony that his literary acquirements were more solid and extensive than was common in those days. He was taken by the hand by the late generous-hearted Babu Gunga Churn Sen, who then possessed considerable influence at that station. Digambar's early associates at Berhampore were Babu Gunga Churn, the late Raja Dukhina Runjun Mukerji, Rai Koonjo Lal Banerji Bahadoor, Baboo Denobondhu Sanyal, Babu Pulin Chunder Sen and others. The talents with which Digambar had been endowed by nature were not such as could allow him to confine himself to the beaten track of his duties as a mere pedagogue at Berhampore. His natural and acquired abilities had brought him under the especial notice of Dwarkanath Tagore, the most conspicuous Bengali gentleman of his age, and it was as if at Dwarkanath Tagore's feet that Digambar imbibed those advanced and liberal ideas, by acting up to which he afterwards raised himself from the obscurity of a school master to the rank and position of a leading member of the Native aristocracy in Bengal. Dwarkanath Tagore, who took a very keen interest in Digamber, imbued him with his own principles and views. After a short stay at Berhampore, Digambar, obtained the post of Tutor to Raja Kissen Nath Roy, of Cassimbazar, (the husband of Her Highness Maharani Surnomoyi C. I.) then a minor under the Court of Wards, and it was during his service in this capacity that the first gleam of fortune fell on him. While acting as Tutor to Raja Kissen Nath, that the latter, with the generosity and liberality so characteristic of him, made a noble gift of a lac of rupees to him. But, though such a magnificent gift was ample enough to have made him independent of service for life, and might have unsettled the principles of most men, Digambar would not compromise the integrity of his character by unworthy concessions he was tempted to make by the prospects of rewards so magnificent. His rigid sense of duty cost him the friendship of Raja Kissen Nath, with whom his later relations in life were not of the most satisfactory character.

After his connection with Raja Kissen Nath had terminated, Digambar passed much time at Murshedabad, where he found profitable employment for the capital he possessed in the pursuit of the silk-trade. In this trade he achieved most remarkable success—his trade mark D. M., we believe, having given special value to the silk of Berhampore, which was then in great demand. The silk-trade added to his fortune. After the China war, the silk trade in Berhampore fell off considerably, and Digambar removed to Calcutta, where during the Mutinies, when it was generally believed that the British Empire of India was almost at an end, and Government paper was at a ruinous rate of discount, Digambar who was thoroughly master of the situation, speculated, to a very considerable extent in Government paper, and, as was to have been expected, realised a more magnificent fortune than the most judicious and successful employment of his available capital in any other way could have yielded. His extraordinary share of common sense, which had taught him the art of making, as distinguished from earning money, also taught him when to be content with what he had made.

But with the acquisition of an ample fortune, the labours of his life had not terminated. Having done enough for himself, he now sought to employ the leisure at his command for the benefit of his fellow-men. He was, we believe, a member of the Indigo Commission in Bengal. And during the Orissa Famine he not only rendered great service to the Government by the valuable advice he gave, but proved the practical value of that advice by the measures he subsequently took, when he himself began to own estates in Orissa, formerly the property of Babu Kali Prossonno Sing. Digambar was the officiating President of the British Indian Association during the famine of 1874 in Bengal and Behar, and the views embodied in the Memorial then submitted by the Association to the Government, were principally his views, and they were acted as in all cases; and with perfect success too. The facts and figures which he brought forward to support the statements in the memorial were singularly accurate and precise, and had been arrived at by so close a study and application to enquiries on the subject of famines that his health seriously suffered from his labours, and he was forced to take rest in retirement; which was quite uncongenial to his active habits of mind. Nor was this the last public service he rendered during his valuable life. The mortality that, year after year, had been sweeping away the populations of several districts in Bengal, had stirred the sympathies of his benevolent heart and active and enquiring mind; and he set himself to the careful observations of the probable causes by which that mortality was brought about. His theory, that the epidemic fever, which prevailed in Bengal was wholly and solely attributable to the obstruction of the natural drainage of the country, asserted itself, in spite of the contrary opinions of the professional men whom the Government thought fit to consult; and after years of unprofitable discussion and lengthy correspondence, the Government of Bengal was large-minded enough to accept the soundness of that theory, and to enjoin the observance of an efficient system of drainage as a preliminary measure to the introduction of a more perfect system of sanitation. *Finis coronant opus.* Raja Digambar Mitter lived to see his views put into practice.

Having related the salient facts of his memorable life, we desire to guard our opinion of it by our frank avowal of the great personal esteem and regard we have felt for him during a close personal friendship that has only been terminated by his lamented death. His career is full of instruction. With neither opulence, nor social position, to help him, Digambar Mitter, by the mere force of an undoubted character for intelligence and perfect integrity, raised himself from obscurity to a conspicuous position among the most conspicuous men of his time. And this end he attained not by sycophancy and subservience, but by an independence of spirit and conduct which were valued more highly on account of their uncommonness. We have already referred to the extraordinary common sense with which he was endowed; but that common sense was perfected by an experience that was as large as the sympathies of his great heart. The popular estimation of his personal character for intelligence and integrity of character was so assured that not only was his advice most freely sought for and given on all occasions to the wide circle of his friends and acquaintances, but, in many cases of litigatiön, the assistance of his sound judgment and impartiality was solicited and used to arbitrate between conflicting claims. His strength of mind was such that for years he bore the death of his only son with a fortitude of spirit that was almost incredible. His deep but unshown sense of it was proved by his end in a career of usefulness. In such high esteem were his sound sense and vast experience of life held that both the Government of India and the Government of Bengal freely applied to him for advice on all questions that affected the interests of the people of Bengal. During the time he filled a seat in the Legislative Council of this Province, he rendered most eminent services to his country and countrymen. He was the first, and yet the only Bengali gentleman that has held the important office of Sheriff of Calcutta. Though among the wealthiest members of the Native Aristocracy, it was not his wealth, but his abilities and high character, that won him the distinction he enjoyed. A spiritualist by religion, Digambar's spiritualism was of such pure and elevated character that he firmly believed the end of his mortal life was not, and would not be, the end of his life of usefulness. To such a man, death could have had no terror, but, rather, the prospect of a renewal of the beneficent life he had always led. Though his public charities were not conspicuous for the amounts he bestowed, he proved the earnestness and sincerity of his love for his country and countrymen by supporting, during years, so large a number as eighty students, who, came to pursue their education in the great schools of the city. He provided them with daily food and the shelter of a home, helping them, in fact, to educate themselves for the mission of propagating the principles of Western civilization among their less favoured brethern in their distant homes. If such an act be not the very essence of charity, we fear we do not, and shall never, understand the true aim and ends of charity. His rare goodness of heart was proved by unostentatious acts of kindness to all men. He was one of the Honorary Secretaries to the District Charitable Society, in which he had an endowment, called after his name. His sympathies were large and Catholic.

Essentially a self-made man, Digambar Mitter owed the distinction he had achieved in life neither to birth, nor to the favours of fortune. Every step in the upward course of his life was achieved by himself, and, though the outset of his career was marked by great vicissitudes, the close of it was as brilliant as he himself, or his dearest friends could have wished. His character for unimpeachable integrity and sound judgment was so well and widely established that he was selected to be executor to the estates of such men as Roma Persad Roy and Gopal Lall Tagore. The independence of his spirit was never so conspicuous as during the time he filled a seat in the Legislative Council of Bengal, where his opinions were always outspoken. His abilities and worth were so rightly estimated that he was appointed President of the British Indian Association—a position of the highest trust and distinction among the landed aristocracy of Bengal. His manners were perfect. Frank and sociable, his address was so prepossessing that he won his way at once to the heart of all he came contact with, either in the way of business or in social intercourse; and it is, perhaps, this trait, above his many great and good qualities, that constituted the secret of his great success in life. His social qualities were conspicuous far more than Hindu hospitality, and his house was always open to the numerous European and Native friends who took delight in his agreeable and instructive company. As the zemindar of very considerable estates, both in Orissa and in other provinces, he was most kind to his numerous tenantry, of whose conditions, wants, and grievance he was most particular in inquiring from his agents. The estimate of his life and character which we have ventured to offer in this necessarily hurried sketch, was formed after many years of close observation and study.

So highly esteemed was Digambar both by the Supreme and Local Government, that he was often consulted on great occasions of public emergency, such as the famine and the dreadful mortality which the epidemic fever in some of the Bengal Districts caused among the populations of those districts. His theory in respect to the causes of this epidemic fever was so sound that, in spite of the opposition of the professional men, it was eventually accepted by the Government; and Sir Ashley Eden, who knows the country more, perhaps, than any other Lieutenant-Governor who has preceded him, has insisted on the introduction, and maintenance of a proper system of drainage as among the most urgent and important wants of the Provinces under his rule. For this service alone Raja Digambar Mitter will long be remembered by generations yet unborn. Many of our countrymen have, perhaps, been more distinguished by brilliant qualities; but few have gone to their well-earned rest after a life of such disinterested, useful, and unostentatious labour, rendered purely and simply from love of his fellow-men, as Raja Digambar Mitter. Among the few Bengalee gentlemen to whom the distinction of a Companionship of the Star of India was awarded he was one. He was made Raja on the proclamations of the Empire of India at Delhi on the memorable 1st January 1877.

APPENDIX--F.

II.

(The Bengalee, 26th April, 1879)

One by one some of our best men are passing away from amongst us. One by one they are leaving the scene of their labours, where their names will long be remembered, where their memories will long be cherished. We know not whether a great curse is on the land ; we know not what awful visitation is upon us. By an inscrutable decree of fate, those whose lives have been a blessing to their countrymen, those who have been the foremost in the great fight that is now going on, for social and political regeneration, have, with but rare exceptions, been snatched away from our midst, at a time of life when they had but made themselves masters of the situation and when their experience and ripe judgment would have rendered incalculable service to their countrymen. Ram Gopal Ghose, Hurrish Chundar Mookerjee, Dwarkanath Mitter, and others whose names might be mentioned, were all cut off at a time of life when the memory of their great services had raised still greater hopes in the minds of their countrymen, and when their ripe judgment and mature experience would have materially contributed to the solution of the great social and political problems of the day. European history has made us familiar with the names of great statesmen and of great patriots who after a life of eminent service, and at times of unexampled sufferings, have descended to their graves, having outrun the allotted span of human existence. One of the most curious facts of European life and one which has often struck us as very remarkable, is the longevity of European statesmen, who from the very nature of their duties, have so many anxieties to endure and so much hard work to go through' and who, therefore, of all men, would be supposed least likely to be blessed with the blessing of longevity. Talleyrand, Guizot, Thiers, Brougham, Wellington, Russel and Palmerston, the foremost statesmen of this century, and one of this brilliant group, no less distinguished as a statesmen than a soldier, all died at an advanced age. The foremost European statesmen of the present day are all old men. With the traditions of European statesmanship they have inherited the longevity of European statesmen. Prince Gorstchakoff the Russian Chancellor of the Empire is 79 years of age, having been born in 1800. Prince Bismark is 64 years of age, having been born in 1815. Lord Beaconsfield is in his seventy-fifth year and was born in 1805. Mr. Gladstone is four years younger than his great rival, having been born, in 1809. The question at once occurs—why is it that our foremost men die at a comparatively early age? It cannot be hard work alone that kills them. European statesmen have much harder work to go through. The long debates in Parliament, at times extending from the early hours of evening to the early hours of day-light, the excitement of Parliamentary contest, the anxieties of office, must constitute a much severer strain upon the constitution than all the hard work which our public men have to go through. Or is it the climate and the hard work combined that kills off our best men so early? The question is far too important to be summarily disposed of in the course of an obituary notice like this. But it is impossible to deny, and the reflection is painful in the extreme, that the generation which has derived the greatest advantage from English education, is short lived as compared with the generation which has gone by and which was content to walk in the ways of its fathers. It would be absurd to connect English education with the fact to which we have referred. English education is no more responsible for it, than it is for cyclones and famines and storm-waves. The struggle for existence has greatly increased. The competition in life has become much keener. In this keen struggle, in this arduous contest, considerations of health are sacrificed to the desire to live any how. An increasing population, in a society where every man must marry whether he has the means to support a family or not, has made the position one of increasing embarrassment and has added to the keenness of the competition. Be the solution of the problem whatever it may, it is impossible to shut our eyes to the terrible problem itself—why is it that we are a short-lived people as compared with our fathers—and which sooner or later must claim a solution at our hands. Raja Digambar Mitter died at the comparatively early age of 63, in the full possession of his intellectual powers, when he might yet have rendered great services to his countrymen, and enhanced his claims to their gratitude.

Raja Digambar Mitter was born in the month of July in 1816 at

Connagur in the District of Hooghly. His father Babu Shib Chunder Mitter sent him to a Patshala where he received the rudiments of his Vernacular education. After having been for sometime at the Hare School, that nursery of our best men, he joined the Hindoo College. There he came under the influence of that celebrated teacher Mr. De. Rozerio who so powerfully influenced the thought of the foremost young men of that day. After a brilliant career at College, Babu Digambar Mittra was nominated when nineteen years of age, a teacher in the Nizamat School. But he was soon after appointed Head Clerk in the Rajshai Collectorate. And it was probably while performing his duties in this humble sphere that he laid the foundation of that comprehensive knowledge of the revenue system of the country which was of such great use to him in the management of his Zamindaries as well as in the efficient discharge of his duties as a public man. We are now approaching that period in the life of Digambar Mitter when he was to lay the foundation of his future fortune. Raja Kissennath of Moorshedabad, whose widow is the celebrated Moharani Sarnamaye, appointed him his tutor. The grateful pupil in recognition of the services of his teacher made a gift of a lakh of Rupees to Babu Digambar Mitter. It was this lakh which Babu Digambar received, that became the *nucleus* of his vast fortune He invested the money in silk trade. He prospered in the trade and soon after he took to indigo planting. But he was not very successful in indigo planting. With the fortune that he had been able to realize from the proceeds of his trade, he purchased Zemindaries, and eventually settled in Calcutta. Henceforward Babu Degumber Mitter appears before the public not as the astute merchant or the sagacious Zemindar but as one who felt a deep interest in all such movements as were calculated to promote the welfare of his countrymen. The British Indian Association had been established in 1851, and Babu Digambar Mitter became its first Assistant Secretary—an office which the Hon'ble Kristo Dass Pal now so worthily fills. He always took a leading part in the deliberations of the Association and was one of the foremost of its members. In 1864, when a Commission was appointed by Government to inquire into the causes of malarious fever, Babu Digambar Mitter was named a member of that Commission. It was while serving on that Commission, that he hit upon the real cause of malarious fever in Bengal and propounded that theory with which his name will always remain inseparably associated. All sorts of theories had been started, all kinds of doctrines had been laid down to explain the causes of an epidemic which was decimating Bengal, and had converted some of its most salubrious districts into the hot-beds of disease and death. The theories did no good. The doctrines were found to be wholly illusory. The disease raged in all its virulence. The sufferings of the people knew no bounds: they died by hundreds and thousands. Whole villages were depopulated, and yet the fell epidemic continued to rage with unabted virulence and cast its depeening shadows over the face of the land. It was at such a time, after a most patient investigation in which he spared neither time nor money, that Babu Digambar Mitter offered his well-known explanation of the cause of the epidemic fever in Bengal, an explanation which has now been universally accepted. He explained that malarious fever was due to subsoil humidity arising from obstructed drainage. Open the natural outlets for the drainage of your villages, and the fever will disappear. It was not for one moment to be expected that a theory started by one who was not a medical man, who had never received a medical education and had probably never read a medical book in his life, in explanation of an epidemic that had yet baffled all explanation, would be received unhesitatingly and without question by the members of the medical profession. The theory shared the fate of all correct theories which have the misfortune of being new. It was laughed at, ridiculed and cried down, in turn. But Babu Digambar combined, and in a rare degree, the sagacity and penetration of a shrewed man of the world with the enthusiasm of a reformer. He was not to be daunted because his theory had not been accepted by the Government or by the public. Having convinced himself of its accuracy he set himself with a degree of energy that was truly remarkable to the task of convincing others. People must listen to his drainage theory whether they wished it or not. People must listen to his arguments whether they liked them or not. The world was to have no peace till it had accepted his theorv or had finally refused to do so. Something of the spirit of the apostle of a new faith animated Babu Digambar Mitter, and his perseverance was eventually rewarded by the triumphant establishment of his theory and by the acceptance of it by those who had refused to consider its merits. The theory was recognised in the Embankment Bill; and the Government of Sir Ashley Eden has definitely adopted it. We repeat that the labours of Babu Digambar Mitter to ascertain the cause of the epidemic fever of Bengal; and his persistent and energetic effort to bring about the acceptance of that theory by the public and the Government in the face of much oppositon and of no little cavil, will constitute the most lasting monument of his patriotism, and public spirit, and his surest claim to the gratitude of his countrymen. In 1865, Babu Digambar Mitter was appointed member of the Bengal Council. So highly were his services appreciated in the Council, that he was thrice nominated by three successive Lieutenant-Governors to this honorable office. He rendered many valuable services in connection with the Road Cess Act. He was opposed to the Act, as he regarded it a violation of the Permament Settlement. But nevertheless when the Act was passed, he loyally submitted to it and helped to make it successful in its operation. Babu Digambar Mitter took great interest in the District Charitable Society and was the Secretary to the native Committee of the Society. Babu Digambar Mitter while he had always been willing to help all public movements with his money, was not slow in the unostentatious performance of Acts of private beneficence. He entertained in his house about eighty poor students who were supported by him. We know how highly the boon was prized by those who were its recipients. We are glad to learn that this charity will be continued, and we understand that a provision to that effect has been made in his will. In 1875 Babu Digambar Mitter was appointed High Sheriff of Calcutta. In 1876, he was made a Companion of the Order of the Star of India. And on the first of January 1877, on the occasion of the Proclamation of the Imperial Title, Babu Digambar Mitter was created a Raja. On the death of the venerable Maharaja Romanath Tagore, Raja Digambar Mitter was elected President of the British Indian Association. But his highly useful career was fast approaching its close. The hand of death was upon him. The iron frame sank beneath a complication of maladies which he had at first refused to take notice of. It would be difficult to fill the void which the death of the Raja has created in Native Society. Such a combination of practicai sagacity with high literary accomplishments as was seen in his case is very rare, especially in India. We hope the life of such a man will not be without its influence upon the rising generation of his countrymen. Raja Digambar Mitter possessed in an eminent degree qualities which could not but ensure success, in life, It was his earnestness, practical sagacity and indomitable energy of purpose, which raised him from obscurity and placed him in the front rank of life, The possession of the same qualities except under exceptional circumstances must lead to the same results. This is the lesson to be learnt from the life of Raja Digambar Mitter and it would be as well in an epoch so barren of great examples, to treasure up this lesson in our minds.

Lightning Source UK Ltd.
Milton Keynes UK
UKOW01f0218010917
308357UK00016B/365/P

9 781333 466695